SMOGTOWN

SMOGTOWN

THE LUNG-BURNING HISTORY
OF POLLUTION IN LOS ANGELES

CHIP JACOBS &
WILLIAM J. KELLY

THE OVERLOOK PRESS
Woodstock & New York

First published in the United States in 2008 by
The Overlook Press, Peter Mayer Publishers, Inc.
Woodstock & New York

WOODSTOCK:
One Overlook Drive
Woodstock, NY 12498
www.overlookpress.com
[for individual orders, bulk and special sales, contact our Woodstock office]

NEW YORK:
141 Wooster Street
New York, NY 10012

Cataloging-in-Publication Data is available from the Library of Congress

Book design and type formatting by Bernard Schleifer
Manufactured in the United States of America
FIRST EDITION
ISBN 978-1-58567-860-0
10 9 8 7 6 5 4 3 2 1

CONTENTS

ACKNOWLEDGMENTS

BEFORE WE OPEN THE DOORS TO *SMOGTOWN*, WE WANT TO THANK THE MANY people who gave *us* a tour, or at least pointed us in the right direction. Special credit goes to South Coast Air Quality Management District (AQMD) librarian Hiawatha Norris and her assistant Lora Trapp for retrieving files and tracking down obscure materials, and to district spokesman Sam Atwood for answering our inquiries. We also owe a major debt of gratitude to Gladys Meade, a legendary California clean-air advocate who granted us interviews while recovering from a serious illness. Jim Birakos, the district's former communications chief and deputy executive officer, has our hearty appreciation, for knocking the dust off his files and memories from that brown-air period. Others deserving our appreciation include former and current California Air Resources Board chairs Mary Nichols, Tom Quinn, and John Dunlap, in addition to Bill Sessa, the board's ex-longtime spokesman. Former AQMD executive officer James Lents gave us tremendous insight, as did Ed Camarena, the district's onetime-enforcement boss. To all those other officials not listed here, please know your contributions show up in these pages and in our thoughts.

We're equally appreciative of the archivists at our local institutions, particularly Shelley Erwin at the California Institute of Technology Archives, Simon Elliott at the University of California at Los Angeles' Department of Special Collections, and Bruce Carouchet at Los Angeles County. The folks at the California State Archives and the University of Southern California Regional History Collection came through for us, as well, organizing dozens of boxes of documents for review. So did the capable people at the California State Library, the ARB Library, The Ronald Reagan Library, and the Los Angeles and Pasadena public libraries.

Finally, we would like to thank The Overlook Press, particularly editor David Shoemaker, and our agent Mitchell Hamilburg for believing in this story in a time of green rethinking.

Chip Jacobs & William Kelly,
December 2007

PREFACE

WHATEVER SCIENCE TELLS US ABOUT SENSE-OF-SMELL HARBORING OUR most enduring memories, any longtime Southern Californian knows that barraged lungs have a recall all their own. We were both youths here in the 1960s and 1970s, and our bronchial tracts remember the clotted skies that draped our hometowns in a mist of hydrocarbons, soot, lead, acidic gases, and particles that made entire mountain ranges disappear. They can't forget the stabbing ache during sandlot baseball games, where you sometimes ran the bases feeling dizzy, or going to grab the morning paper and inhaling gasoline vapors. All our moms could do as we straggled in from the outdoors was to dispense aspirin, maybe a damp washcloth, and tell us to rest; the forecast called for letup in a week. Luckily, we didn't know any better, so when the patio furniture faded and the flowers browned, when asthma, bronchitis, even cancer, unexpectedly decked our loved ones and acquaintances, we figured all big American cities lived saddled like this. We didn't know then that the government that had vowed to give Los Angeles back its famous sun had practically self-immolated in its failure to deliver. In our boyhood reveries, we only knew that when temperatures rose and the landscape receded, you were supposed to breathe warily until you got indoors.

With those memories in our respiratory DNA, we bring to you L.A.'s greatest crisis as survivors of it. Our parents' friends stored gas masks. Our P.E. classes were canceled on account of hovering hydrocarbons. To us, Orange County got its name from the color of its atmosphere, not its indigenous fruit. Moreover, though, we now recognize smog's capacity to pounce again, no matter the massive gains that put light blue back in the horizon. Civilizations always seem to create ashes faster than anybody can sweep them up.

For reasons you'll discover, air pollution was a devil at once ironic and insidious. Over the decades, it became an almost natural state requiring unnatural vigilance. Hundreds of thousands of people died from it, mostly from slow acting diseases, in a toll dwarfing local losses to war, traffic accidents, and gang bloodshed. Versatile in its mischief, it also provoked murders, suicides, mental disorders, faithlessness, and a reactionary itch for blame. It unleashed corporate skullduggery and tainted science, idling movie productions and beloved pets along the way. Presidential candidates hacked in it, hikers cursed it, comedians made jokes about it, and airline pilots disparaged it for obscuring UFO sightings (really). How far did it penetrate our world? Check out the statistics showing the Dodgers were more likely to win when the air hurt. Type in the four-letter word "smog" into the *Los Angeles Times* database, and you'll get back more than *75,000* hits covering the years 1940-1970. When rock singer Commander Cody sang, "I'm lost in the ozone again," we understood. It was our ozone, too.

Your authors met in the early 1990s, when Chip was a cub reporter, William the spokesperson for the beleaguered-yet-revered regional agency charged with reversing this destruction. It was a period when the air had grown alarmingly toxic again after years of steady improvement, as Los Angeles and Houston were battling *not* to be crowned the planet's air-pollution capital. Frustrated regulators here ordered mandatory carpooling, smokeless barbecue briquettes, oil-free paints, and other crackdowns, while business asked, "Why blame us?" and environmentalists hollered, "What about the poor?" In many respects, it was déjà vu from our boyhoods. Tens years later, scarred by the fact the murky air remains, we decided to pen the L.A. smog phenomenon.

Be forewarned, though, this is not your father's environmental tome. Down at the library you'll find a mound of books exploring smog policy, smog chemistry, smog law, and enough automotive engineering to bore Mr. Goodwrench. Neither is this a campy, low-brow take on the subject. (There's eBay for that, or 1971's *Godzilla Vs. The Smog Monster.*) What you'll find here, instead, is a broader social history with splashes of science, regulation, and culture mixed in. As denizens and writers, we focused on the human element in all its wheezy urgency. Along the way, we hope we extracted some lessons for a world looking to green over its damage.

You might be surprised about what we can learn from a pair of L.A. lungs.

—CHIP JACOBS & WILLIAM KELLY
Pasadena area, California
December 2007

1
STATE OF SIEGE

THE BEAST YOU COULDN'T STAB FANNED ITS POISON ACROSS THE waking downtown. Cunning and silent, its gray mist engulfed buildings and streetcars, obscuring the sun and killing all sense of direction as it assaulted Los Angeles' citizenry with a face-stinging burn. Though nobody realized it then, the mystery cloudbank would rattle the planet—making "green" a cause, not just a color—but first there was the suffering, a city full of it. Inhaling the viscous stuff socked folks with instant allergies whether they had them before or not, eyes welled, throats rasped, hands grasped for hankies and for answers. On July 8, 1943, crowds from Grand Avenue to Union Station muttered surprise at the abruptness of the confounding haze, later mouthing anger at whoever was responsible. The pall, which seemed to have lunged from everywhere and nowhere at once, was a real day-wrecker. After a few hours, what had been a steamy West Coast morning in the town that had shredded notions that one place couldn't have it all felt more like a party crashed by industrial fire.

Peoples' attempted escapes from the noxious cloud bred hair-raising street drama. Blinded drivers jerked from side to side to avoid collisions. Mothers snatched up frightened children into ornate lobbies for shelter. If it was hard on pedestrians, it was hellish for the beat cops supervising public safety, let alone for any dangling window-washers. Whatever had summarily blanketed downtown was reminiscent of a harsh, pea-soup London fog. Then again, this was Southern California, where fabulous sunshine was a birthright. Try telling that to the beast.

From within the horn-honking turmoil spread a wild rumor that the cloudbank meant war—chemical munitions the Japanese had lobbed in a sneak attack. With Pearl Harbor and the Imperial Navy's shelling of Santa Barbara, might this be the first salvo against L.A.? Was mustard gas next? By hour two, the tendrils of the murky climes had thickened and widened, edging toward the northern foothills, where the big-spenders lived against the national forest's piney backdrop. An irritating haze had intermittently gripped the central city since the turn of the century. Never a crisis before, it was fodder for blue ribbon committees and the reason for a drawer full of ordinances targeting smoke, soot, and odors. Now the stuff had re-materialized with a vengeance and, maybe, an agenda. Deprived of the sweet air they'd taken for granted, tens of thousands of Angelenos hacked: the thin and sickly, the corpulent moneymen of Spring Street, jug-eared Boy Scouts, grimy trench diggers, haberdashers, transplanted Okies. A judge furious that acrid air had invaded his courtroom threatened to adjourn for the day, the docket be damned.[1]

City health inspectors instructed, even shushed Angelenos not to overreact. A focused crackdown, they said, should make the hijacked sun reappear. Engineers suspected that a rogue factory had leaked the gases, which the freakishly warm weather then trapped around the city. To officials' delight, easy breathing returned the next day with the sunny skies. Relief and even corny humor rippled through the City of Angels. The *Los Angeles Times*, then Southern California's archconservative conscience, joked that the onslaught was the product of "sulfurous fumes from a heated meeting in the mayor's office" over streetcar-strike negotiations.[2] The laughing, however, was not universal. One councilman, risking the Cassandra crown in a land of optimism, warned they had better stem the recurring attacks or brace for the city frittering into a "deserted village."[3] *Balderdash*, replied Los Angeles Mayor Fletcher Bowron, a judicious, owlish man whose forte was legislative nuance and stem-winding speeches. Angelenos had chosen Bowron and his progressive, good-government plank after a police and vice scandal doomed his predecessor. Bowron could sense people's jumpiness about whether the fume-beast might spring again, so in August the mayor provided a fatherly guarantee. There would be, he promised, "an entire elimination" of the vexing plume within four months.[4]

So began the official campaign to make Los Angeles' air sparkle uninterrupted. If you had predicted then that the airshed would remain hideously unhealthy sixty-five years later, somebody might've questioned your lucidity, perhaps even your patriotism. It was all about belief. When smog collared the city in the early 1940s, local government assessed it a moderate nuisance as fixable as a pothole-chewed boulevard. Los Angeles—America's newest industrial powerhouse, not just its redoubt of Hollywood cool—had, after all, a military to arm and a neon future to invent. After the first batch of rulemaking accomplished little, a troupe of politicians from Bowron to eventually Ronald Reagan enacted progressively tougher rules that they expected would give the people back their sky. Smog, though, had a knack for dragging these expectations into exasperation, for inverting cheery promises into broken ones. As the years passed, the chemical air humbled many of the countermeasures against it with tenacity and guile, sowing discord

among its victims, be they aggrieved family men or scapegoated industrialists. They knew smog would have its say into
whether Southern California represented a land of the future
or a civic flash-in-the-pan, and influence it would. Just when
you thought it had lifted, it would strike harder, smudging the
West Coast dream with a vapory char.

Not to fear, big voices proclaimed. America's technological
ingenuity had throttled the Axis and now was putting astronauts into orbit and push-button appliances into kitchens.
Science held the answer to pure air without requiring disruptive lifestyle changes. Los Angeles, as such, converted itself
into the world's first-ever laboratory for smog destruction, its
millions of inhabitants the test subjects. But, that's getting
ahead of the story.

*   *   *

In the summer of 1943, the city's engineering department
readied itself to apprehend the guilty. Out in the field, testers
collected a hodgepodge of airborne samples—ammonia,
formaldehyde, sulfuric acid, dust, chlorine—that would've been
impressive if the men had not been so baffled about their origin.
Most Angelenos, sweating rent, their focus on family and overseas combat, were disinterested in the chemistry of what was
making them sniffle and tear. They just wanted their outdoors
back. Regrettably, when Los Angeles' City Hall finally fingered
the source of the returning fumebank, it fingered the wrong culprit. This rashness had some justification. Southern California's
dry, crystal-fresh air was the dominant characteristic of the
upbeat metropolitan personality. It was God-given advantage,
central to lifestyle and commerce, worth practically any defense.

L.A. consequently burst into the unchartered world of air-
pollution abatement less like Raymond Chandler's shrewd

detective Philip Marlowe and more like gunslinger John Dillinger. When spot inspections, triangulated coughing, and grimy drapes all pointed in the same direction—a Southern California Gas Co. factory east of downtown—authorities assumed it was the sole villain. Blame the obscure Aliso Street plant for shooting phenol and benzol from misfiring generators, they said. After a September 9 episode of wickedly gray air—the *Times* dubbed it a "daylight dimout," the day thousands "wept, sneezed, and coughed" from "man-made hay fever"—Bowron snarled that he'd put an end to it. His men would slap code violations on the plant if the irritating fumes continued. The only reason inspectors had not already padlocked the factory was that it was a cog in the rubber-manufacturing cycle the military needed.[5] Plant grit blistering the paint-jobs on nearby cars unnerved the mayor about its effects on delicate humans. Managers of nearby hotels and restaurants harbored their own fears, aghast to find that the air had splat black, greasy residue on their curtains and furniture. "The problem is fumes," stressed councilman John Baumgartner. "There is no question that the main cause is the butadiene— so why beat around the bush?"[6] Determined, city attorneys burned the midnight oil to return the city—including its dirty sofas—to normal.

The Feds were perspiring, too. They understood that Los Angeles, with its $9 *billion* in military contracts, was an armaments-production hotbed—not some backwater in revolt. They dispatched Col. Bradley Dewey, the U.S. "Rubber Czar," to the West Coast for emergency consoling. The squat, white-haired Dewey could work a room. Speaking inside the starch-linen environs of the California Club, he told the assembled audience that the gas company was close to perfecting new fume-cutting equipment that'd make things right. It had to; the factory was irreplaceable. With the bulk of the world's natural rubber supply in the hands of the Japanese military at the time, the U.S. armed forces had become desperate for synthetic versions of it. Military brass had selected the West Coast, with its strategic location and manufacturing base, as the nexus for expanding production of the versatile, stretchy material. With that in mind, the Aliso Street plant had undergone a $14 million conversion that enabled it to mass produce crude butadiene, which then was used as feedstock in artificial rubber. Dewey stressed the connection between that operation and the plight of American combat troops overseas. After softening the crowd up with patriotic guilt, he promised breathable improvement by December. If not, he said, "You can call me a bum and I will close down the plant myself."[7]

Dewey's peace mission convinced Los Angeles and Pasadena to drop their prepared injunctions against the gas company. For the rest of '43, with the factory offline for retrofits and the city bearing down on other flagrant smoke sources, the skies shimmered again in pale-blue majesty. These basic steps, the *Times* chest-thumped, had liberated the town.[8] As if on punchline, the murk returned.

When the groans subsided, civic government mobilized with a battery of new entities and proclamations suggesting an offensive against a conquerable adversary. The Los Angeles County Board of Supervisors, a powerful board of five unglamorous "little kings" who oversaw the county's unincorporated sections, appointed a "smoke-and-fumes" commission. In 1945, they shotgunned through a county ordinance limiting smoky effluents from backyard trash-burning, rubbish collection, diesel truck exhaust, and orchard heaters called "smudge pots." The county grand jury acted next, convening to investigate the stuffy, poker-room conditions flaring around the region on hotter days. L.A. City Hall took it even further, christening a new department: the Bureau of Air Pollution Control. Government rustlings were good for the public outlook. For the folks at the L.A. Chamber of Commerce, salesmen of the gangbusters economy, they were, conversely, a cause for slight uneasiness. They preferred a go-slow approach where industrial cleanups were voluntary.

Whatever the method, it needed to be snappy, because the gray overhang was shrouding more communities than ever before. In the mid-1940s—when smog took a backbeat to issues of housing, crime, and traffic—people's hankering for yesterday's air went beyond aggravated sinuses and runny noses. It was about what they couldn't see on the bad days, including landmarks or even a street sign a half-mile away. A wistful aesthetic about such lost scenery trickled into neighborhoods, riling up old-timers and nature lovers sentimental about the beach-to-mountains panoramas characteristic of so few places in the world. To them, the blocked skies were tantamount to acne on a beauty queen. It hadn't been that long ago those homeowners had bragged about being able to make out Catalina Island twenty miles offshore on a cloudless day. Now washed-out hues supplanted those memories. Heavy smog bleached the terrain, making it seem as if somebody had swiped the boldest colors from nature's palette. Instead of misty morning light, a blah brownish-gray filled windshields and bay windows. Spectacular sunsets of brilliant orange and noble crimson blurred to dull peach. Lush, emerald-green hillsides and jutting cocoa-colored mountains ebbed to silhouetted nothingness. No need telling that to the forestry department; it abandoned a lookout tower in Monrovia, just east of Pasadena, because fire-spotters couldn't see much from sixty feet up anymore.[9] The timing was ironic. Just as Hollywood magicians were perfecting Technicolor to infuse lifelike colors into movies, the outdoor canvas languished in dispiriting monochrome. On some mornings, the top floor of L.A.'s signature City Hall pierced the clinging filth like a cork bobbing in diseased water.

For writers, it was post-Industrial Age-noir. "Like a dirty gray blanket flung across the city, a dense, eye-stinging layer of smoke dimmed the sun," ranted one scribe in September 1946.[10] Slowly, a fringe of agitated suburbanites vocalized doubts that a few plant adjustments and regulations would revive L.A.'s picture-postcard vistas. In Altadena, a free-spirited hamlet northwest of Pasadena, the gunk chased residents indoors. "You can see the fumes, just crawl up the hills," explained property-rights leader James Clark. The district attorney's office, acting then as both smog cop and public guardian, had advised the Altadenans to relax; the "obnoxious fumes" had mainly a psychological effect. Clark, responding cleverly, invited the D.A. to travel there, then, to "get (his) lungs full of psychology."[11]

Curmudgeons notwithstanding, there was no wide clamoring for hearings or action. Los Angeles' middle class was still sanguine about the future in 1946. One denizen, expressing the popular sentiment, believed that the same "capable leadership and patriotic endeavor" marshaled against the Axis in World War II would defeat this new "common enemy."[12] Good Samaritans offered their assistance against the foe. Earnest requests for fresh air swept around as well, including a petition from thirty Pasadena City College students displeased that they were inhaling dark particles in their gym class. Publicity-chasers eagerly pawed at their opportunity. One young couple relayed a heartwarming story about how they were protecting their newborn by taking him up above the grime in their private plane. Right behind them was a pair of British and Dutch aviators on a cross-country tour. They claimed they could barely see where to land. Once they had, they evidently found a phone to call the *Times*.[13]

Nobody had to communicate the fact that the root cause of the gray air was proving harder to pin down than first imagined. Public engineers, having exonerated the butadiene plant after smog wafted even when the facility went offline, subsequently veered in another direction. Their focus was still enforcement, not chasing theories. One doozy had emanated from the president of the American Institute of Chemists, Gustav Egloff, who speculated that the improper combustion of gasoline-related products might be causing the mist.[14] Ignoring that possibility, the engineers charged that oil refineries and smelters in a lunchpail industrial grid south of L.A. city limits were responsible for the bulk of the "the fumes epidemic." Harry Kunkel, the city's wrinkled "air pollution control" chief (before there was much control), reckoned his men were onto something. The vapors there had already overcome twenty-three truckers, which didn't seem to be a coincidence. When Kunkel, a former World War I military pilot, inspected a nearby Long Beach foundry, the bleachy stench reminded him of French battlefield gases. Following his instinct, he bailed out of there fast.

Kunkel stayed on at his job past retirement to attack the mystifying crud.[15] His office, in fact, rolled out the planet's first "smogometer," a machine that extracted foreign-matter from the air. Dandy sounding, it was barely useful, as was the case with most analytical instruments of the era. Kunkel's meatiest contribution was putting his office's manpower into the effort.[16] The Los Angeles Police Department chipped in with recruits itself, and Bowron asked the 200 chemists in the Civilian

Defense Corps to help, too. In one sense, officials were militarizing the offensive by assigning so many tangential people to it. The head of the school district even said students would join the effort.[17] The D.A.'s office also sought aerial reconnaissance, and secured it by commissioning a squadron of private pilots to scout and report smoking chimneys and burning dumps. For all that, what leaders really desired was rulebook authority. Among other suspicions, they believed military contractors were hiding behind the war to skirt blame for their emissions.[18]

There were just so many complexities, in particular the apprehension the fumebank stirred with its relentless drift toward the suburbs. Like a damaging high tide, it rolled in and ebbed out, leaving some communities unscarred, others regularly abused. Citizens living downwind of the smokestack towers a half-county to the north and east often felt clobbered by them. In Azusa, a rural, hillside city northeast of downtown, severe air had already prompted two small evacuations by 1946. Bedroom towns in and around the foothills of the San Gabriel Mountains were so alarmed about the creepy tendrils that they pointedly told the L.A. politicians to either discipline their industries or brace for a "relentless" backlash.[19] Seeking consensus, county supervisors organized a meeting with twenty-six cities in the spring of 1946 about a uniform anti-air-pollution law. Nothing concrete emerged, and in October, hundreds of "aroused" Pasadenans held a protest march. It wasn't a full-scale uprising, but the message from the suburbs was powerful: united they stood, wheezing they'd fall. L.A. authorities immediately sent out the message after the demonstration. Vernon, South Gate, Torrance, and El Segundo—nondescript manufacturing cities that had flouted cleanup calls for their refineries and steel mills like defiant teenagers—were polluting on borrowed time.[20]

Southern California, so it seemed, still trusted that a crackdown was all that was required to make the weather pleasant again. Experts trekked in to furnish advice: Dr. Edward Weidlein, head of Pittsburgh's Mellon Institute, came, as did members from the U.S. Bureau of Mines. They were of little help. Still, most people thought that L.A. had time to spare, assuming that "get-tough" policies and engineering breakthroughs would purify the airshed. For now, it was just periodic misery, neither metereological curse nor foreshadowing of unhappy days ahead.[21] In a way, it was understandable. Los Angeles had rearranged nature in the past, so why not again?

Consider how it imported a natural resource to its parched terrain. In 1898, then-mayor Frederick Eaton realized his city had nowhere near the water it'd need to prosper, and appointed his buddy William Mulholland as superintendent of the just-formed Los Angeles Department of Water & Power to handle the predicament. The two men spotted the liquidity they needed a couple hundred miles north in the Owens Valley area, where runoff from the Sierra Nevada Mountains was abundant. Eaton lobbied President Teddy Roosevelt to halt a federal irrigation system for farmers there, while the cagey Mulholland, doling out bribes and misinformation, won the water rights needed for an aqueduct. The channel was as complex to design as the Panama Canal, and it certainly was historic. When workers completed it in 1913, the aqueduct expedited the city's annexation of the rural San Fernando Valley and other development ambitions. Los Angeles grabbed so much water that Owens Valley felt betrayed. In 1924, armed farmers from that area dynamited part of the system to register their fury. Strained relations between the two areas persist to this day. Nonetheless, Mulholland said of the water pouring from his engineering feat, "There it is. Take it." He had demonstrated that a city could bend nature to meet its demands. Before and after this water-grab, men here dredged massive harbors from silt, dragged a cosmos-searching observatory onto a mountaintop, smashed flight-speed records, and harnessed ocean currents for electricity.[22] A near-religious devotion to technology had made Southern California's nature seem malleable.

*   *   *

From the late 1930s on, Los Angeles had been riding a hot streak almost unprecedented for American cities. It hadn't been an overnight success. Explorer Gaspar de Portola claimed the city and environs for the Spanish Empire in 1781 when Los Angeles was just a sleepy spot for cattle ranching. After earning its independence from Spain in 1821, Mexico hung on to the dusty province until the U.S. Army captured "Alta California" in 1846. Development-wise, though, it was still siesta-time for L.A.; Northern California's gold rush monopolized the excitement. It was the Southern Pacific and the Santa Fe railroads that recognized the astonishing promise others had missed, building lines that precipitated a land boom in Los Angeles. When that land-acquisition waned, the discovery of oil deposits in 1890 lured a second wave of settlers and investors. One group of them hailed from the New York City movie industry. Enthralled by the cheap land and dry weather ideal for year-round shooting, they packed their Kodak cameras and makeup bags and plowed west like so many other dreamers.

Between the arrival of the first transcontinental railroad lines and the appearance of D.W. Griffith and Cecil B. DeMille, the region's dry, crystal-clean air became its unofficial billboard. Soon it'd be a cottage industry, a franchise of sorts. Marketers peddled Southern California as a haven where spirits weakened by asthma, bronchitis, tuberculosis, and alcoholism would regain their strength. Health sanitariums popped up in Sierra Madre and northern San Diego County, in Riverside and Palm Springs. Famous drunks and the hopelessly sick supposedly became their old selves here. Fairytale-castle vacation resorts then seduced millionaire East Coast guests with advertisements about sun-splashed bliss. They rhapsodized that the balmy weather and shoreline-to-alpine landscape reminded them of lower Spain, even Greece. Writers, advertising men, and the miraculously recovered picked up where the travelers left off, praising the land as if it were a mythical concoction.[23] These believers evidently skipped the diary of Spanish explorer Juan Rodriguez Cabrillo, who sailed into what is now San Pedro Harbor in 1542. Watching Indian fires darken the sky, Cabrillo had a name for the inlet—*la Bahia de las Fumas* (the Bay of Smokes).

Centuries later, nothing would transform Los Angeles from a middling city with potential to a regional behemoth like global combat. With a federal-money pipeline for warplanes and other weapons well trenched, hundreds of thousands of people from the Midwest and the South ventured here. New companies and corporate branches hotfooted in. Diversification soon flexed with textile, tire, and furniture factories. By 1949, the L.A. economy hauled in more fish than Boston, produced more cars than anyplace outside Detroit, all the while constructing 240,000 new homes and apartments in a four-year development geyser.[24]

This wellspring of investment sprinkled magic on the Pacific Coast. Trend-watchers predicted that with America's westward tilt, California would "radically influence the pat-

tern of American life as a whole" with its modern, freewheeling style.[25] As one outsider enthused:

> Even on his first, casual, hundred-mile drive, the pilgrim
> achieves a kind of stunned tranquility, and gazes unblink-
> ingly at palace-studded mountains, rat-proofed palms, and
> supermarkets as big (as hangers for Air Force bombers). All
> this has given the lie to the starched double-doubters who
> cried that Los Angeles was a gaudy but impractical con-
> traption which would inevitably collapse, trapping swarms
> of blondes and bare-toed yogis in its wreckage . . . Los Angeles
> has its own brand of magnificence. It is amazingly clean,
> awesomely spacious. It has ramshackle houses, but in com-
> parison with other big cities, no slums. Its great boulevards
> wind through miles of windblown trees, bright flowers and
> sweeping, emerald-green lawns.[26]

America caught the West Coast bug. Southern California,
long a magnet for the restless and repressed, would soon con-
tain a population larger than Montana, Idaho, New Mexico,
Utah, Colorado, and Nevada *combined*. People were here for
the jobs, here for their slice of the dream, and natural beauty
gilded connections between the two. The Mediterranean climate churned out mild winters, low humidity, and long
"Indian" summers promoting outdoor life so convincingly, in
fact, that many newcomers seemed to overlook the fact that
they'd moved into earthquake country.

The eclectic topography further enhanced the feeling of
magnificence. Moving west to east, the counties seamed
together California's long shoreline with flatlands, foothills,
and desert. To the north was agricultural Ventura; swampy
Long Beach sat roughly one hundred miles to the south. The
coastal plain, extending from Long Beach up to Malibu, gently
transitioned easterly into two enormous floorbeds side by side

in the San Fernando and the San Gabriel valleys. Rimming them to the north like a headboard were the brown-flecked San Gabriel and San Bernardino mountain ranges, which rippled east to west. (Behind them lied the sandy desolation of the Mojave high desert.) South of all that, near Palm Springs, were the San Jacinto Mountains. Gazing down from space, you'd notice that this mountainous contour formed a splendid bowl conducive, unluckily as it would turn out, to unmoving air. Not surprisingly, this landscape hosted a zoological grab-bag of wondrous varmints: the Western toad, the Monarch butterfly, coyotes, bears. Around the animals, the fertile land grew practically anything, especially juicy citrus and leafy vegetables. Variegated trees and flowers such as Coastal live oak, Torrey Pine, wild hyacinths, blue elderberries, and even wisteria sprouted thick and strong, to say nothing of the trademark palm tree that'd one day line the area's swankiest boulevards.

All the Ivy League intellectuals and civic bosses of rival cities could muster in response was disparagement of Angelenos as a collection of boorish philistines. Favorably for these critics, smog served up reams of material twenty years before Johnny Carson roasted it in his nightly *Tonight Show* monologue. By pointing to the skies, they burst the L.A. balloon. Harvard sociologist Carle Zimmerman opined about a "completely lost" populace unable to rescue itself.[27] The *St. Louis' Globe-Democrat* gleefully inferred that air pollution was Los Angeles paying the piper for its whirlwind growth and Sunset Strip vanity. "Angelenos can't see their own mothers across the street" courtesy of air pollution, yet no one worries about darkness because of so many klieg lights advertising hot-dog stands and plumbing-supply houses. Locals, the *Globe* added, resisted discussing smog with outsiders, because they'd deluded themselves it would lift.[28] As much as the stereotypes infuriated L.A.'s Establishment, the *Globe's* needling was a tipping point. A month after the Globe's jab, *Times* publisher Norman Chandler assigned veteran reporter Ed Ainsworth to write an air pollution series as a "public service."[29]

Unmentioned in the series was how the landowning *Times* was servicing its own economic interests along with those of the hoi polloi, and it was just as well. Chandler, son of the walrus-mustached ex-colonel who'd founded the paper, resembled an aging lifeguard with his strong build and copper skin. More genteel than his empire-minded father, he might've been the most influential person atop the banish-smog bandwagon. There weren't many patriarchal options. Southern California was an amorphous confederation of cities and interests devoid of *Rockefellerian*-institutions or clubby machine politics. "No one can force anybody down anybody else's throat," Chandler liked saying.[30] Dubious as his premise was in a town where entities like the California Bank and the Merchants and Manufacturers Association called many shots, there was a transcendent truth to decentralized power—and an obvious downside to it. There was no central leader, no formidable bureaucracy. The *Times*, as the loudest voice around, was one of the world's first environmental soliders, and Chandler was its General Patton.

Over the next months, the perceptive Ainsworth chaperoned readers through trash heaps, refinery boilers, chemical factories, and every other operation unofficially indicted for the scourge. "For years now," Ainsworth began, "the sun has been something of a mystery." To him, governmental unaccountability, "fumbling," and duplicative efforts had been busts. They'd achieved as much as "punching a smoke cloud with bare fists." Without a countywide law, he said forget about success. Part muckraking journalism, part educational text,

Ainsworth introduced the area's residents to chemistry-lab nomenclature they'd eventually learn like street names. As the series became popular, the paper invited readers to send the identities and addresses of polluters to the *Times'* "smog editor." By today's standards, it was patchy reporting but ripping-good entertainment. Ainsworth described how I.A. Deutch, the man recruited from smoky Chicago to lead the county's Air Pollution Control Department, ran his fanny off looking for clues and culprits in a "Sherlock Holmes Atmosphere." Ainsworth noted the bombshell working next to Deutch in a crowded little office as they chased the trail of what Ainsworth nicknamed "Algy Aldehyde," an obscure compound believed to make eyes water. He told how Deutch's subordinates had to conceal jars measuring fine particles because naughty, young boys liked chucking rocks at them, and about the clampdown on diesel trucks he described as "lumbering monsters of the highway." His stories signed off like serialized movie potboilers, where the screen fades to black as the detective closes in on the killer: *"To be continued."*[31]

Los Angeles' oil industry was smart enough to realize all this activity would train the crosshairs on it. A mélange of ferociously competitive petroleum giants, wildcatters, and independents, the sector embraced an early strategy to preserve this lucrative market: stay informed.[32] It was no accident that the chairman of the Western Oil & Gas Association, a pivotal trade group, also quarterbacked the chamber of commerce's smoke and fumes" commission, where he heard ear-loads about dangerous hydrogen sulfide and skunk gases. The D.A., in a blast at these manufacturers, filed thirteen smoke-abatement lawsuits, including two against well-known outfits—Standard Oil's coastal refinery and Vernon's Bethlehem Steel Corporation.[33] As word about the industrial crackdown spread, distant politicians hoping to save the day flung in unsolicited suggestions. Some of them were obvious long shots. Senator Joseph McCarthy (R-Wisconsin), future commie-hunter and then head of the Senate's War Assets Investigating Committee, encouraged the county to relocate its entire chemical industry from its vaporous climes to the open arms of Henderson, Nevada. He believed Nevada's cheap land and vacant plants could free L.A. of its albatross.[34] No one took McCarthy up on it. Petroleum executives maintained their guard.

In December 1946, with the crud striking again and weird reports coming in about pollution-gnawed crops and forests, reinforcements hit town. No, not the Feds, nor the state; neither of them had much substance to offer. The *Times* had coaxed St. Louis professor and mechanical engineer Raymond Tucker to L.A. for an analytical examination about why the problem was occurring and what would reverse it. St. Louis residents in the 1920s and 1930s had wheezed dirty, carbon-thick air until the city's politicians appointed Tucker smoke commissioner. With the help of both the local newspaper and smokeless coal, he'd returned easy breathing to the Midwestern town. To the *Times* he looked like a battle-tested gem.

Tucker's report, prepared after a feverish two-week visit, keenly, if not originally, connected the manufacturing jetsam with L.A.'s warm, stagnant weather patterns. Industrial operations that had nearly doubled during the previous five years, he noted, had unloosed a fearsome foursome of smoke, dust, fumes, and odors originating from smokestacks, cooling ponds, boilers, and storage tanks in the industrial zone. Couple this with a population explosion—the county ballooned from 900,000 people to 3.7 million just in the pre-war days— and it was little wonder the Mediterranean-like climate had turned traitorous. The professor had seen the enemy, and it was the undiscouraged cascade of companies producing oil, lumber, food, soap, paints, and warplanes migrating here, along with smoldering dumps and smelly locomotives already around. Against this prosperity, Tucker singled out sulfur and its chemical cousins as the top concerns. Marginal amounts of floating compounds found mostly at morgues and metal-finishers were secondary worries.[35] Car and truck exhaust also were minor accomplices, as L.A. vehicle traffic actually had declined between 1941 and 1944. "Although it is quite possible that the automobile does contribute to the nuisance," Tucker explained, "it is not in such proportion that it is the sole cause."[36] Had Tucker dug deeper, correlating smog with the demise of Southern California's rail system in what was already America's car capital, he might've more emphasized the role of the automobile. Yet with Los Angeles' thirst for unequivocal answers, he never did, and this diluted his otherwise pioneering legacy.

The media publicized the professor's findings with front-page fanfare normally reserved for assassinations or post-war parades. If you want sapphire skies again, the Missourian lectured, it required a tough-love regimen extending from factory equipment to the private household. It meant a prohibition on backyard trash burning and a chemical audit of every smokestack. It meant resisting the temptation to heap blame on any one industry when they were all complicit to fluctuating degrees. Tucker's doctrine would become environmental dogma for sixty-plus years. *"Any air pollution program,"* his report said, *"must attack the nuisance at its source. The atmosphere cannot be controlled but the discharge of contaminants into the air can be."*[37] The flaw in Tucker's manifesto was its presumption about corporate behavior: that large outfits geared for efficiency would alter their production methods in the absence of compelling evidence they were at fault. His other error was in failing to persuade area leaders to enlist crackerjack scientists to analyze the interactions of the contaminants already identified. If they were incapable of inflicting such eye-watering, view-blocking harm, shouldn't that mean a return to the drawing board?

Helpful as that recommendation might've been, civic back-slapping over the professor's wisdom is what filled the public square. County supervisors tripped over themselves lauding him and the *Times*. Pasadena assemblyman A.I. Stewart fed the cheerfulness with his discovery of a loophole in the state code freeing manufacturers and dumps to emit any amount of smoke or fumes they deemed "reasonable."[38] Even before Tucker's report was printed, Stewart had introduced the aptly numbered Assembly Bill No. 1 to create a countywide smoke-abatement district vested with police powers under the state constitution. Industry hackles rose swiftly. Farmers wanted exemptions for their crop-warming smudge pots. The railroads fulminated that new regulations would bog down interstate commerce. Oil and power interests complained about having to seek permits every time they expanded or fine-tuned their equipment. The headstrong were everywhere.

It wasn't only business that Stewart was confronting, either. For generations, the county's patchwork cities had coexisted under the tacit canon of "home rule." Essentially a gentleman's agreement, it stipulated that proposed state laws of major consequence had to receive the blessing of the individual communities they'd affect pre-submission—and there hadn't been united agreement for Stewart's legislation. Mayor Bowron, in particular, had stewed over it precisely because cities would have no policy voice; it'd be the county supervisors in charge of the new district.[39] Still, Tucker had shown the way out. Police every source no matter how miniscule, and do it with arms linked.

*   *   *

As Southern California debated how to establish a pollution district without halting its salad days, gruesome accidents caused by blinding street conditions took many to early graves. There'd been causalities of spirit, and now there were causalities of the flesh. On January 24, 1947, for instance, two young people died in separate accidents when the motorcycles they were riding on collided with automobiles in the midst of a disorienting smog/fog whiteout. Another man unable to navigate it perished when he slammed his automobile into a Red Car trolley.[40] A wholly different image of L.A.—formerly modern dreamland, now emerging dystopia—began to crystallize.

Unease about community health percolated alongside these consequences. Troubled parents and hypochondriacs wanted guarantees that the awful way they felt did not signal disease or chronic illness ahead. Physicians curious about the effect of unleashed gases on industrializing cities, meanwhile, recognized the unique test case at their doorstep. Most of them were troubled. An army germ-warfare doctor glum about air quality and slum housing foresaw Los Angeles overrun by rheumatic fever. Dr. Bernice Wedum, a specialist for that disease, followed up by announcing that neither she nor her colleagues would continue shipping their patients to L.A. to recover. "Your smog," she chastised, "[is a] serious public health matter."[41] It was a gutsy stand to take. In those days, medical stories about the short and long-term effects of breathing L.A. air frequently carried a jocular tone that neutralized many residents' innate fears. One story in particular was a pop-culture kneeslapper, even if the city's boosters, some of them demeaned as "sunshine-sellers," wished it'd never appeared. A transplanted East Coast man, it seems, had approached his L.A. doctor with an atypical medical dilemma. He said he needed a new glass eye to match his remaining real one, because pollution rendered it bloodshot so often. The *Associated Press* ran the story of the one-eyed man around the world.[42] Besides feeling mocked, state health officials realized something from this anecdote: they had better start making plans about how to study what biological harm smog portended, because the knowledge gap was immense.

Dr. George Kress, chairman of the Los Angeles County Medical Association's air pollution panel, was one of the first local physicians to trumpet anti-smog convictions. For the severely ill and the elderly, Kress said, heavy air pollution might be a fatal catalyst, since it appeared to restrict oxygen in the blood stream. If you had TB or asthma or heart problems, an approaching smog attack was a prudent time to book a trip. He called the stuff a "disease breeder."[43] A group of "militant mothers" from South Central L.A. voiced their own misgivings, begging for environmental justice decades before activists would create that concept. They wanted the smog exiled, and the burning dumps—riddled with hospital waste, ash, rotting tires, and rats—shuttered. They were saddling their kids with never-ending colds and infections. The mothers estimated that 300,000 disenfranchised people like them were suffering as a result of reckless garbage policies. These were under review, thanks to smog, but the mothers wanted action now. When one group of them met at a local school to discuss it, a miasma of smog and trash fumes made them throw hankies over their mouths.[44] All around the county, parents were noticing their children gasp, lose sleep, and struggle to focus at school. Bundles of letters about it began clogging politicians' mailboxes.

If L.A.'s upturned weather had set it apart from the rest of the country before, it was now becoming *literally* isolated. General and civil aviation might've been the first profession systematically handcuffed by air pollution's infiltration.[45] In February 1947, a Palm Springs beauty pageant teetered into a roll-call contest when only ten of thirty contestants boarded flights able to pierce the sub-climate. Pilots landing at the future Los Angeles International Airport could sympathize. They had to bone up, and fast, on instrument navigation, because poor visibility often enveloped the runways until the planes were just above them. One young pilot unable to locate the airstrip was fortunate to find a "hole in the smog" to make an emergency landing around the slack-jawed sunbathers at Santa Monica Beach; years later, a bewildered aviator put down on a strip of future freeway in Pomona.[46] By the late 1940s, the fumebank clung so regularly that the federal government agreed to permit mail-ferrying helicopters in the L.A. Basin to fly by instruments. Aviation became downright unfriendly. Even the skywriting companies got no pass. Authorities falsely accused them of further junking the air with their vaporized-oil letters. Once episodic, smog was grounding more planes than ever before.[47]

Perhaps the most damaging blows to L.A.'s image were the bitter farewell letters by relocating citizens published in newspaper letters' sections and elsewhere. Why? Because, the pot-shots were a harbinger that something profoundly askew *was* afoot, that Los Angeles wasn't just a bobby-soxing, house-building orgy immune from cyclonic bust. "Better the snows of Iowa than the smogs of Los Angeles," one retiree wrote. Denver was frigid, but at least it was unpolluted, huffed another. The chairman of New York's largest bank groused he'd had to abandon his normal winter vacation spot in L.A. to salvage his wife's inflamed throat.[48] Meantime, a La Jolla man and his wife said they'd fled L.A. after fifty-eight years "with pity in our hearts for all the poor souls who have to live and take it."[49] Some homeowners who stuck around fed off this dissent, which cloned more of it. "You may not relish being referred back to your first year chemistry," one Pasadenan wrote to his city hall. "But maybe all of us, including the $20,000 expert, should clean house by starting to think all over again."[50]

Whatever their qualms were over smog's future, local politicians were hip deep in them. They were unsure of how a control agency would operate, let alone how disruptive it'd be to civic personalities. The surliest gadfly continued to be the mayor of Los Angeles himself, still apoplectic that the epidemic was occurring on his watch. Bowron was incensed that eighty percent of the floating garbage originated outside of Los Angeles in small industry towns he could not control. Had the governments of those towns been as aggressive as L.A. City Hall, Bowron said, "Our smog problem would be pretty well licked by now."[51]

Up in Sacramento, the state capital, wrangling over Stewart's bill was bare-knuckle politics. County counsel Harold Kennedy traveled there with William Jeffers—a rough-hewn ex-railroad executive now heading the Los Angeles Citizens Smog Committee chartered by the *Times*—to help blunt opposition. Leading it were the oil companies, which angled for escape-clause language that would allow them to continue emitting what they wanted.[52] Two events immediately went against them: the sudden appearance of a new, scalding smog, and Kennedy's unwillingness to cater to special interests. They had assumed that Kennedy, far from the standard staid bureaucrat, would be sympathetic to their objections, and their assumption was wrong. Kennedy and Stewart, in fact, snitched to the *Times* about industry machinations. Out came an editorial asking if corporate wealth justified "the oppressive clouds of smoke and fumes?" The *Pasadena Star-News* sermonized as well, predicting to its fidgety readership that the loopholes would make Stewart's bill flaccid.

Feeling the heat from that obstructionist tag, executives from the major West Coast oil companies—Standard, Richfield, Union, Texaco, and General Petroleum—gathered in the old Richfield Oil Building in downtown Los Angeles to mull over their choices. A Union Oil executive told his peers that he saw wisdom in retreat: thwarting steps against a potential health crisis, he said, was bad business and unjust. With Kennedy and Jeffers in the room, and hundreds of millions of dollars in equipment and future revenue on the line, the mood flashed with tension. Following some "frank" (read: contentious) discussion, the oilmen held a roll-call vote and it wasn't close. The companies would allow Stewart's legislation to pass. They risked appearing as heavy-handed profiteers if they did otherwise.[53] Soon, Chamber honks, the California League of Cities, the California Fruit Grower's Exchange, and even the Automobile Club of Southern California were all endorsing the legislation.

On June 10, 1947, Governor Earl Warren, future chief justice of the U.S. Supreme Court, signed into law America's first unified smog agency. An area catapulted by seemingly interwoven advantages—brilliant weather and unbridled development—simultaneously celebrated and held its nose as the Los Angeles County Air Pollution Control District was born. "This has been," exuded Jeffers, "the most amazing campaign I've ever seen."[54]

Given the dearth of expertise on the issue, there was little surprise that the county cherry-picked a military man to run the new district for an $11,000/year salary (about $102,000 in 2007 dollars). Louis McCabe, of Graphic, Arkansas, had had quite a career, first as an engineer and U.S. Army standout, and then as a fuels expert with the U.S. Bureau of Mines. When he stepped off the Union Pacific train to Los Angeles, however, he alighted into crummy breathing. "There," someone told him, "is your job."[55] McCabe said all the right things—he'd seek industry's cooperation "rather than waving a big stick" at them—to all the right crowds. He had a forty-seven-person staff, a then-$178,000-budget, and high expectations of figuring out how such wildly disparate compounds became such a menace.[56] The balding, bespectacled McCabe enjoyed his brief honeymoon period. His cute, four-year-old daughter, who'd been scared that her new city was lightless, drew "aws" when she boasted on a clear day that her daddy "must have been doing a good job."[57] Reinforcements were arriving for him—nominally, anyway. At the Los Angeles Police Department Academy, buzz-cut recruits learned how to detect smoke violations using the visibility-measuring "Ringelmann chart," a French-developed diagram that gauged the opacity of smoke emissions by matching their color with shaded illustrations spanning from gray to black on the light spectrum. It was the L.A. smog-fighter's equivalent of a Geiger counter. Thirty black-and-white, *Dragnet*-style "patrol cars" also bolstered McCabe's new legion. All the major local universities were rushing into research projects, as well, and in some cases product pitching. USC promoted an $18,000 "blink-reflex" apparatus—think clunky welder's helmet—to observe people's reactions to unpleasant materials.[58]

The *Times* tried insulating McCabe from the start, realizing his rules soon would ruffle companies unaccustomed to stiff regulation. His job, the paper editorialized, was a "thankless, unspectacular task" unlikely to have a storybook ending.[59] Actually, there'd be no ending. During the next decade, assigning or ducking responsibility for the pervading wisps would rival the NFL's newly arrived Rams as Los Angeles' next contact sport—a ferocious, hard-hitting brand of politics that let nobody out of bounds.

The APCD's most wanted emissions were sulfur compounds, and the oil-burning industries and other plants that generated them were its primary targets. McCabe, invoking his "fair but strict" credo, yanked the permit of a noncompliant South Bay steel plant in January 1948 to underscore it. Pollution officials attentive to the coming backlash reminded people that their rules had not yet knocked a single company out of business. The argument wouldn't hold. McCabe secondarily wanted municipal trash burning stopped, and the district attorney made it official by announcing that all public-dump burning would end on or before July 1. Opposing city fire chiefs, concerned about increased fire hazards, asked who this guy thought he was? So did some city governments confused over what they could do with their trash except bury it in covered trenches. Whittier, a smallish community southeast of Pasadena, threatened to secede from Los Angeles County and join neighboring Orange County over the order. After tempers receded—County Supervisor Raymond Darby called Whittier's threat "childish nonsense"—the breakaway talk ended.[60]

McCabe plucked the other low hanging fruit that he could. He hired a weatherman and printed 50,000 "What the County Is Doing about Smog" leaflets. He doled out consulting gigs to brainy, accomplished men, such as former Caltech professor Arnold Beckman and Morris Neiburger of UCLA. He arranged specialized hearing boards for railroads and diesel trucks cited for violations. He gave the volunteer

"Flying Vigilantes" a more militarized name as they continued their sorties: the "Smog Aerial Observation Corps."
County supervisors then gave him the regulatory sinew he'd
sought, requiring that any entity installing or operating
smog-producing machinery worth more than $300 file for a
permit first.[61]

The soapbox was one thing for McCabe, the brass tacks of
policing block-long plants quite another. At a closed-door
meeting with thirty of the region's top industrialists before
McCabe's office chair was warm, executives sought from him a
rulemaking timeout. Refiners, in particular, wanted relaxation
on sulfur capping. An APCD regulation stipulating that smokestacks not belch emissions with more than 0.2% sulfur by volume was too Draconian—they wanted it at 0.35, or 0.3 at the
worst. Think about the consumer, they said. Burning the kind
of low-grade oil the APCD recommended was so prone to problems that higher consumer electricity bills were good as
mailed. McCabe acted unfazed. It disconcerted him that every
sector except oil had begun slashing its smoke and fumes. In
his engineering mind, petroleum-burning industries discharging sulfur dioxide made the Southland vulnerable to a lethal
smog episode. Everything else was "minor."[62] For the Western
Oil & Gas Association, these were fighting words. It asked
McCabe whether he realized its members "were merchants of
fuel" for thousands of square miles and could only curb effluents within "reasonable tolerances"? Besides, where was the
substantiation that they were responsible?[63]

Rather than cower, McCabe advanced. He boldly relocated
the APCD into the heart of the suspected smog-production
dungeon on Santa Fe Avenue in Vernon— a move tantamount
to the FBI moving in next door to the mob. The new headquarters featured a lab, a dark room, an engineering office, and

momentum. No self-perpetuating bureaucracy here, McCabe told a Chamber group nervous about overkill. "The problem will be eradicated within two-three years."

As his confidence demonstrated, it's vital here not to confuse the fumes' jarring entrance with a metropolis biting its nails over it. Regard it more as nail polishing. The movie capital of the planet was nothing if not image-obsessed, so opportunistic entrepreneurs and beauty watchers had no difficulty commoditizing hokey anti-smog products. These goods illuminated a wing-it-style commercialism with a subconscious current: things *would* return to normal, so look your best until they do. Even before the lab whizzes appreciated what they were up against, chatty columnists recommended that ladies ward off the effects of swollen smog-face with eye-relief pads soaked with lotion or witch hazel.[64] A gal who ignored this advice reportedly contracted a painful coating on her eyeballs. "Girls," one beauty diva asked, "how often do you look in the mirror after a hectic day in the secretary pool or the supermarket to see puffy, inflamed peepers gazing back at you?"[65]

Not exactly the sound of a metropolitan juggernaut quivering about its future, is it? Los Angeles for years had been a city seeking identity, a region in flux. Now it juggled two personalities at the same time: a sunny, hopeful boomtown, and a dire, gritty Smogtown.

PARADISE OBSCURED

2

BY DISAPPEARING FOR PERIODS, AND THEN SWOOPING DOWN AND returning at will, smog—the unsolved phenomenon—was jamming a subplot into Los Angeles' postwar story. Excitement about ranch house-filled subdivisions and blueprints for Buck Rogers-style freeway interchanges had to cohabitate with days of blotted sunshine. Rival cities envious of Southern California's luster—towns like St. Louis and Boston—took delight at this contradiction, wallowing in *schadenfreude* over the grit regularly swallowing L.A. during the late 1940s. The real dilemma for the still-confident town was that no one could explain the phenomenon credibly, let alone solve it, at a time when the American way bubbled over with technical breakthroughs, be they radar, polymers, antibiotics, or atom splitting. Since people needed to latch onto something, amateurs' theories, left-field speculation, and periodic hysteria poured into the explanatory void. The resulting intellectual tumult socked government with even more pressure, with Louis McCabe's reign— at this point brief, and already reaching its end—reflecting a man cognizant of how society, like nature, detests a vacuum.

As McCabe's successors would learn, goodwill about fresh leadership on the smog front had a way of curdling into community distrust over why the nitwit hadn't yet found a remedy.

It was a hard sell begging for patience while the expertise accumulated when thousands were hacking and sniffing for days on end. Polluted Los Angeles was a histamine nation. In previous times, the Establishment had been able to ride out the attacks, because conditions had always snapped back to sunny normalcy. This was the case in 1903, when a daytime haze forced downtown streetlights on in a scene some citizens mistook for an unanticipated solar eclipse.[1] Half a century later, it was a different milieu. Astronomers' unsettling assertion that smog-associated dust and gases had ventured into space, even reports about foul air plaguing other urban centers, carried little currency with the locals. So up stood Conrad Hilton, president of the eponymous hotel chain, to give notice that the topsy-turvy climate had sliced hotel occupancy in half.[2] Up rose the bereaved widow asking why her husband died abruptly. The nuisance was dawning into crisis, a crisis of the unexplained. Emblematic of the transition was a paranoid feud between the reserved McCabe and an obstinate gentleman from Pasadena. By the 1950s turmoil, their dealings seemed prosaic.

Where McCabe's newly minted agency saw glimmers of progress, George L. Schuler saw a smokestack-scalded atmosphere where the fix was in. Schuler, an ex-Pasadena city councilman and mechanical engineer who'd conducted his own two-year study of the situation, bombarded officials with his handwritten ravings. "Dust mop, sky writing and smudge pot propaganda is just making conversation," he wrote. "The real offender in the smog nuisance is the sulfur burning refineries."[3] Schuler was sure that kyboshing sulfur emissions would end the scourge. Let it continue, he said, and plow new graveyards. Sulfur poisoning, he asserted, had easily doubled fatal heart attacks in Pasadena from 1939 to 1948 as part of the 10,000 people he purported area smog had killed. When Schuler compiled the dead, he counted six neighbors on his own street, as well as some unexplained murders and suicides, three young prizefighters, and several racehorses. "We cannot sit by like children and allow Dr. McCabe and the oil industry to set maximums which are ruining the health and shortening the lives of millions of people," he wrote. "We have reached the end of this buck-passing, fence-straddling and dereliction of duty by public officials." He threatened to mail incriminating evidence to the newspapers unless he got action.[4] Schuler caused such a fuss that McCabe had to pen a calming letter to Pasadena's city council explaining that L.A.'s ground-level sulfur compounds were one-third of Pittsburgh's and just half that of Chicago's. McCabe even invited Schuler down to the lab for a tour, probably because Schuler knew enough to terrify his community without truly comprehending the subtleties of the danger.[5] Their indirect back-and-forth over deadly gases appeared to have subsided by the spring of 1948. It was just as well, since McCabe had other George Schulers to try to neutralize.

McCabe's primary mission was bigger picture, and by the fall of 1948, his cleanup campaign had edged into a more aggressive posture. His Flying Vigilantes described how white, feathery plumes at daybreak near the refineries interlaced and darkened into a monolithic cloudbank that digested the landscape on a northwestern bearing by mid-morning. The major oil companies disliked the attention engulfing them, retaining a highfalutin' scientific think tank to conduct experiments to help determine what was responsible for the beastly air. If it were only a biased nonprofit dogging him, McCabe might not have felt like pulled taffy. Yet, he knew he needed the manufacturers' cooperation, and they were raging in open memos and at private gatherings that he was crucifying them. Citizen leaders caterwauled about flimsy progress. Wedged between polarized sides, he kept remarkable sangfroid.[6]

Just as Congress launched its prosecution of the "Hollywood Ten" for invoking the Fifth Amendment over their communist affiliations, McCabe gambled on several "frank" closed-doors dialogues with his adversaries. At a posh downtown club, where petroleum executives vented about feeling like prejudged criminals, he reiterated his disinterest in playing policeman out to ticket them. Soon after that failed peace effort, the decisive showdown everyone knew was inevitable unfolded at Pasadena's historic Huntington Hotel, where some of Smogtown's nastiest battles sparkled under exquisite chandeliers. Inside the room, the mood was contentious, each side intransigent. Oil executives, most notably from Richfield Oil and Union Oil, upbraided McCabe for acting despotically by overemphasizing sulfur dioxide without empirical backup from the district's technical wizards. Undaunted, McCabe insisted that the oil companies were "substantial" polluters who needed to scrub as much of the contaminant from their operations as possible. For him, that was the only path to reconciliation. The *Times'* Chandler, in attendance with Caltech president/physicist Robert Millikan to defend the APCD, warned the corporations that the paper would continue its anti-smog coverage without "fear or favor" of its effect on any industry. McCabe, by now receiving tempting out-of-state job offers, had shown up equipped to defend himself, however. He passed around the table embarrassing photographs of refinery smokestacks belching fumes, including a General Petroleum plant that the company claimed was offline. After the meeting, with Big Oil backed into another concessionary corner, McCabe agreed to stay on the job until he bore better news.[7]

For all the millions of words (etched on thousands of felled trees) about L.A.'s quest to distill air pollution's makeup, one parable stands out. It was an allegory about six blind Hindus that appeared in the closeout report of the APCD's predecessor agency. In this amusing metaphor, six sightless men were challenged with describing an elephant based on the part of it the pachyderm they were touching. Not surprisingly, they all extrapolated incorrectly. And so with smog:

> The citizen whose house turns black overnight believes 'smog' to be fumes which react with lead paint," the report noted. "The aviator who has difficulty in landing in the blinding, murky pall that so frequently hangs over the Los Angeles Basin cusses the visibility-reducing manmade components of smog. The resident of the foothill cities who is awakened at three in the morning by offensive garlic-like odors condemns the refinery which spews mercaptans into the atmosphere. The downtown shopper whose eyes burn and tear is bitter against any sources which produce lachrimating substances. . . . Just as the elephant cannot be cleaned by washing his trunk, so will it be impossible to make Los Angeles a desired place where people can live and work in comfort and amenity if (smog) control is limited. . .[8]

Simply put, air pollution impaired one's field of vision. (Smog, it's worth noting here, is a dated slang contraction for "smoke and fog." In low-smoke, seasonally foggy Southern California, people repeated the simple term out of ease and habit, not appreciating that they were mislabeling the trait for which L.A. would become infamous.)

McCabe, aware of the public's confusion, took his case to the people for validation. He repeated in his own "special report" about the imperative to slash sulfur compounds because of their capacity to inflict widespread harm in a toxin-saturated atmosphere. And it was the L.A. oil industry emitting the bulk of the 822 tons of sulfur dioxide per day, his agency charged. Invisible to the eye, heavier than air, oxygen-rich sulfur compounds could transform in sunlight to create a mist abrading everything in its path, he warned. Forms of it even generated light-blocking particles that left behind a surreal blue haze. Evidence scooped by planes, rooftop inspectors, university scientists, and new super-magnifying photography corroborated his belief.

Compelled to prioritize in an increasingly blame-driven environment, McCabe concentrated on sulfur, no matter its relatively low quantitative presence in L.A. and the community's schizophrenic opinions about it. In June 1949, he tapped it "the most important problem."[9] As one scientist recalled, deduction was a reason to fixate on it:

> . . . In Pittsburgh and St. Louis, the air pollution villains were indeed soot and sulfur dioxide. As there was no soot in the Los Angeles area, obviously (then) sulfur dioxide must be the obnoxious pollutant. It was well known . . . that sulfur dioxide does, in fact, cause eye irritation and coughing. . . . So, rightly or wrongly. . . . McCabe set out on a campaign to reduce smoke, fumes and sulfur dioxide.[10]

Climaxing a year of "intensive investigation" by the district, the *Times* editorialized, the truth was "out in the open" about sulfur dioxide's culpability. Comments that the pollution drive had languished, or that McCabe was too timid to confront industry, it said, was defensive malarkey.[11] The firewords, indeed, were just starting. Now that McCabe was rousting the public to view Southern California's multimillion-dollar petroleum production as the barrier to blue skies, Big Oil hit back vigorously with proxy organizations in what would be a much-copied tactic by others. Using the Western Oil & Gas Association as its mouthpiece (and the Stanford Research Institute as its scientists), researchers claimed they found more sulfur dioxide in the skies *before* World War II than at the time of their current research. They added that since 1946, many refiners had already switched from sulfur-bearing fuel oil to natural or refinery gas. Nobody was burning acid sludge anymore, either. Despite those hard facts, the oil association wrote bitterly, "It is obvious to any citizen we still have smog. . . . We doubt whether the real cause of smog has yet been discovered, or that your report charging the petroleum industry as the principal offender is justified by the facts so far presented."[12]

In 1948, the oil barons had no monopoly on pique and confusion wrought by the puzzling fumebank. Superior Court Judge Clarence Hanson was beside himself when smog seeped into his courtroom so thickly that it enveloped the witness stand. With a jokester's timing, in fact, the murk had arrived during a proceeding *over* air pollution; specifically, whether fumes from Whittier's burning dump were slinging grit towards neighboring Monrovia, Azusa, and Glendora.[13] The judge refrained from denouncing the ridiculousness of the situation, and in actuality, he didn't have to. From teeming downtown to shady suburbia, it was obvious that the popular mood was dipping into fitful impatience. Smallish cities and bedroom communities weren't as accepting anymore that the upturned weather was a fleeting pest that would eventually trickle away. *Look* magazine labeled L.A. smog "evil," and it sure felt sinister when it tormented entire neighborhoods for a week at a time like a permanent new weather pattern. L.A. was becoming a town of improvisers, the bad days coming with a protocol, where school kids were hustled indoors and sanitariums kept their windows sealed. Some asthma patients even watched their fingers go blue with a hemoglobin defect. They were just one line of sufferers.

*   *   *

Confirming that smog could care less about city borders, farmers in the mid-1940s began noticing that their crops were perishing as a result of their very surroundings. Weather, as Mark Twain famously observed, was unchangeable. Agriculture was a staple native industry. A nurseryman in Temple City, in the central San Gabriel Valley, witnessed the blotching first— his petunias were sick, silvery, and mottled. Nearby, in South El Monte, a farmer heard so many complaints about his discolored lettuce, endives, and celery that he stopped harvesting them. For others like him, the atmosphere was becoming nothing short of a financial horror.[14] One grower suffered $30,000 in dead crops within twelve hours of the vapors' arrival.[15] His wipeout tale would soon be the common plight for many hoeing what had been one of America's most bountiful agricultural plains. Some weeks it'd lose $250,000 of crops. The Southland's food basket would never fully recover.

Along L.A. County's eastern border, in what is now the ever-expanding Inland Empire, people on Sunday drives would stop their cars to gape at the acreage of droopy, dying produce. The damage, while shocking to soak in, was research fairy dust for plant pathology studies under Dr. John Middleton at the University of Riverside's Citrus Experiment Station. Stippled, desiccated vegetables were his students' cadavers. Over the years, they parlayed their findings into a hallowed subspecialty of how dirty air affected—or revealed—crops' frailties and immunities. Most easily strangled, they ascertained, were spinach, lettuce, and beets, which ailed under a silvery glazing, as well as alfalfa, oats and celery. Onions and turnips fared better in acidy air, with broccoli, cabbage, and carrots the next most resistant, followed by radishes and tomatoes. University researchers suspected that the "delicate mechanism" by which plants absorbed water and nutrients was being impaired on an immense scale, likely because of the permeability of plant tissue.[16] While the iconic Southland orange and other citrus crops were better suited to withstand the corrosive airshed, they wound up being fluky survivors. Thus in 1953, the Orange

County Agricultural Commission concluded what area farmers already knew: smog was as lethal a crop killer as frost.[17]

By 1954, experts estimated the loss to Southland crops at $3 million, to say nothing of the emotional wreckage to multi-generational agricultural families. Around D-day, farmers in the area grew 47,800 acres of vegetables; by the time of John Kennedy's assassination in 1963, three quarters of that acreage had no crops on it. Many growers, perhaps even the last great spinach farmer, eventually gave up, while others tried rearing resistant goods or moving to unspoiled fields to the north and south. Developers later would plow under many of those abandoned tracts, transforming them into subdivisions built at break-neck speed. Talk about your incredible shrinking choices! In less than twenty years, smog would eradicate ten types of vegetables present in L.A. during WWII.[18] The spectrum of locally grown cut flowers—gladiolus, chrysanthemums—withered with them. Take the carnation. Smog made the flower "sleep"— industry euphemism for saying it died before its time.[19]

Air pollution in coming years would fell much bigger targets. In Burbank, it decimated most of the city's pepper trees and many of its Carolina cherries. The loudest mourning, though, was for the Ponderosa Pines, which had stood tall in the San Bernardino National Forest roughly sixty miles from Los Angeles since the area was in Spanish hands. Field reports told of all three million Ponderosas quietly dying. Near the mountain city of Crestline, the pines changed from "evergreen to everbrown," their needles falling out in morbid clumps.[20] There was no calculating that loss.

The souring gestalt was so contagious by the fall of 1948 that you'd be hard-pressed to make it through a whole day without hearing about the browning effects of Southern California's postwar air. Exasperation over it kicked up fervor for independent action if not to replace government's fumes crackdown, then to supplement it. From living rooms and local five-and-dime stores emerged citizen "seeing-and-smelling committees" vowing to make a dent in the problem. Individual cities drew up their own action plans. A place that lived for escapism, if not a Brown Derby steak-and-martini dinner, also knew how to broadcast its pathos in the glitziest manner. During Christmastime, 1948, the *Times* released a documentary film, *Smog*, into the theaters with red-carpet fanfare. Actor Victor Jory narrated it; a hotshot cartoonist named Walt Disney animated it.[21] The film was unquestionably more optimistic than the unflattering ink from out-of-town journalists. Unlike the *Times* and *Examiner*, which salivated to unlock the mystery of pollution's origin, the non-California writers had a different assignment: to narrate the saga of paradise delayed.

Time magazine in the spring of '49 punched the L.A. Establishment in the kisser with it. "AIRBORNE DUMP" said little others already hadn't; it just said it in America's most venerable magazine. *Time*, repeating the lost-luster angle, observed that the City of Angels had replaced its halo with a "hat of dirty grey smoke" where you couldn't even drink coffee blithely: Maxwell House Coffee's $75,000 bean-roaster was a smoke threat.[22] An earlier *Colliers Weekly* piece headlined "THREAT OF DISASTER FROM SMOG HANGING OVER LOS ANGELES" was not as damaging, just more lurid. Comparing Los Angeles' air quality, what with its 800 tons of daily airborne sulfur, to Europe's most lethal smogs, *Colliers* assessed "it could happen here." The embattled Dr. McCabe, it said, had stepped into a "first class whodunit." People were getting sick. Oil was under siege.[23] And nothing changed.

And yet everything had. Smog had ear-flicked the popular

mindset; humorists referencing Horace's Greeley's "Go West" motto might've instead advised youths to "Go indoors!" Moviedom felt it. The subtropical weather that had lured film-makers and actors to Burbank, Studio City, Melrose Avenue, Hollywood Boulevard, and the Fairfax area had gone haywire, and it was costing the region's premiere industry plenty of coin. Directors were now nixing outdoor shoots regularly. When entrepreneurial-minded actors Roy Rodgers and Russell Hayden scouted for a new production center, L.A. smog shunted them to the eastern-deserts' hinterlands. In "Pioneertown," a director could shoot a Western without worrying about the sheriff's coughing jag during a gunfight. One production company had sat idle for three weeks waiting for powdery skies. Hedda Hopper, America's ranking gossip columnist, sympa-thized with the pretty peoples' blues. "Bing (Crosby) didn't complain about the smog, but it had affected him so he looked like he had pink eye," she wrote in December 1949. "Too many of us have stopped fighting about the smog. And that's bad."[24] Transport yourself back to that era, and you can picture Humphrey Bogart, Jimmy Stewart, and Katharine Hepburn, even pilot/mogul Howard Hughes, stepping outdoors for java or a smoke only to have smog drive them inside harping about "the old days."

Downtown, L.A.'s two big dailies competed so intensely against each other on the topic that both made air pollution a dedicated beat. The *Examiner* assigned the hot potato to 1924 Pulitzer Prize winner Magner White. The *Examiner*'s star reporter penned muckraking stories and policy critiques paint-ing the anti-pollution drive as ineffective and sodden with political grandstanding. One of White's pieces took aim at the local universities for their lack of scientific contribution and the supervisor's policy paralysis over dumps.[25] Perhaps because of Chandler's initiating role, or his clever, humanizing style, the self-deprecating Ainsworth seemed to cast a bigger impression. Joking tongue-in-cheek where others presented tiresome detail, he admitted in a column that the vapory tentacles wrapped around Southern California had him by the collar, too.

> *My lot has not been an easy one. While other reporters were going on airplane rides, or covering the World Series, or finding out about cop-connected murderers, I was out studying the relative number of tin cans in dumps as compared with old girdles and blown-out auto tires. . . . I have come to be recognized as one of the world's greatest experts on the safest way to grope through smoke and fumes. . . . At night, I dream of little smoke devils chasing me.*[26]

Up the coast in stylish San Francisco, commoners were getting a taste—and a fright. They taped their windows. They called City Hall, their congressman, the cops. They suspected a rogue Japanese warship was lobbing chemical shells at the East Bay. What else could explain the stale gas hanging over the refinery district for days, unleashing pounding headaches, nausea, raw throats, and worry? When officials ruled out warfare, San Franciscans speculated the odors might be emanating from onions, wet dogs, or dead fish. A legislative hearing later revealed where the eye-watering fumes had originated. They'd risen from automobile traffic clogging the Berkeley area prior to a University of California-Washington State football game. The bumper-to-bumper conditions and scorching temperatures around the Bears stadium that day mimicked Los Angeles conditions. San Francisco lawmakers who'd felt blessed before not to have Southern California's gunk clutching their skyline now had to fend off panic from their own voters.[27] All the same, one town back east would've gladly swapped San Francisco's or L.A.'s stink with its own predicament.

*   *   *

The unidentified man from Donora, Pennsylvania, could take no more as he walked home, presumably from a factory job, that night in November 1948. Something tainted he was breathing sent him into a choking seizure. Barely able to contemplate his last moment, the man squatted down on the curb, fell over, and died on the spot. He was the first of twenty to expire when his grungy, little industrial town was shellacked by a four-day-long haze. Donora's toxic air was an untimely confluence of fog, U.S. Steel Corp. smoke and fumes, other plants' effluents and locomotive gases, all of them marinating overhead. The poison mostly took elderly residents with heart or asthmatic conditions, though nearly the whole town became ill. In sooty Donora, poor wind circulation and the hilly terrain turned into a pastoral death chamber, hospitals overrun, pure oxygen the only real treatment. The slaughter reminded doctors of the heavy mist from Belgium's Meuse Valley, where a gas-fog blend in late 1930 transformed to sulfuric acid that killed sixty people and hundreds of horses and cattle.[28]

The Pennsylvania massacre became Los Angeles's preoccupation. McCabe, grilled by the supervisors about the probability of such an accident here, explained repeatedly that Southern California's topography and spread-out manufacturing base provided sufficient ventilation to make such a buildup remote, no matter what scare-mongering publications like *Colliers Weekly* assessed. The politicians accepted his explanations. A cluster of community activists and worrywarts, flustered by what they breathed and what they heard, disagreed. Donora stuck to their minds.

Their stubbornness seemed little more than Philco-radio static next to the crackle that occurred when William Jeffers, a former wartime rubber czar and a patriarchal figure in L.A., abruptly quit his chairmanship of the Citizens' Smog Advisory Committee. He resigned with bombast, publicly lashing McCabe for condoning "politics and big business" that let the powerful off the hook while danger lingered. It was Bowron, surprisingly, who tried to shield McCabe, despite still being upset about his puny say in regional smog policy. To him, McCabe was a "fine, conscientious" leader who wouldn't hesitate to "step on toes and meet resistance." Just back from a trip, Bowron said the whole nation was gabbing about L.A.'s blemish, and there was no time for backbiting. The *Times* again tried tempering emotions, remarking on what a shame it was that a patriot like Jeffers would develop such a wild hair. The flattery fell limply.[29] Jeffers, a cigar-chomping ex-Nebraskan with a Dick Cheney-like scowl, was now a whistleblower. He suggested voters should "get rid of the supervisors" unless they started acting aggressively, and hoped to spearhead a 1,000-person protest against McCabe's department—the bureaucracy he'd helped launch.

McCabe still bet that one-for-all spirit would trump rash emotion. Speaking with youth clubs, grand jury members, civic organizations, and neighborhood leaders, he compared his formative moves to painstaking bridge engineering. It'd be "eighteen months before noticeable improvements." He tried selling perspective: there were 1,500 county industrial plants in 1939. Nine years later, there were 8,500. Skeptical L.A. councilman Kenneth Hahn asked why no plants had closed with the rulebook tightening. McCabe answered he lacked the statutory truncheon to shut down firms, and that the permit system needed time anyway. When a sickly woman queried him whether she should move, McCabe stoutly told her no. "We are going to lick smog," he said.[30] Eyes rolled.

McCabe got a lot right during the smog-ignorance era. One of his most inspired decisions, if one hardly known, was hiring a decorated University of Illinois chemistry professor named H.F. Johnstone to size up the situation in the fall of 1948. Johnstone, whose advice would echo for years, maybe more than St. Louis Professor Raymond Tucker's, was dumbfounded that so little chemical analysis was transpiring. There'd been no rudimentary effort to separate aerosol particles and particulate matter for dissection. Nor was anyone contemplating whether the bluish haze that had just recently materialized originated from a different source than the eye-watering clouds of yore. There might be more than one type of smog!—a theory that was both illuminating and troubling. Adding to this "confusion," he said the APCD was in catch-up mode to strengthen the "lax and uncoordinated" regulations that smaller, non-California cities would never have cottoned. Johnstone also doubted that sulfur dioxide was the bogeyman, not finding enough of it to absolve gasoline and diesel fuel. Above all, he coached McCabe to act judiciously, "never on loosely-based opinions," and to hire top-drawer men of unimpeachable integrity. It'd matter. Lastly, he emphasized that victory was impossible without sacrifice, whether that meant banning heavy manufacturers from population centers or maintaining "public sentiment" when conditions improved. Johnstone concluded that if folks desired yesteryears' air, they had to do more than bellyache to the nearest politician. They might need to give up something.[31]

Unfortunately, public sacrifice was precisely the message Southern Californians a few years removed from World War II and the Great Depression preferred not to hear, and McCabe paid for it. Indeed, 1949 would be the "year of investigations." Before January was over, the California legislature already had launched an inquiry into the district's management after some lawmakers declared the APCD was flunking its mission. The resulting majority report by an assembly governmental efficiency committee recommended no drastic changes to McCabe's agency; the committee's minority report, conversely, lacerated the board of supervisors for not devoting enough time to their pollution-control duties.[32] Coinciding with those split opinions was the impaneling of the county grand jury to determine whether Jeffers' broadside hinting of favoritism and "smog politics" had merit. No sooner had those allegations been debunked in a formal review—one from the previous year had rapped the supervisors for "nebulous thinking" on policy yet complimented McCabe's seriousness[33]—before Pasadenans and others began demanding summary relief. Weren't the skies supposed to be pristine by now? Whatever McCabe tried, subpoenas, anonymous tipsters, grumpy retirees, and the frustrated hounded him as if the painful weather were his doing. *The Los Angeles Herald-Examiner*, the Hearst-owned tabloidesque daily, waved a similar populist flag, slamming officials for "clumsy, half-hearted attempts" to extract Los Angeles from its darkness. Unlike the Establishment-hewing *Times*, the *Examiner* was unimpressed by McCabe's initiatives. One of its headlines went for the jugular: "OFFICIALS SPEND FIVE YEARS ON SMOG WITH NO RESULT."[34]

McCabe, sturdier than his milquetoast appearance implied, refused to knuckle under. On the contrary, he suggested in a 1948 update a smog beast in retreat as manpower and mind bore down on it. In only a year, his district had concocted a plan to attack industrial sulfur dioxide with water scrubbers, baghouses, and other industrial exotica, and precipitated the closures of the county's fiery dumps. He'd overseen more plant inspections than a battalion of meat inspectors could, and prodded 355 steam locomotives to switch to diesel fuel. Dotted in the APCD's first progress report were more pessimistic nuggets that would breed chaos later, specifically L.A.'s shaky technical understanding of invisible smog-forming gases. Despite those analytical gaps, McCabe pronounced that no other American county was capping dust and fumes as exhaustively as L.A. was.[35]

Protective scientific-journal editors around the country, the authoritative *Chemical and Engineering News* chief among them, seconded that, lionizing McCabe's performance as verging on groundbreaking. "The essential wisdom of (his) course has been demonstrated beyond dispute," the *Journal* hooted, "despite the criticism of certain individuals and groups who apparently were not familiar with what was being accomplished."[36] The APCD, they said, not only had to invent the smog control wheel, but the spokes, axel, and drive train. McCabe had midwifed a new technical discipline on the fly. His men, among other triumphs, had developed a "freeze-out" photographic procedure where they induced air samples into connected thermoses packed with dry ice and reactant chemicals that dropped them to -300 degrees.[37] Out at UCLA, cameras were able to zoom in on particles *1/25,000* of an inch.[38] Practical benefits were arriving, too. Using ingenuity and some district expertise, the Hancock Chemical Co. was able to recapture from its operations about 100 tons a day of sulfur dioxide, which it then converted to pure sulfur that it resold for agricultural products and to other factories. A German-run plant in the Persian Gulf had conceived the process, and McCabe's cleanup brought it West.[39] Journal editors said that informed people should be impressed, even dazzled with how much he'd done in such a short period. For the American Chemical Society, McCabe's achievements were "remarkable."[40]

*   *   *

Smattering praise could only affect so much. In the spring of 1949, with the world riveted on the Berlin Airlift, McCabe announced he was departing. He was resigning his director-ship satisfied that he'd given the district its roadmap and technical bearings. While the soft-spoken, ex-army colonel explained he'd never intended to stay on as smog czar, his news caught the supervisors off guard. He'd only been in place two years. After hitting a few more milestones, he planned to return to the U.S. Bureau of Mines, which was sallying into the smog-study business itself and needed a relatively seasoned pro like McCabe in the command booth. "There are no mira-cles to be performed," he explained of his departure. "There will be the problem of holding the gains made."[41] A smognoscenti never spoke truer words. It *would* be a problem, and McCabe felt the burden, if not the burnout.

It had been six years since the July '43 attack, and the air did not feel appreciably better. Whatever statistical firepower the APCD wielded after 16,500 inspections, easy breathing was still hit-and-miss. A heavy, gray September underscored that. Figuring the pollution drive required continuity, county super-visors named Gordon Larson, McCabe's old lieutenant, as L.A.'s new smog chief. Though his engineering background paralleled that of his old boss, and his experience certainly made him fit for the post, Larson faced a more spooked con-stituency. Even the superintendent of public schools talked openly about pollution disrupting the region's education sys-tem.[42] Assemblyman Stewart, whose legislation created the APCD, also was discouraged. He anticipated that politicians' irresistible second-guessing of the smog fight ahead would foster an ambience of perpetual mistrust. "The most tragic thing today," Stewart cautioned, "is destructive criticism which influences the ordinary citizen to think the government is going to hell."[43]

Public opinion reflected a chasm about what had to be done or undone. Lack of concrete science was lumped in with the fright factor. People horrified about a mass-casualty event suggested smog cops carry white mice or canaries to alert them *when*, not if, the atmosphere reached poisonous proportions. They suggested inspections of the oily fumes evaporating from the La Brea Tar Pits in the Miracle Mile section of Los Angeles west of downtown.[44] These notions weren't as loopy as they sounded—at least not compared to what passed for scientific speculation at the time. A state health official had already questioned whether the thousands of California turkeys nervously milling about the barnyard prior to the Thanksgiving ax were kicking up dust that made matters worse.

Poor Fletcher Bowron just wanted into the conversation after the grand jury refused to pursue his allegations that the district applied its rules unevenly.[45] In September 1949, unable to get his way, Mayor Bowron threw a public tantrum that'd been churning inside him for years. Bowron fulminated, in a prepared statement that splashed across the headlines, that it was time to stop hearing anecdotes about seas of "yellow, smelly" fumes where beautiful valleys used to appear. It was time to stop constant silverware polishing, or having his office number morph into a grievance hotline each time the aerial crud returned. At L.A. City Hall, it was regularly driving civil servants home sick.

Smog is bad in Los Angeles, and the fault does not lie with the city administration. There has not been sufficient improvement in two years, and the people have a right to know why . . . Smog, particularly the eye-irritating fumes, is of industrial origin. There can be no question about that . . . Are the industries that are the real offenders so powerful financially that someone is afraid to regulate them properly?[46]

Bowron's jeremiad rung loudly, riling up civic cleanup organizations that were sprouting by the week. There were trade front groups, coffee-klatch committees, community Establishment-bashers, and academic dabblers. Even more vested was the Pure Air Council of Southern California, which touted itself as a "militant organization," when in truth it was a para-governmental front defending the APCD against criticism that it was too passive. Larson, Stewart, and other founders pined for more of everything: citizen involvement, research, education, "smog-complaint" stations, and respect for the district's slide-rule-calculating, clipboard-toting brain trust. Besides this wish list, they also seemed to be signaling that all those bravado predictions by leaders like Bowron and McCabe about ending the blight in a few years were overly optimistic, to put it mildly. Over at the board of supervisors, there was head scratching over why Bowron, the area's predominant politician, a man armed with the facts, would say what he had.[47] Was it justified? Was it pandering fears?

Politicians' squabbling further demoralized civic boosters, who reacted by pumping out press releases announcing the L.A. dream as splendid as ever. The All-Year Club asserted that even with the smog and traffic, three million "satisfied" tourists visited the region a year, nearly twice the prewar levels. Evidently, it was still a hot destination, because those out-of-towners spent roughly $400 million in L.A. in 1949. The East Coast elite could eat its heart out. Real estate, the coin of the realm, was going to endure, too. Smaller developers and

hoteliers improvised a role for air pollution: as product coun-
terpoint. Whether it was at a dude ranch in the Mojave Desert
or a custom-housing tract in Ojai, the theme was the same—
continual sunshine. Near San Diego's hoity-toity crowd, the
Casa de Manana jingle was direct. "Did someone say smog?
Never heard of it—not in lovely La Jolla."[48]

Even the commercialism and vows of relief ahead could
not obscure anxieties about the most chilling unknown: how
much, if at all, were air contaminants eroding community
health? City health officers furnished little, except publicly
advising people about drinking fluids during smog attacks to
replenish tear ducts. Inside the medical world, Los Angeles'
situation was shaping up as an important sample group for
epidemiologists. Most significant for them was an oppressive
smog attack of September 29, 1949 that wags dubbed "Black
Friday." It had statistical heft. Where thirty-seven Angelenos
would've normally perished from heart or respiratory ailments
that day, the stained air brought the toll to fifty-five, according
to Clarence Mills, an experimental-medicine professor at the
University of Cincinnati. He termed the eighteen additional
fatalities "excess deaths," as in preventable.[49] Two months
later, as the unrelenting murk kept "public officials and the
local citizenry in a fighting mood,"[50] Mills amplified on his
watershed research. He said his calculations indicated that air
contaminants caused "significantly higher death rates" for
people with heart or lung diseases.[51] This terse and disturbing
conclusion was all he'd say. For patients at the world-
renowned Rancho Los Amigos hospital in Downey, which had
a foundry close by, clean air was a life-or-death proposition.
Rancho's polio patients sometimes strained so hard for breath
that nurses needed to suction their throats.[52]

Smog killed Southern Californians indirectly, and instantly, too, in violent traffic incidents peppering the back-page news over the years. Just before Christmas 1949, a heavy morning pall caused two streetcars to collide in a dramatic crash that injured twenty-two people, two of them seriously. No one is sure, outside of urban legends, how many more people would perish in pollution-blinding car accidents. For accuracy, you'd have to wait until L.A.'s future freeways were built and suburbia completed, and, even then, the California Highway Patrol and local police probably lost count.[53] Four-legged creatures met their makers among the early victims, and you'd have been surprised at the mourning for "Mr. Riley," a celebrated tomcat who adopted the posh Beverly Hills Hotel as his home. The feline had lived his three years like the ultimate party animal, brawling, mating, and dodging doormen, all the while licking up plates of chicken liver that hotel guests illicitly fed him. When he got sick in late 1949, pneumonia triggered by air pollution, Mr. Riley's last meow carried meaning beyond his old haunt.[54] A cat today, people tomorrow?

More sobering was a white-knuckle scenario where the lives of tens of thousands of Angelenos hung on crisis decision-making if stagnant winds coincided with an insidious bad-air buildup. In December 1949, in what would be first tremor in a long-running political ruckus over prevention, the question broke loose over how to keep Los Angeles from becoming the next Donora. Evacuations were not on the table. County supervisors, acting as the APCD board, split over priorities symbolic of the time: continued clampdown or a more tempered approach until the science hardened up? Supervisor John Anson Ford wanted all oil refineries closed if signs pointed to a catastrophe, assuming someone could quantify what that was. Supervisor Leonard Roach, emoting New Deal sensibility, said, it'd be "a sad thing indeed to throw thousands of

people out of work during the approaching holiday season."
The hearings did reveal that the APCD had an emergency plan
it'd kept under wraps. Whether it envisioned asking the
refineries to shut off their smokestacks wasn't clear, because as
Supervisor William A. Smith stressed, "it's much more than a
matter of turning off a valve." Experts spoke up. The most
vaunted was Dr. Irving Krick, who'd gained celebrity for predicting clear weather for the Allies' D-day invasion at
Normandy. If Krick could formulate what historians believed
was a world-changing forecast, imagine what he could drum
up for smog predictions? True to his reputation, Krick testified
in December 1949 that methods were available to predict a
pollution siege one to two weeks before its arrival, just as his
firm had predicted this current one. Krick, a bushy-haired, ex-
academic known for his piano talents and lead-foot driving,
was baffled as to why forecasts hadn't been explored when
they might be integral in blunting a killer smog. Krick, some-
what ahead of his time, believed the radio and newspapers
should be part of a notification chain alerting the public. After
Krick's statement, meteorology quickly became a district
forte.[55] Before then, Krick gave Angelenos another Donora-
harkening reminder. He testified that a toxic-air incident in
L.A. could kill 6,000 people.[56]

Thus, as the heroic forties faded to the consumer-and-
Cold-War fifties, Los Angeles' smog-comprehension deficit
was not only precarious but also open to interpretation. What
made the chemical air so repulsive? How long would it harass
Southern California? What harm was it causing living organ-
isms? Could it be vanquished by industrial crackdowns, merely
lightened by cunning engineers, or did you have to just outlive
it until a magic bullet answer appeared?

Uncertainties and all, when McCabe returned to the area

for an air pollution symposium, he returned as the federal smog-control guru hired in part on the strength of his professionally lauded APCD tenure. Now that he no longer drew a paycheck from the district, he could reveal the secret dynamics he'd confronted there. McCabe, in the now-it-can-be-told-department, confirmed the deliberate corporate resistance others had denied. He said industry *was* stalling on fume-trapping equipment more cleverly than the public realized. "We have failed because industry believed that air pollution control would cost too much," McCabe told the conference. "Engineers were assigned to write diverting papers on the minutiae of the problem and the trade journals editorialized on the unreasonableness of the do-gooders."[57] Larson spoke at the symposium too, though his speech lacked similar revelations. Instead, he espoused an evolving philosophy that a young Martin Luther King would have applauded. "The growing feeling is that any community is entitled to clean air."

The refiners were as unhappy with Larson's rhetoric as they had been with McCabe's, still feeling unfairly blamed after all their research. For them, it was time to throw a sharp elbow. The same month as the symposium, Western Oil & Gas Association members said they could no longer keep "their mouths shut" while their sector did more than any other trying to understand the baffling weather. They had spent $10 million on equipment, and given $500,000 to a research institute, even as they were being set up as the whipping boy for "every misinformed person claiming to be an expert on smog." A region whose population nearly doubles in ten years is bound to have a corresponding thirst for more oil.[58] And more oil equaled more emissions.

There was no disputing it anymore: air pollution was jeopardizing Southern California's future, if not its cohesion.

You needed to look no further than Pasadena, where activists wanted an industrial shutdown during staid weather, and made plans to recall all five county supervisors over their displeasure.[59] As future analysis would show, they had a right to be incensed. While the APCD beat its chest in 1949 about eliminating 35 percent of the suspect contaminants, experts later realized the district had underestimated, by a stunning two-thirds, the real tonnage of emissions contributing to dark skies. It wasn't 741 tons. It was about 2,000 tons! A county historian phrased it this way:

> Not only was it doubtful that material improvements had occurred; the situation seemed to be worse than it had ever been. "When . . . improvement does occur," observed the Committee On Air and Water Pollution, "it will not be necessary to demonstrate it with statistical data. It will be apparent to the man in the street . . ."[60]

Was it any wonder that every time the district hailed better air that it provoked a flood of protesting citizen letters about the abyss between data and breathing? Neither was it a shocker that when the county grand jury hinted about its subjects for 1950, it said it was dropping ongoing investigations of gangsters. Its new focus was on the LAPD, on "unsolved sex murders" like the Black Dahlia case, and on that other unsolved caper—the one that really made you gasp.[61]

DUTCHMAN OVER THE PACIFIC

IN A FRAGRANT LAB BENEATH A SLEEPY UNIVERSITY, A DUTCH BIO-chemist with a knack for discoveries couldn't stop daydreaming about the simplest of pleasures: intoxicating air. For months on end, Arie Haagen-Smit and his assistants had labored in their underground lair extracting the fumes from raw pineapples, all in an attempt to isolate what gave the prickly-skinned fruit its zesty flavor. The average stiff munching canned pineapple might not appreciate it, but the micro-chemical payoff from unlocking nature's flavor secrets could be huge, potentially Nobel Prize huge. So "Haagy," as his fellow California Institute of Technology professors called their twinkled-eyed, genteel friend, endured the processing of 6,000 pounds of imported Hawaiian pineapples to meticulously wring a few tablespoons of sample. He smirked at the needling about how he'd look in a grass hula skirt. Fond of his work as he was, he was still human. Gradually, his trail blazing experimentations had begun to feel like common drudgery.

One broiling morning in 1949, head woozy with smells and equations, he decided to treat himself to a short break. He burst out of Kerckhoff Hall and into the sunlight hoping for tonic for his lungs. In his ten years in Pasadena, he had heard all about the city's sweet, cathartic atmosphere. Yet when the hawk-nosed scientist inhaled that day, what he drew in did not seem pure, and it definitely wasn't invigorating. It was harsh and bleach-tinged, a bronchial sucker punch. Haggy, forty-nine, coughed hard. As history would have it, it was the hack heard around the world.

Padding back to his fluorescent-lit lair, he could not shake the taste of foul air. Though he still had pineapples to juice, the air had rousted his curiosity. Haagy knew from the papers that smog had people frothing, and that the government folks in charge seemed to career from one guess to the next. The science behind some of their mantras—"Where there's smoke, there's smog"—was just as preposterous. Out-of-state experts recruited to save the day weren't much better. They consistently assumed that pollution everywhere was the same, consistently getting it wrong.

Arnold Beckman, a colleague of Haagy's on the Caltech chemistry faculty, also watched the herky-jerky science with a skeptical brow. He did not accept the conventional wisdom that L.A. air pollution evolved from sulfur dioxide, as so many impressively titled people had asserted in the mad rush for answers. Beckman knew that compound oozed a distinct gassy odor that he had never sniffed in the grating air. This was Chemistry 101. Where legitimate science went missing, shaky explanations appeared— sometimes, for example, up the thigh. Women across America had begun donning nylon stockings in those days to give their gams sculpted sex appeal. When that hosiery ran, sheared, or nearly dissolved with noticeable frequency in the L.A. air, one bunch chirped it was evidence too gripping to ignore. True, nylon fabric does weaken in contact with sulfur trioxide. Even so, Beckman and a USC professor thought this connection almost laughable, and believed the situation demanded rigorous clinical analysis. They needed to act. Sometime in the late 1940s, they arranged a meeting with McCabe before he bailed out of the L.A. smog caper for his waiting federal job. If they'd really wanted on his good side, they should have brought him barbed wire to ward off his encircling critics.[1]

"The poor chap," Beckman recalled, "was being harassed from all sides." Smog was fast becoming political putty, malleable for vote pandering and showboating. "What's the matter with McCabe?" the chairman of one advisory committee had clucked. "He's been on the job for three months and pollution is just as bad as ever." Pasadena politician Warren Dorn couldn't resist either, telling voters he had the answers as he campaigned for county supervisor. "Elect me and I'll get rid of smog." Not surprisingly, McCabe was skittish when Beckman buttonholed him about further study. *Study?* McCabe asked incredulously. "There was no time" for that. No, people demanded action.[2] His livelihood might depend on it.

McCabe eventually warmed up to Beckman's pitch, and Beckman said he had the man for the job: a fellow Caltech professor named Arie Haagen-Smit. Not only was his chum Arie apolitical, he was a virtuoso in his field. Haagy had something else, too. Like Beckman, he was already acquainted with the L.A. Establishment, because he was a member of the chamber of commerce's Scientific Committee. The chamber couldn't wait for an atmospheric reprieve. Pictures of secretaries galloping to their cars with handkerchiefs over their faces and heartbreaking quotes from bankrupt farmers were stigmatizing PR. Who'd want to live here, columnists asked, if you couldn't make it to the grocery store without a gas mask? A persuaded McCabe told Beckman he'd hire his friend. Haagy accepted the challenge, probably unaware the Establishment's pitchforks would soon be chasing him.[3]

Haagy did understand how to pry smog-truths from the Periodic Table. To do it, he walked a few feet, tossed open his ground-floor windows, and, during a few days, pulled 30,000 cubic feet of Pasadena air through a trap chilled with cool air. From that sample, he distilled frozen water vapor, extracting a few drops of chocolate-colored, rancid-smelling liquid he felt blessed to have. He then did to them what he'd done experimenting with pineapples, garlic, radishes, and the beatnik herb, marijuana: he passed air over the drops to wring their acids, and converted those into telltale derivatives. Dashing a little sodium hydroxide here, some ether there, he slid the derivatives through a column of silica. *Voila!* Fifteen fluorescent bands revealed themselves like magic. With his disciplined methods, he had captured smog in a test tube.[4] The intriguing results rolled around in Haagy's mind until he could scribble a crude formula. He had a hunch. Chemical reactions of undetermined complexity had to be junking the air through oxidation, which any seaman knows as rust. Whatever was rusting the climate had to be manmade, too, and continually produced. Back in his Caltech lab, he exposed plants sealed tight in a box to oxidizing materials. They keeled over dead. This got him wondering about the unsavory byproducts of iodine when they're burned off potassium by a category of elements called "volatile organics compounds." The more iodine escapes from potassium in experiments, including ones measuring chemical reagents, the more oxidation results. Six months later, these disjointed fragments fell monumentally into place.

The transplanted egghead, working between classes with so-so equipment, had accomplished in a few months what none of his American counterparts had done in the six years since the Aliso Street gas attack: he had identified the elemental properties of Southern California smog. The economic implications of it were seismic. With science, not conjecture, he'd indicted the automobile and oil businesses—industries that eyed the region's ever-bulging population as the most fertile car market the world had ever seen. The electrifying aspect of Haagy's work was so transcendent that it prompted Gordon Larson, McCabe's successor, to publicize the findings, first to the supervisors, then to the public. There was delirium before the gravity of the situation sank in.

The unknown solved, Haagy hoped to return to his pineapples. Like many, he cast air pollution as an annoying gnat. The notion that it might jar asthmatic convulsions, imperil the elderly and young, or provoke cancer cells to grow was Chicken-Little-thinking to him, not fit for serious minds. "Smog is an aesthetic and economic nuisance," he'd say years later. "Don't believe stories that death in the form of smog stalks the streets of Los Angeles."[5] It was one rare occasion in which he was wrong.

Soon, Haagy testified before a special state assembly committee just glad that someone had finally focused on car exhausts. Legislators, after all, remembered the filthy sheen over Berkeley from the traffic heading in and out of that football game. In L.A., though, Haagy's theory had made him at once surprise hero and marked man. The oil lobby initially had greeted him with a shrug of its shoulders, evidently convinced that his findings were a maverick's left-field postulation. When Haagy's idea showed legs, the hopeful dismissiveness balled into concentrated vengeance against him. Industry-sponsored research accelerated. Front men got busy. Orchestrating the counteroffensive was the Stanford Research Institute (SRI), the supposedly independent Bay Area think tank with an unclear connection to the blue-blood university but a fat contract with

the Western Oil & Gas Association. Corporations that would
become behemoths Unocal, Atlantic Ridgefield Oil Corporation
(ARCO,) Texaco, and Dutch-Shell dominated the membership.
Remedies for the common weal and assistance for its oil clients
precipitated its interest. "Knowledge stored up in the minds of
scientists," the SRI's 1950 L.A. air pollution report hailed, "is of
little direct benefit to the community. The knowledge must be
understandable and available to all who are interested."

The SRI's critique of the L.A. smog situation amounted to
a technical defense of a client hoisted up the public petard.
The Institute agreed that an interlocking chain of molecular
reactions was behind the phenomenon, pointing the finger
back at sulfur as the possible instigator. The oil companies,
with hundreds of millions of dollars in plant investment in
L.A., required a more pointed response than that. They'd
heard about Haagy's earlier experiments with smog, when the
war was just over and he had become fascinated with why rubber goods splintered like dead wood under the L.A. sun. Tires
were most troublesome, lasting about two-thirds as long as
elsewhere.[6] Investigating this, Haagy had timed how long it
took for strips of rubber tubing to crack after exposing them to
oxidized air. In this way, Haagy's instincts about oxidation
mortified them. Years later now, the decision came thundering
down: someone had to shut up the professor.

The SRI dispatched a researcher to present its views at the
unlikely institution in the thick of the smog-science competition: the California Institute of Technology. Caltech hadn't yet
made anyone forget about the Ivy League, but the smallish
school had a stronghold in micro-chemical analysis, a distinc-
tive niche in a young field. (Only a fool back then would make
air pollution a career, a mutt specialty in short demand requiring smarts in chemistry, engineering, meteorology, and public

administration, if not public psychology.) Standing in a darkened auditorium, not far from where Albert Einstein had resided as the frizzy-haired emeritus of American physics, the SRI man swung rhetorical brass knuckles. While no one remembers his name or his own credentials, they can't forget his audacity. He described his own lab work as a setup to discredit Haagy's. How, he asked contemptuously, could such an esteemed mind arrive at such faulty, premature conclusions? Surely he was "guessing." SRI scientists, he explained, had tried duplicating Haagen-Smit's experiments and the air they produced was "no more irritating than fresh outside air." By the Institute's math, "automobile processes," garbage-burning, and ordinary heating exhaust stewed the worst of it. Thousands of compounds aloft in the atmosphere acted and reacted in a still-unexplained transformation, so it was reprehensible blaming Big Oil for an aerosol cocktail that modern science only had begun studying. Without more research to apportion the blame, the SRI wasn't buying Haagy's theory. Nope. It was merely pointed opinion by a scientific Lone Ranger.[7]

Beckman had invited Haagy to the SRI speech that he probably suspected would skewer his pal. If Beckman was trying to goad his coworker into action, he got what he wanted. Listening to the SRI man smear his reputation in front of peers and students, the levelheaded Haagy was Krakatoa inside. His carotid arteries throbbed near eruption. "I could almost feel Haagy's blood pressure rise," Beckman recalled. "He was furious—the validity of his work was being questioned." Stomping from the lecture, Haagy was not his normally unflappable self. Instead, he was muttering, "I'll show them who's right and who's wrong."[8] And that's what he did. He embraced the improbable. He had found a cause that'd wrench him away from plant-growth assays and why fruit flies had red eyes. Before, solving nature's puzzles had been "real sport and excitement." Environmental sleuthing had rated as a dry "assembly of facts." He'd preferred non-confrontational challenges, where he could "hightail it back to his lab."[9] Everything changed after the SRI hatchet job. People torn over the prospect that Haagy's jump into urban pollution might torpedo revolutionary hormone research were powerless to make pineapple-flavor research his obsession again.

A year removed from anonymity, Haagy in March 1949 agreed to become the APCD's star consultant. With the "SRI dogs" hot at his heels, he threw himself into his new work for the next eighteen months.[10] Once he'd finished near the tail end of 1950, he'd not only reconfirmed that unburned gasoline was Southern California's predominant smog-maker, he'd demonstrated why the SRI had been unable to duplicate his results. They'd skipped critical lab procedures. Haagy, realizing his enemies hadn't flinched, next surprised them with his own bit of preemption. He and a student built a phone booth-sized "smog chamber" in the APCD parking lot using Plexiglas and greenhouse frames ditched at a local junkyard. The $350-contraption, a lot of dough in that era, knocked leafy, green plants in the test group into lifeless stalks within days. Haagy and the district invited the public, anyone, to enter the chamber to see the dying plants for themselves while getting a dose of the eye-scratching, nostril-offending fumes that Haagy's insight was able to reproduce. "It was sort of a PR deal," he admitted, if not a *take-that* slug at the SRI.[11]

The implicit message behind the laudatory headlines—"PUZZLE OF SMOG PRODUCTION SOLVED BY CALTECH SCIENTIST"—was of a red-eyed town poised for deliverance.[12] Around Christmas 1950, Haagy tied the strands together in a masterful

article he penned in Caltech's *Engineering and Science* magazine. Historians would frame it a bombshell. Interestingly, the
chemist led off his explanation with a warning. The common
assumption that L.A.'s sub-atmosphere was an "unlimited
reservoir" for man's refuse was a fallacy of the "machine age."
With this one sentence, buried within an explanation of how
iodine blasted off the potassium-iodine molecule in the oxidation guillotine, Haagy condemned the gods of growth. Postwar
L.A. had bloated with so many people spread over so wide an
area that the region essentially had turned nature against itself.

The paradox was rueful irony: what helped make Southern
California so attractive to the sick and snowbound also con-
signed it to never-ending susceptibility. The mild climate and
diverse topography, in fact, compressed smog into the low
atmosphere (the troposphere), below the clouds, essentially
straight into the lives and respiratory tracts of the populace.
Others had dwelt on this, just none as compellingly. The
vapors from the "great city," Haagy wrote, began swirling in
the predawn hours along the coast as the last of the moon-
beams lit the Pacific. A gentle offshore breeze then blew the
exhausts across the basin on a northeasterly bearing, where
they stagnated over what would be the area's most populous
suburb, the San Fernando Valley. At night, the winds reversed
course, sweeping the fumes back toward the coast barely any
cleaner than they started. The local mountain ranges ringing
the basin on three sides behaved in this cycle as an unwanted
dam. They blocked the sullied air from escaping toward the
best place for it: the cacti and creosote of the uninhabited
inland deserts to the east.[13]

Haagy confirmed that while the mountains trapped smog
vertically, the warm air aloft acted as a cauldron lid locking the
filth in place. High-pressure weather systems, which parked

over the Southland's basin for much of the year, imitated a ceiling that pressed the smoke, fumes, and manmade particles close to the earth, preventing them from rising up and billowing out on the jet stream. Meteorologists had coined the syndrome a "temperature inversion." This is where a band of warm, stationary air creates a canopy over a layer of cooler air, whose heavier density prevents it from rising. It relented a few times a year, typically when heavy storms marched through. The inversion, whose base usually squatted 500 feet to 1,500 feet above the ground, always returned afterwards. Just like smog. Hence, L.A.'s sunny climes were great for your tan but murderous on air purity.

On the cliffhanger of where it originated, the professor furnished an explanation as spellbinding today as the 10-cent hamburger age.

> At one end of the scale we find the petroleum industry, where a few refineries are handling many thousands of tons of material every day. But the half-million automobiles driving around in Los Angeles contribute their share of pollution, too. Together, they burn approximately 12,000 tons of gasoline daily. Even if the combustion were 99 percent complete, which it certainly is not, 120 tons of unburned gasoline would be released.[14]

Intuitively, the European's theories clicked. Peoples' eyes watered because of the oxidized particles spritzing around their head. Those same particles also just happened to be small enough to block visible light, which left the terrain a dull gray. Hydrocarbons descending from the winds blotched and damaged crops in battered farmland. And it was ozone—the harmfully volatile cousin of oxygen that popular culture worshipped as healing—acting as a dark knight. When Haagy had piped ozone over gasoline-filled beakers, the pungent fumes that filled his lab forced people to flee the room. "It was just luck," Haagy admitted. "We hit the jackpot with our first nickel."[15] In another experiment, the combination had caused a small lab explosion that supposedly pitted the professor's glasses.[16] "When automobiles and the petroleum industry are controlled," he reasoned, "smog won't bother us anymore."[17] For Haagy, there were no two ways about it. While factories, city dumps, backyard incinerators, and other sources certainly notched unsavory elements skywards, they were negligible compared to capitalism's lifeblood: gasoline. It all had a devastating wallop of truth.

Still, truth depends on its acceptance, and the Great American Automobile stood relatively unimpeachable. Haagy's announcement that invisible gasoline vapors reacting chemically in bright, continuous sunshine to create ozone, aldehydes, and other smog ingredients was *prima facie* evidence too mind-boggling for the public to easily accept and too threatening for the industry to go unchallenged. When conventioneers attended the SRI-sponsored First National Air Pollution Symposium in Pasadena in May 1952, talk of hydrocarbons and ozone was peripheral. McCabe, speaking as a federal official, was more worried about a kangaroo court. "I do not mean to imply that improperly operated and obsolete motor vehicles should be allowed to pollute the atmosphere—they should not be—but neither should folklore be encouraged that will place the onus of metropolitan area air pollution on the automobile, without proof."[18] *Folklore?*

The *Times'* Ainsworth realized how bizarre this all was, having the public APCD and the private SRI vying for the population's trust in news articles and white papers impossible for people to miss. Ainsworth might not have known the difference between ionization and oxidation, but he recognized that corporate interests had an ax to grind, if not future billions in sales to protect, over smog's origins. As a reminder, he told a *Times* colleague to view any material the Institute distributed at the conference dubiously, because the oil companies employed the SRI. "I recommend we be very careful in editing and handling [their] handouts on the session," he said. "They need watching, [and] are employed by the oil companies. Stanford Research is a private corporation on the Stanford campus."[19]

As the convention at which he was not invited to speak got under way, Haagy watched the local media gobble up his myth-shattering findings. An aura of excitement and anticipation throbbed from his achievement. The American imagination then was captivated by modern science—space travel, robots, nuclear power, deep-sea diving—as a national pride and the path to the good life. While the SRI argued that the L.A. atmosphere was a chemical potpourri, the *Times* and other media sprinkled rose petals at Haagy's loafers. "Going on in the air, under the effect of sunlight, are billions of miniature 'atom bomb' explosions, a chain reaction of violence and chemical fury," one article hyperventilated. "Out of this maelstrom emerges a constant discharge of highly irritating substances affecting both human eyes and the tender structure of growing plants, plus an enormous byproduct of ozone. . . . For a long time, it had been known that the Los Angeles atmosphere contained large amounts of ozone, but its origin until now was not definitely known."[20]

As Haagy's experiments proved, hydrocarbons had been smog's tripwire all along. The European scientist wasn't even the first technical person to ponder this. In 1947, the ACPD's start-up year, an unnamed engineer had cut through the patter about garbage fumes and crumbling nylons to write his superior that the scientific literature had clues worth chasing. Nitrogen oxides and hydrocarbon compounds "in the exhaust gases of internal combustion engines. . . might quite reasonably be among the most potent tear-producing substances around," the engineer typed. That year, city and county health investigators arrived at similar conclusions. Inexplicably, neither the APCD engineer nor the investigators who later transferred to the agency were encouraged to continue exploring the theory. Ainsworth himself had written about aldehydes as a reason for eye and breathing irritation in a December 1946 story about diesel bus fumes,[21] as well in an article about exhaust tests in the Second Street Tunnel downtown. Nonetheless, it was as though the hydrocarbon theory just vanished until Haagy showed up. Was it poor leadership? Was it ego, technical overload, or institutional corruption? Pacifying a nervous countryside was tricky.

Just having evidence could be corrosive to the conscience. When Haagy's oxidation ideas went public in January 1951, a UCLA physiologist named Herman Roth wrote a confession to Ainsworth. The implications were explosive. Roth divulged that the same conclusions that Larson had touted as "startling" revelations weren't novel at all. Scientists had homed in on unburned gasoline in the smog cycle a full four years earlier while Roth was at the USC School of Medicine, but this information never came out. The October 15, 1947 study Roth cowrote involved the "first comprehensive attempt" to measure why some people were sensitive to air pollution's health effects while others were not. Curiously, the county-contracted study did not mention gasoline.[22] Roth said "political considerations" from the supervisors was the reason, without specifying what that reason was. "It is necessary for me to admit [this] with bitter regret that certain portions of that report, which are material, were omitted. . . ." Roth wrote. They'd squandered valuable time and public goodwill since. "We were also requested to delete reference to the possible danger of an accidental release of a large mass of some toxic substance into the air during a period of marked inversion. . . ."[23] Roth, unsure what breaking this silence would accomplish, seemed to fade into the background after his admission. Either Ainsworth never wrote about it or it was simply forgotten.

For Haagy, celebrity status gave him a big dose of ambivalence. Paul Mader, Walter Hamming, and other APCD chemists who had zeroed in on the effects of raw gasoline vapors received few hosannas. Same for the prolific Frits Went, a fellow Dutchman and Caltech botanist revered for his understanding of how plants and the environment interacted. Air pollution circa-1951 was no longer just smog. It was, as his detractors and champions clarified, "Haagen Smog." He ridiculed the sobriquet that he was "the father of smog," asking who, then, was the mother? Later, when quizzed by reporters about playing the Brahma bull, he was fatalistic about the career effects. "It was a case," he observed, "of being handed your own death certificate. There just was no arguing with anyone."[24]

*   *   *

Arie Haagen-Smit was born in 1901 on the cusp of a technological century during which the world's largest nations simultaneously learned to advance the sciences as never before and to kill with brutal efficiency. His native Holland wasn't big. No, it was merely beautiful, ice-swept, and class-driven. It was good to be him, a child of fate, as Haagy's father was the chief chemist at Holland's national mint. When the boy tired of playing hide-and-seek amid towering bricks of gold and silver, he was able to watch his dad conduct metal-purity spot-checks and other experiments. Science was his toy chest.

In high school, young Haagy mastered three foreign languages, taught himself calculus, became a formidable boxer, and trained to out-row the bigger kids on Holland's frosty canals. Everybody belittled mathematics, his favorite subject, as a dead-end vocation, which nudged Haagy into majoring in chemistry for his undergraduate and Ph.D. work at the University of Utrecht. His curiosity led him into plant hormones and the organic chemistry department hired him. His group achieved surprising early success, unearthing a whole class of synthetic chemicals that regulate plant growth. From their efforts blossomed whole shelf-loads of commercial weed-killers and herbicides. Tellingly, Haagy neither sought nor was bestowed much of the glory. By then, it was already evident that his analytical talent was world class, perhaps even world changing.[25]

Circumstance presented an obstacle course for him to highlight it further, however, his wife's sudden lung cancer being the first grievous blow. When she died in the early 1930s, leaving him with a baby son, he became a single dad and virtuoso chemist with an unsettled future. The heartache passed, and after a respectable time he met a woman who snuggled into his second soul mate. Maria, who everyone called "Zus," was younger than him and a botanist by training. They married in 1935 in the tense prewar days. Watching the Nazis' maneuverings, the young couple made plans not to be among the conquered. Once the red tape for their visas unstuck, they fled their homeland because they didn't want to live under Hitler's thumb.

Their American welcome mat was Harvard University, courtesy of a biologist impressed by Haagy on a trip to Holland. As a visiting lecturer the money was insultingly low, his field of research dull. Still, Harvard was Harvard, and the Haagen-Smits arrived in snowy Massachusetts in 1936. Thomas Hunt Morgan, the famous Caltech geneticist who'd also met Haagy in Europe, suggested he not get too comfortable. Morgan had assembled a coterie of young talents to work on plant hormones in Southern California, and promised Haagy a mainstay role as an assistant professor. After pondering his future, Haagy accepted Morgan's carrot.[26]

If Hollywood casting agents ever sought a real-life scientist for a part, Haagy would've fit the bill of well-packaged brilliance. His sharp nose presided over an arrowhead-shaped face lit by penetrating blue eyes, which usually hid behind Clark Kent-style glasses. His mouth was frequently pursed, and his head of lacquered dark hair lent him a hunky flair. At work, Haagy had a steady manner that belied how strange it must've been as a thick-tongued truthsayer challenging America's petro-economy. At Caltech, he was a student's teacher and eager administrator, sometimes taking home at night a suitcase full of papers instead of the standard valise. People said he was a combination of "Old Dutch Cleanser and St. George," perhaps because they didn't know what to make of him. Beckman did. At an awards ceremony for Haagy, he credited his friend with "absolute integrity and a delightful sense of humor" endearing to peers in "those hectic early days."[27]

In Pasadena, Haagy befriended five other Holland-born scientists on the university payroll. Having the "Dutch Mafia" around was comforting because the salary wasn't; Caltech was just trying to survive the Depression. Haagy seemed fine with a bare-bones existence, though. Just as in Utrecht, what thrilled him were plant discoveries and flavor experiments. The most nerve-racking aspect to his life was the dread of not knowing the fate of his family and friends in the Nazi-occupied Netherlands.[28] As a newcomer to America, he was too sheltered to recognize that a more personal warfare was circling. Once he entered L.A.'s pollution bog, big ideas not only made him enemies with the SRI and the automakers, but rendered him something of a pariah at Caltech. His theory put heat on the university, and some of his peers probably urged to tell him to pipe down or he'd be looking at a professorship in Idaho. Colleagues' whispers and chuckling sometimes greeted him when he'd grab lunch at the Athenaeum's faculty dining hall.

Beside all that notoriety, there also was grumbling within some citizen groups that by his linking smog with the tailpipe, he was indicting The People. A handful asked if there was a plot by "interests" to blame the "little man's automobile and incinerator." Implicating the citizenry, justified as it might've been, was perilous—a columnist said it was like giving "castor oil to a small child"—when many believed it was the fault of refineries burping contaminants under the "cloak of night."[29] If that wasn't enough pressure, some businessmen peddled the alternative theory that ozone was not a product of refiners or cars but the West Coast's natural stratosphere.[30] By most accounts, Haagy was quite alone in his ideas, if never weak-kneed in his convictions. Years later, he admitted to the despair beneath his I-told-you-so vindication. "I didn't have any public relations agent, but they had. It was very unpleasant. . . . At first [the oil and car industry] were very quiet. Then they laughed at me and tried to discredit me. Then there was a war. . . . They said my work wasn't scientific. But you can't beat the truth."[31]

Haagy shook the landscape again in May 1952 with another valiant article targeting Southern Californian's favorite machine. The internal combustion engine that powered the family Oldsmobile, the teenage hotrod, the commuter car, and the diesel truck made the state hum and Detroit's automakers wealthy. Haagy, however, argued that little-publicized changes in gasoline formulation by the oil companies during the war years to boost crude-oil yield—by adding paraffins and olefins in the refining process—had backfired meteorologically. The new gas unleashed more unburned hydrocarbons than before, though how much was not apparent. Every day of the work-week, he estimated 2,000 tons of hydrocarbons and 250 tons of nitrogen oxide puffed skywards. Most of the light particles originated directly from engines blocks and tailpipes. These vehicles, Haagy stressed, were each "little gas crackers scurrying around the basin,"[32] because each lost approximately ten to fifteen percent of their engine power from incomplete fuel combustion. By 1955, when county-driven vehicles slurped a staggering 4.6 million gallons of gas daily, the unused fuel drenched the air more than ever.[33] By Haagy's math, 120,000 to 250,000 gallons of unburned fossil fuel—enough to fill the tanks of thousands of commuter cars—evaporated into the smog-production chain. To him, it was "astounding."[34] The sloppy handling of gasoline by refilling motorists and restocking gas stations, which slung another 250 tons upwards daily, represented two other leaks to plug. Fumes wafting from skimming ponds at South Bay refineries were another fissure in a leaky dam of them. "Until changes in the composition of the present-day gasoline have been made," he reasoned, "it is necessary to handle modern gasoline as a potential irritant, and losses have to be prevented wherever possible."[35]

Crunching fresh climate data, he also identified the path

by which those fumes and vapors raked the populace, when temperatures were high and the inversion layer exerted itself. At 8 a.m., in the teeth of the rush hour, the smog drifted northward, pinching through the hills separating Pasadena from Los Angeles, until it covered the San Fernando and San Gabriel valleys by early afternoon. This pattern repeated Monday through Friday around sunrise, when somnolent equipment droned to life. Automobiles operating throughout the day then spread more fumes, which dispersed on light, four-five mph, mid-altitude winds. Another lasting revelation: the faster a car was traveling when it began braking, the greater the emissions its engine disgorged.

Haagy's integrated theories steadily won converts in states not named Michigan. The SRI's oil-exoneration struck the media as untrustworthy afterwards. How, they asked, could the Institute have spent $1.25 million to research smog and still profess to know practically nothing about its chemistry? The year 1953 generously provided a reminder of the debate's import. A five-day barrage of tainted air knocked L.A. refineries, gas stations, and the Big Three automakers on their heels with stories accusing them of doing little to plug emissions. Thousands of people hunkered indoors. High-smog days used to be snickered at as "Black Mondays." Forget that. Now it could be any day, or every day. Not that Southern Californians en masse were ready to condemn their beloved sedans. Haagy was right. Until L.A. bird-dogged the small reservoir of unburned gasoline leaching out, any day could be black.

*   *   *

Every time a thick fumebank rolled in, it was a brutal time to be L.A.'s smog chief. Ask Gordon Larson. Just a few short months after he replaced his old boss McCabe, Larson became the consensus bureaucrat to loathe. A marathon twenty-one-day run of murk in November 1949 did his image no favors. Mild improvement during the next several years had optimists hopeful that the worst was over. Unfortunately, the beast roared again in fall 1952, hanging around for 77 out of 78 consecutive autumn days.[36] Larson tried blunt talk. Progress was thorny with $1 billion in new industry since 1948 and two million cars. As long as these existed in a still-air basin, he said, there'd always be always be a Dr. Jekyll component to the weather—lovely on some days, wretched on others. Larson believed that bringing smog to "acceptable levels," where people's bodies didn't suffer grievously, was more realistic.[37] His pragmatism involved pressing on four fronts: refineries, auto exhaust, trash burning, and industries' location. Larson risked heresy with unmerciful activist groups when he suggested that Big Oil wasn't the biggest threat, as it had taken "huge steps" toward green operations. And they had. The petroleum sector, ragged from criticism, was indifferent to the compliment. Angelenos had kicked it around for a long time. "The people in this county must not believe that they will ever have clean air unless most of the four million of them move away," said one independent refiner.[38]

Haagy, at least, was the Elvis of his field. A piñata received better treatment than Larson did. At forty-one, he was a trim, balding, West Point-trained engineer with what one co-worker deemed "the most awful job you could possibly wish on your enemies." Groups gnawed him, as they did McCabe, for being either too knee-jerk aggressive or too kid-glove lax. When he preached patience, an increasingly hostile community said they'd already displayed it. They needed results they could inhale and see. L.A.'s new mayor, Norris Poulson, was there to tag-team him, tearing into Larson for publicizing a list of the city's smog offenses—a list that Poulson had originally sought administratively. Larson, when asked about the pervasive antipathy, said he lived beleaguered because of it. "It shocks me. I think about it nights. I find myself getting up in the morning . . . hoping, wondering if the situation is getting better."[39] Gaunt and exhausted, Larson slipped painfully in the meat-grinder of a crisis with no end, just as others would.

Twenty miles away, much of Pasadena's citizenry wanted Larson frog-marched from office no matter the statistics his agency pumped out to stem the public vitriol. These citizens were unimpressed that the district had curbed overall contaminants by 600 tons per day and nearly halved sulfur dioxide emissions, or that it had sent 300 charged violators to court.[40] Pasadena refused to give him any quarter. It was a city obsessed, what with dirty wisps barreling down on it from smokestacks and industry foreign to their tree-lined suburbs. More than any other small town, Pasadena's preoccupation brought fits of temporary madness. Leaders there toyed with naming their own smog commissioner, vilifying APCD "pollutocrats" as worthless.[41] A pair of local newspapers launched a crusade to recall *all* five Los Angeles county supervisors for "stall, runaround, and double-talk" in their role as APCD board members.[42] Adding to that peptic civic mood was word that the air was even affecting Caltech geologists' lead measurements of ancient rocks.[43] At one public meeting near the school, Pasadena activists unfurled a one-word banner inked for Larson. It read, "RESIGN!"

With their own necks exposed, the supervisors did the predictable: they voted to cashier him. Larson's sternest critic was Supervisor Herbert Legg, who was unhappy with the APCD's spotty research and shoddy board communications. Larson's beat-down signified more than just another ex-military man bested by smog. Tumbling out of his firing was a collective vexation that after all this time and money, L.A.'s efforts still were no match for air pollution's stranglehold on Southern California. Beckman, just then launching what would be a wildly successful instrument-making company after his invention of the pH-meter, hustled down to the County Hall of Administration to praise Larson's record and ask for a sane rethinking of his dismissal. Supervisor Roger Jessup, likewise, asked the board why it should crucify Larson before it pinpointed someone better to take the job. No "cure for smog" would be arriving soon, and he advised his fellow politicians to stop telling people as much.[44] Then again, the alternative was so grim that political indifference— or worse, silence—was its own liability. Lose ground in the fight, twenty-three University of California physiologists contended after spending time at the Riverside plant-study center in late 1953, and "parts of Southern California might have to be evacuated."[45] Out in L.A. again for a conference, McCabe added his voice. He asserted the only reason disaster hadn't hit was *because* of Larson's blitz on established sources under the APCD enforcement flag.[46] It was all too late. "It is my opinion," Legg said, "and has been for some time that our Air Pollution Control District is not geared for the job ahead of us."[47]

Larson was gracious, even relieved, about being the sacrificial lamb. He consented to stay on as chief until his replacement came. If one came. The supervisors burned through about a dozen prospects, most of them too savvy to take the job. Lt. Gen. Leslie Groves, who'd overseen construction of the atomic bomb, wouldn't do it, and neither would Gen. Lucius Clay, who'd commanded U.S. forces in occupied Germany.[48] A California health official rejected the offer, as did a former university official. Larson remained boss by elimination. It might've been this juncture when dark humor became the smog laugh track for Southern California's new cynicism. This editorial ran as an imaginary want ad:

> *Man or woman wanted to take over top-paying administra-*
> *tive position with a reliable organization. . . Must, above all,*
> *have thick skin, preferably at least three or four inches*
> *thick. . . Must be polite and temperate, and willing to take*
> *unending abuse from a large body of customers, many of*
> *whom call at midnight and say, "Why the devil aren't you*
> *on the job?" Future uncertain, but plenty of thrills guaran-*
> *teed. Knowledge of how to get rid of smog not necessary—*
> *only a firm belief that it can be spent out of existence.*[49]

The finger-pointing was caustic for public confidence and the body politic. In an area better known for its progressive movements and tolerated eccentricities, L.A.'s air pollution dynamics were at turns contentious, personal, venomous, silly, and distracting. Einstein's quip that politics were more challenging than science resonated during this era of accusations. The mood certainly was set for upheaval and mistrust when six APCD researchers charged Larson with "maladministration" and corruption in early 1954. Among the allegations were falsified payroll records, excessive coffee breaks, doctored research, lousy morale, squashed studies, and even a shoving match. Immediately, almost 100 district workers bopped up to defend Larson.[50] A subsequent 2,700-page county inquiry did, too. It concluded almost every charge as groundless. One of Larson's main accusers, in fact, turned out to be one Meier Schneider, a man colleagues described as a troublemaking "busybody" with "diarrhea of the mouth."[51] Larson, salvaging the honor he could while acting as the district's temporary chief, fired the malcontents four days after the county exonerated him.[52]

Soon enough, Warren Dorn, Smogtown's original demagogue, stirred the pot again when he accused the district of easing back on refiners that he claimed were blackening the air to hazardous concentrations.[53] Reactionary newspapers raked in good money perpetuating controversies like this. A *Pasadena Independent* column illuminated the feisty mood by mocking Larson's superiors. "Find the fear, the indecision, the stupidity and the confusion and you've found the cause of smog. And where you do you find that? Right in the Board of County Supervisors, a collection of political frustrates whose convictions lack the durability of bubbles."[54] Larson about then probably should've had the good sense to stay away from Pasadena. Not surprisingly, when he attended a meeting in the city of Craftsman architecture and The Tournament of Roses parade, a grandmotherly advocate immortalized herself by waving an indignant finger in his face. Next, some 4,500 Pasadenans and other Valley residents jammed Pasadena's civic auditorium area for an overflow rally. Speakers at the foot-stomping event demanded another grand jury investigation. People wanted succor, wanted their mountain views back, the mayor said, "even if it means making the most radical kind of adjustments in our economy."[55]

Just as it is today, it's easy to criticize, harder to fix. Still the beast fathered a new type of trans-regional class divide not dictated by race, religion, or tax bracket, but split between source emitters and angry sufferers faraway.

*   *   *

In October 1954, Governor Goodwin Knight hurriedly flew down to L.A. to assist with one of the worst multi-week smogs ever recorded. Local authorities had been so unnerved about it that they took the unusual step of temporarily diverting commercial air traffic from LAX to Burbank and blockaded ships from entering San Pedro harbor. To keep cars' exhaust and panic down from what it expected to be a mass rush home, the California Highway Patrol, legend has it, went on alert at freeway on-ramps. Knight asked the refineries during the surge if they would temporarily halt their operations to gauge what effect it had. They snubbed him by answering "No." Knight, forsaking brinksmanship and by-the-horns leadership, took the middle path, leaving zealots unsatisfied. He allotted $100,000 to the Department of Public Health to begin examining smog's influence on human biology. The previous October, Knight had commissioned a blue-ribbon panel led by Beckman to see how to strengthen the air district. The committee endorsed a broader research menu and tighter industrial controls. It also wholeheartedly concurred with Haagy's focus on gasoline. Want to know where most smog came from? they asked. Check the garage.[56] It was not a people-pleasing message. Knight understood that, just as he knew what a complex problem L.A. had as weather and car effluents alloyed. "Smog," the governor reasoned, "is a scientific and engineering problem and not a political or legal one." Numerous judges later, and expediently, parroted that line.[57]

Such was the whammy for California's elected leadership. You couldn't imprison the beast by executive order, pound it into submission with artillery, negotiate for better terms, whistle for a holiday break, or shame it into hiding. Leaders looked inept in its grip. Poulson, for instance, appeared weak and almost irrelevant by putting his energy into seeking federal tax breaks for adapting industry on tax day in April 1954. He was a worried man. The mayor, riffing off U.S. census numbers, said that in 1950, a quarter-million people had settled into L.A.

neighborhoods largely untouched by the soupy skies, while 71,000 vacated polluted enclaves.[58] A dysfunctional pattern that one observer phrased as "senseless clamor" swirled among the proliferating interests after an attack shooed them indoors. They'd decry the conditions, argue responsibility, rhapsodize for unrealistic changes, topping it all off with saccharine sentiments for a better tomorrow. For the men in charge, smog really was "political dynamite."[59]

It blew up on Larson for the last time in a tiff with Poulson over a contentious phone call. There'd been suggestions that maybe the district should retain him. Not anymore. The mayor claimed that Larson had urged him during that October '54 episode to prepare an emergency declaration. Pressed for his recollection, Larson passionately disputed he'd said that, explaining he was just warning the mayor of the weather forecast and expected "calls for action" from other officials.[60] Poulson wouldn't drop it, branding Larson a liar. Even supervisors who'd championed him before had to ditch him now, replacing him temporarily with the county's chief administrative officer.[61]

For Larson, it was a winter to forget. Not only had he lost his job, but also his wife accused him of physical abuse during the holidays. He formally resigned in June 1955, as an obscure bureaucrat with a prospector-type name took the reigns.[62]

*   *   *

Besides igniting recrimination and personal attacks, Haagy's lab heroics also fostered offshoots that, over time, added meaty expertise about smog's composition and behaviors. His efforts certainly helped inspire a starburst of Bunsen-burning chemists and engineers who hankered for their own mighty discovery. Well-funded entities associated with corporations or the region's major universities—organizations such as the SRI, the Air Pollution Foundation, and its near-namesake, the Southern California Air Pollution Foundation—employed a majority of them, organizing them into groups with officious letterheads and countless subcommittees. They glommed initially around the role of hydrocarbons, generally dubious that auto exhaust was the crisis' breeder, before branching out into subfields. Bundled together, these organizations would've occupied a large industrial park, where smart, lab-coated men in a strange new frontier tested gadgetry and hypotheses. The Air Pollution Foundation, a private organization flush with oil money, ran thirty-four projects. Among them were the "Howdry catalytic muffler," then billed as a magic stopper for car exhausts, and a climate study involving 100,000 punch cards fed into a primitive computer.[63] A few years after its christening, the foundation announced a recalibrated goal. It wanted the APCD disbanded or downsized because it'd "rat-holed" $15 million in taxpayer funds as "nothing but a propaganda mill." A citizens' activist group that backed the district saw ulterior motives in the foundation's obstreperous stance, suggesting later it was shilling for oil and car interests fiercely opposed to reformulating gasoline to reduce annoying emissions.[64] Ideologically aligned with the foundation was the Southern California Air Pollution Foundation, which in 1954 had a $1.8-million budget from members such as Southern California Edison and Union Oil. Electing USC's president and then UCLA's chancellor as its chairmen gave it a prestigious sheen. Both groups fervently sought citizen sacrifice, not accelerated regulation.

Even so, the SRI remained the big contrarian on the block. A.M. Zarem, a young "war-problem" researcher, led its fifteen-person staff inside downtown's General Petroleum Building.[65]

While air pollution was one of its main topics, the Institute also studied rubber, bubbles, antenna design, and missile electronics. As late as August 1954, the SRI was resolute that it was the basin's villainous sun and indolent breezes that transformed otherwise harmless chemicals into a photochemical dungeon.[66] It recycled this message to the media, academia, symposiums, officialdom, anyone. When, in 1956, it shifted its local operation to a 38,000-square-foot lab in South Pasadena, the SRI crowed it was the second largest research organization of its kind in America.

Haagy, however, made them feel miniscule. After a number of severe smogs, the SRI leadership recognized that it would look dishonest and transparent continually downplaying hydrocarbons' effects, even if many non-partisan scientists were unsure about the role of un-combusted petroleum products. Begrudgingly, the Institute admitted automobiles were "the primary source of air pollution." Before this acknowledgement, though, there already had been another one. Zus Haagen-Smit, Haagy's second wife, in 2000 retold an enlightening vignette about an SRI employee—maybe even the man who gave the scorching Caltech speech. Without specifying where or when it occurred, she said the man passed her husband a note on the sly. It read, "You know where my livelihood comes from. You know I have to say these things." Typically, Zus commented, "you don't put something like that down on paper."[67]

In late 1956, in fact, the SRI apparently saw benefit in teaming up with old adversaries. It proposed an APCD research contract to ascertain whether unstable molecules called free radicals were a source of some of the eye irritation and plant damage. Asked his input, Haagy scoffed. The district had well established that it was olefins and nitrogen dioxide responsible for the eye-smarting fumes. Between its offensive against him and the Institute's "delayed acceptance" of his breakthroughs, he strongly recommended the district "steer clear" of any association with the group. They did.[68] Automakers did not capitulate as willingly. They conceded gasoline vapors were a problem, yet insisted that L.A.'s sub-atmosphere had its own "peculiar" nature unrelated to their tailpipe emissions. Garbage burning to them had as much to do with air pollution as their gas-guzzling machines.

Haagy barely was around to toot his own horn as many of his ideas underwent double and triple corroboration by others. By the mid-1950s, he again ditched his professorial blazer, this time to assist power-maker Edison burn its oil more completely. His determined gait next showed up in the South Bay, where he encouraged refiners to install "floating roofs" over their skimming ponds to stop oil vapors from evaporating. He was testing dangerous stuff inside his smog chamber and around these factories. "Sometimes," he remarked, "I've had the skin peel off my hands from chemicals, and I've had to say to myself, 'I must be more careful.'"[69]

Almost no matter what he did, Haagy remained captive to his own genius. Johnny-Come-Lately chemists regularly bothered him about why they'd been unable to replicate his lab results. One of his fondest pleasures, he admitted, was chatting with stewardesses during flights because they did not recognize him enough to pester him about his deductions. His enemies were impressed, or at least cagey enough to try to co-opt him. In the dead of the Michigan winter in 1955, there he was at the GM Research Lab sharing his story with the Society of Automobile Engineers. "It was like inviting a Trojan horse into the meeting," he chortled. He must have made an impression inside those enemy walls because auto executives were soon coming to see him.[70] Not that they started moving double-time on smog-control devices. Nonetheless, they seemed to know he was onto them. (The most he ever took from the carmakers were some of their gift ties.)[71] Outed by him or not, Detroit adored Southern California in the Ozzie and Harriet age, (when the songwriter who'd compose the iconic "I Love L.A." was still a pup). The area contained more automobiles per capita than any other place on the planet. Each week, for an indeterminate period in the go-go 1950s, 1,700 new vehicles joined this sumptuous market—allowing on average seven percent of their fuel to escape un-combusted. This, in essence, gave smog its growth hormones.[72]

Intellectually, the brick-by-brick mortaring of the L.A. smog bureaucracy bored Haagy. The drag of leaking fossil fuels on a teeming metropolis was a hypothetical no more, and he could see that air quality regulation was going to be a shambling progress of regulation and negotiation ping-ponged among lawyers, politicians, and technocrats. Haagy's previous conviction that once the automakers focused on engine and tailpipe exhausts smog would dissipate in two years wobbled. He now perceived the carmakers as sandbaggers. Since Detroit wasn't fully trustworthy, Haagy wanted the politicians to pick up the slack with hard-nose rules. They listened to him. Later he became one of them as a state air-quality general of sorts. Despite the honor, he always was better at science.

Come the 1960s, what he really desired was a fresh challenge. He found it right there in the driver's seat. Carbon monoxide—a poisonous fume also produced by incomplete combustion—would be his next hurdle. Gauging its biological effects harbored the kind of scientific urgency ideal for him. Commuters in stop-and-go traffic, he realized, were swimming through the odorless, tasteless gas every day in their cars without recognizing it. Carbon monoxide, while irrelevant in smog formation, was a sneaky assassin. Even 1960s' medicine comprehended it. Red blood corpuscles that normally carry oxygen to the body transport carbon monoxide instead when it's present. Prolonged contact with the gas starves cells, producing loss of judgment, muscular weakness, breathing distress and, if acute enough, death by asphyxiation. The threat was as real as the traffic accidents in Los Angeles and Sacramento that implicated it. California health officers compared carbon monoxide poisoning to a "mild anesthetic."[73] Peak-hour concentrations of it whacked drivers' alertness.

To understand the gas better, Haagy rigged his ancient Plymouth to a portable tester and drove between Pasadena and Los Angeles' Exposition Park during rush hour eight times in 1964.[74] Carbon monoxide registered at 37 parts per million (ppm), slightly over the 30 ppm the state had already set as hazardous. For true measure, he and an aide conducted some of the tests with the windows rolled up and the engine running. Haagy concluded that it was only after eight hours of exposure at 30 ppm that drivers got sleepy. Spending an hour in carbon monoxide at 120 ppm, conversely, was life threatening.

Coughing and sweating, the Dutchman jotted down what he could for a semi-grateful people.

L.A. AGAINST THE WORLD

On a lovely sunlit morning last October, Martin and his wife Evelyn sat at breakfast in the patio of their San Fernando Valley . . . listening apprehensively to the radio. Finally, it came, the same thing they had heard for five days in succession—"Smog Red." Martin swore and his wife groaned as they began revising their plans for the day. Evelyn decided to put off her marketing until nightfall again. Martin telephoned John Eggston, a neighbor. "Heard the report? Guess we'd better drive downtown together." . . . "What about the rubbish?" Evelyn asked her husband as he left the house. The "Smog Red" announcement meant that no trash could be burned until the smog lifted. . . As the two men drove through Cahuenga Pass toward central Los Angeles, they could see the smog lying in wait for them. . . Back home Evelyn watered the wilted flowers and brown-spotted hedges in the garden while she had the chance to be outdoors. By 10:30, the fumes had crept through the pass and were drifting toward her home. She picked up the baby, went into the house and closed all the doors and windows. . .[1]

WELCOME TO THE NEW L.A., THE UPTIGHT HOMETOWN. LOOK NO further than Martin and Evelyn's plight. Neglect to organize your regularly scheduled life around the ozone forecast and the misery was yours! Unless they resided at the desert or beach,

Southern Californians in 1956 couldn't just weather-worship lazily anymore. During the gray-domed days of spring and summer, they had to weather-watch. The recurring smog-bank took a wrecking ball to prior routines, drizzling complications, stress, and discomfort on tens of thousands of families across the socioeconomic spectrometer. Queried in a state survey whether smog bothered them, half of the local population answered, "YES!"[2] At noxious levels, the chemical troposphere drove kids off playgrounds and from sandlot games, throttled picnics, and bothered pets and old people. Airline passengers shook their heads in revulsion as their planes pierced the grungy inversion layer as they prepared to land. Live near a busy freeway, where the ozone concentrated, and you might need a good pulmonary doctor. Gamblers visiting Hollywood Park were smart to haul their binoculars along; opaque conditions sometimes eclipsed their view of the track —from the grandstands.[3] There was no escaping that dreary ceiling. Homeowners trying to sell their places knew to expect a discounted price if they were in an especially polluted zipcode. Even old safe havens lost their immunity. In the once-pristine canyons and neighborhoods of the West San Fernando Valley, smog from local auto traffic tumbled in from gorges near Griffith Park and the Cahuenga Pass.[4]

Those same microscopic pebbles also spritzed emission dust on cars, house exteriors, air conditioning compressors, tool sheds, and pretty much anything else left outside. Something in smog's chromosomes also faded textile dyes and weakened fabrics. Bad for consumers, the bleached clothing, pocked sidings, cracked whitewall tires, and the like became easy profits for retailers able to sell replacements and cleansing potions. Researchers scouring for causation occasionally benefited, as well. After a USC student noticed his tie had changed from a coral color his wife disliked to a bluish-purple color during a single day outside, technicians confiscated his neckwear as if it were a frozen caveman or other long-sought artifact, rushing it to the university's chemical engineering department for priority analysis.[5]

As the masses coped with their own smoggy circumstances, the elderly and sick bolting Southern California hardly made news.[6] Neither was there much alarm when officials tripped across a tenfold hike in absenteeism among government employees in the downtown branches of the Justice Department and IRS.[7] Whether the acidy air seeping into the buildings was responsible for this trend or whether it had just given malingers a fantastic excuse to call in sick wasn't easily known. People might've even chuckled about it had they not been dabbing smog tears so continually. These tears had gestalt for the era. While New York City's iconic images featured forlorn diners and partying at Times Square, Southern California's vintage shots had veered away from normal celebrity portraits. The classic L.A. pose now was the commoners' wince: old ladies wiping tears, cops tamping little girls' faces, even experiment volunteers in fishbowl helmets with pollution tears about to roll.

Inside civic groups and medical organizations, smog's presence in the clip-clop of everyday life continually shoved front and center questions about its effects on health. It was not just about the lungs, either. It was about the brain. L.A.'s brand of air pollution apparently was afflicting certain people with a perplexing condition. It could roust the temper, inciting grumpiness, belligerency, and even violent urges over nothing important.[8] California's mental health director speculated that auto fumes swirling inside the unhealthy air were so poisonous neurologically that it actually shook some individuals' sanity. Dr. Walter Rapaport, director of California's Mental Hygiene

Department, in fact, blamed the "stresses and strains" of inhaling tailpipe exhaust for increasing admissions to state mental hospitals.[9] The chief of the local medical association broadened the concept of pollution-disrupted physiology by claiming it fanned anxiety disorders and cognitive defects not seen in good weather. This so-called "mental tailspin" included "globus hystericus," an imaginary lump in the throat that provoked repeated swallowing.[10] No one tallied how many contracted it. Another frightening proposition was whether smog might inflame homicidal desires. The gruesome murder of a Jehovah's Witness in 1963 by a self-appointed crusader indicated that the theory might hold water. Albert Riviera allegedly killed his thirty-three-year-old victim, Harold Mather, because Mather was driving a chartered bus, and Riviera had taken it upon himself to eliminate those coaches as pollution sources. Riviera, forty-eight, had somehow forced Mather to stop the bus, and then ran him down with his car. Mather, citing his religious beliefs, refused a blood transfusion at the hospital and perished. Riviera went for psychiatric examination.[11]

Corroding property. Murderous rampages. Insane-asylum admissions. Hopelessness. Was it any surprise, then, that Los Angeles' chunky airshed induced new social neuroses expressed from pillow talk to public sermons? The Glendale Betterment Committee, a civic group, communicated in 1958 what others en masse later would: their chance at salvation had bypassed them. The Glendalians brooded that motorists had been "denied mass transit," and the soulless statistics heralding better air quality ahead were awing the average person into a state of numbness.[12] Albion Nelson, a sixty-three-year-old carpenter from Griffith Park, was among the damned, and hardly the last. On a fall day in 1956, he left his wife at the store to return home to give his final day meaning. "This is the only way I know of to accomplish what I have outlived," he wrote her. "Try to live where there's plenty of fresh air so the same thing doesn't happen to you." Nelson, dejected and determined, walked into the bathroom and fatally shot himself in the head with a 22-caliber rifle.[13] How many more suicides followed is an open question. Practically the only person embracing the situation was a convicted burglar esctatic to be out of jail after an L.A. judge mistakenly released him. He'd take sputtered breathing any day over leg shackles. "Everybody's complaining about the smog, but it suits me fine," felon Philip Ward burbled.[14]

*   *   *

S. Smith Griswold, the man who replaced Gordon Larson as smog boss, frequently sounded like an abandoned explorer when describing L.A.'s isolation in the pall. Throughout the early 1950s, California's top politician, Governor Knight, consistently snubbed the region's appeals for state help and cash. Griswold and others petitioned him to have Sacramento take over all or part of the burden from the overmatched APCD, but Knight rejected these requests as soon as they hit his inbox. He was simply unpersuaded that the situation was as grave as increasingly stressed Angelenos painted it. Knight reserved emergency declarations for earthquakes, floods, and military invasions, not a rolling chemical cloudbank that struck him more as a local nuisance to abate—or endure. His intractability made for years of mudslinging, as lesser officials he otherwise could've crushed vilified him.[15] Essentially asking "what now," supervisor Kenneth Hahn upbraided the governor for dodging the "hot potato" of state involvement except when it served his own agenda. Having watched Knight, then up for re-election, travel to L.A. with the California National Guard and civil defense commanders during the smog seize that closed the harbor, Hahn tartly predicted that Knight would reappear only after the next attack "to blow the bugles" again. Knight punched back that the supervisors were the ones with squishy backbones. Why were they so eager to shift responsibility to somebody else when local control was political holy writ? "Even since I've been in public life," Knight said, "I've heard we should keep government close to the people."[16] Translated: Sacramento was not trotting south without good reason.

Before the modern observer throws darts at Knight, it's important to remember that American-green circa 1955 meant money, not budding environmentalism. Gluttonous consumerism and Cold War apprehensions coexisted just fine. Disneyland, jets, fluoride, the Brat Pack, and the Corvette dazzled the popular mind. Smog barely registered outside the complaint line. There was no state or federal EPA, no Clean Air Act, no Natural Resources Defense Council to file suit for the disenfranchised and, largely, no calls for anything of the sort. Griswold, in writing to a senatorial-aide friend, cringed at the meek role of the Feds in L.A., where smog "generated one crisis after another."[17] Washington had given the district virtually no assistance, he said, and of the four people they did assign, two were untrained tenderfeet. So as Ike sermonized about broadening federal involvement, Griswold openly ripped the leader of the free world for an inchoate national air pollution program "heavy on overhead and light on research."[18] Sure, there were minor exceptions. Congressman Carl Hinshaw, for one, promised an applauding town hall audience that "if Los Angeles can't or won't do something quickly, we [Congress] will have to."[19] Given the scraps offered for the West Coast's smog tsunami, Hinshaw's words were shallow bluster.

As of 1957, the federal government had expended a mere $37,000 in L.A. on smog reduction—about $273,000 in today's dollars. Columnists tabbed it "strange parsimony and laggard-ness,"[20] and the neglect extended statewide. In Santa Clara County and San Diego, nobody was researching. San Francisco's air district had zero staff; Riverside's agency had no budget. In Washington's absence, private industry-linked research organizations like the Air Pollution Foundation (annual budget $750,000) and the SRI (with forty to fifty peo-ple studying smog) were far ahead of most West Coast cities and most Western states. When California smog floated into unprepared Arizona, Senator Barry Goldwater replied, with biting wit, "We try to keep it out."[21]

Luckily for Angelenos, the APCD had in Louis Fuller—the #2 behind Griswold—a first-ever enforcement boss chomping to take the fight to emissions. Fuller was an ex-LAPD motorcy-cle captain with a granite face and no soft spot for lawbreakers. Soon after becoming Griswold's lieutenant, he deputized the region's 10,000 police officers to buttress the district's twenty-three-man inspection squad. Second-guessing his predecessors, he asked why so many industries had gotten away with "30 to 80" separate violations sans conviction. "Don't underestimate smog," Fuller warned. "We came perilously close to a major disaster in the onset of last October." During a thirty-month period ending in September 1957, he'd help file 7,541 cases with a ninety-six percent conviction rate that any Texas hang-ing judge would admire. He designated helicopters and Cessnas with sheriff's department colors for overhead coverage. A man sent to jail for igniting a blaze during a debris cleanup seemed petrified of him, saying repeatedly in court, "I will never light another fire again."[22] Fuller, with a little *Dragnet*-style "Joe Friday" in him, made sure to hire inspectors knowledgeable about refineries, chemistry, and industry shenanigans. Any pol-luting business, whether discharging effluents inadvertently or on the sly, would face "serious consequences," Fuller said without exaggeration.[23]

Griswold exuded the same determination, telling people the "distasteful" news they didn't want to hear: smog might get worse before it got better. Industry generally had complied, he said. Carmakers hadn't.[24] It was no stunner that a bus strike, which inundated the roads with 100,000 additional cars, generated predictably ungodly air. Griswold and Fuller also approached the jaws of the beast. Along with Hahn, they directed county lawyers to explore local government's authority to outlaw cars operating without exhaust-catching filters. The idea of the county using its own legal sword to protect its people was tantalizing for politicians coveting self-action. Unfortunately, no matter how many times it was hyped as a regulatory ace, constitutional issues about the fairness of imposing standards on businesses without practical technology and the marketplace to achieve them negated the chances. The supervisors also demanded to know whether they might use their "almost unlimited authority" to keep new pollution-generating businesses out of the basin, and learned the only clout they had was in prohibiting expansion of existing industries.[25] Their search for more iron-fisted control soon led them to the out-ringing areas, where subdivisions were cropping up like wild oaks. Word got back to the APCD that some wily speculators were purchasing farmland that was exempt from anti-burning rules for supposed "agricultural purposes." In a classic land machination, they'd torch citrus groves after gaining title, and then sell the land to residential-home developers afterwards.[26] Builder-types barked that Griswold was over-reacting to the ploy, which seemed to subside after the media publicized the scheme. Griswold acted immune from the complaints. The real problem was millions of dirty tailpipes.

Fuller soon appreciated what Larson had learned. Leading the anti-smog charge meant simultaneously fighting public skepticism and defending your personal honor. At an impromptu APCD meeting, Pasadena's merciless Citizen's Anti-Smog Action Committee accused him of running interference for Big Oil by preventing the group from seeing data on refineries' sulfur-collecting scavenger pipes. The take-no-guff Fuller denied any hidden motives, adding that he'd consult with his lawyer about a libel suit targeting the rabble-rousers. "I'm a little agitated," he admitted. As the finger-pointing continued, the supervisors shouted that the uproar had "gone far enough," and swore both Fuller and Committee members under oath. Activists later apologized to Fuller for contesting his "integrity."[27]

The movie studios presented a different case. They complained that the rule limiting burning to three minutes an hour was crimping the sorts of movie shoots where Roman cities went up in flames or combat scenes concussed with epic, bomb-rattling action. Not everybody felt those laws were onerous. On the San Fernando Valley set of the Western drama Brave Eagle, smog was a backdrop destroyer, blotting out what were supposed to be the blue skies of yesteryear. "Every morning before we leave the studio we say a few Indian prayers that the smog will have blown away," confessed the co-star and part-Cheyenne Keith Larsen. Had his ancestors been dealing with it, "they'd never had been able to see each other's smoke signals."[28] The Motion Picture Producers' Association approached Fuller for a compromise. He refused. He told the studios and TV networks they could appeal their grievance to the hearing board like anyone else.

Besides those district-run hearing boards—and there were multiple ones, broken down by industry—Griswold and Fuller saw their aggressive enforcement creed segue into the general legal system. At Hahn's urging, a superior-style court dedicated exclusively to smaller smog violations began hearing cases in February of 1955.[29] That court and similar ones in places like El Monte began simplistically, targeting private citizens whose cars discharged excessive amounts of smoke. (Because of technical limitations and the state's hesitation to make air pollution an urgent priority, no laws yet existed for smog constituents like hydrocarbons and nitrogen oxide.)

Nonetheless, establishing a dedicated smog court, where penalties started at $50 and/or five days in jail, was a symbolic milestone that Griswold's crackdown was spreading. Before long, local police and the California Highway Patrol had ticketed the drivers of several hundred trucks under the state health and safety code. The widening net for all air contaminants was granting no immunity to individuals, be they blue-collar workers or the rich anymore. Rounding it all out was a new round-the-clock radio system connecting the district with its uniformed enforcement brigade. It scouted for rogue emissions by refineries, woodworkers, steel plants, and asphalt mixers. In Griswold's regime, you emitted at your risk.

*　　*　　*

While Hollywood special-effects crews tried finessing their outdoor shoots, Griswold and others contemplated how to preempt a real-life toxic emergency haunting the region's future. The anguished debate about it pitted California-grown concepts of protective health against well-seated emotionalism. Who were the Joneses to believe: district administrators who downplayed the probability of a sulfur nightmare, or the extremists envisioning carnage so widespread it'd make Donora seem trivial? Against this opinion gulf, a thirteen-man team inside the APCD headquarters tossed around ideas on how to notify the county's millions when the atmosphere tickled hazardous levels. It was one the hardest challenges the district had taken on. No one really knew at what level a toxin went from unhealthy to lethal, just as the varying jurisdictions could not decide who was responsible for protecting exposed communities. Consequently, the logistics of creating an alert network was a drawn-out, unwieldy process, as much pragmatic solution as hard science. For Los Angeles, the world's first beachhead against chronic air contamination, it typified the seeming impossibility of containing an unknown. Each possible answer was either too unpalatable to somebody's interest or too untested to guarantee it could protect tens of thousands of lives in a panic.

To be effective, local government and law-enforcement agencies needed to be able to warn the public at a moment's notice. And in a day when fixed-wired communications meant rotary telephones or desk-sized Telex machines, this presented real dilemmas. Nonetheless, in June 1955 the supervisors approved a three-tiered system reliant on voluntary cooperation by drivers and industry in the first two stages. If the air grew worse, the APCD would alert state government. This refinement, smoothed out from an earlier plan, assuaged fears from citizen groups and some business interests that the APCD was too inexperienced or weak to handle a full-on emergency. The amended alert system, triggered when contaminant standards set by local physicians and scientists exceeded safety limits, still made for instant hullabaloo. The California Manufacturers Association, representative of the state's biggest companies and a mirror of the corporate outlook, insisted that calamity was a "remote possibility," and blanched at the early-warning apparatus.[30] Suburban agitators wanted the notifications to go further. Greetings from 1950s Smogtown.

Those in favor of low thresholds for Los Angeles had a British air tragedy to cite as a powerful argument. In December 1952, Londoners watched a familiar pea-soup fog turn into something terrifyingly unfamiliar. The mist amplified itself into an inversion-trapped cloudbank of sooty, smoky air—instigated by widespread coal burning—that lasted for four days. Visibility was down to almost nothing. Some motorists and bus drivers abandoned their vehicles, sometimes to walk up to road signs to see where they were. Policeman donned gas masks. One newspaper said the sun "hung sulkily in the dirty sky with no more radiance than an unlit Chinese lantern." The Londoners who stumbled into the hospitals with inflamed respiratory tracts and struggling hearts were the first wave of a sick mega-capital. In five days, there were 4,000 more deaths than normal. Another 8,000 perished within the subsequent two months. These so-called "excess deaths" were part of a pattern. London lost another 1,300 in similar coal-related episodes in '56 and '62. Across the pond, New York City experienced three temperature-inversion smogs (in '53, '63, and '66) that killed nearly 700.[31] APCD leaders scoured accounts of the incidents for lessons, sometimes shipping staffers abroad for firsthand accounts. Managing public psychology was more delicate, because the cynicism was becoming as viscous as a stage-two alert. After these other cities descended into their own chemical abysses, APCD experts couldn't keep convincingly repeating the statistical unlikelihood of a death-smog overtaking L.A. It would smack of smug overconfidence—or head-in-the-sand denial.

The district's adopted notification system, based on known health-hazard levels for four base chemicals—ozone, carbon monoxide, nitrogen oxide, and sulfur oxides—was a novelty for manufacturing-heavy America. Its stepped procedures, the nation's first system of the sort, would be an international bellwether for other smoggy lands. But before others borrowed it, the warning plan underwent numerous iterations and even longer second-guessing. In a first-stage alert, if he believed a toxic buildup necessitating preventative action was approaching, L.A.'s smog chief would order all trash burning halted, urge motorists not to drive, and prepare commerce to arrest operations. Picture a bunkering landscape trying not to paralyze itself. Refiners, manufacturers, and other heavy industry would be idled in a second-stage alert, with only essential driving permitted. Radio and TV would transmit public announcements, encouraging carpools for workers to get home. If a third alert sounded, the supervisors would duck into special session to decide whether to ask the governor to declare a state of emergency, including full-scale police action. Should the governor issue one, he could bring the region to a standstill—hospitals and power plants notwithstanding—to allow the contaminants time to disperse.[32] And thanks to additional legislation by Pasadena assemblyman Stewart, smog now was officially "a natural disaster." Like flood, fire, war, and earthquake, a contaminated troposphere now could warrant martial law-type actions after Governor Knight signed legislation amending the California Military and Veterans Code in a low-fanfare ceremony.[33]

That triumph notwithstanding, informing people who were away from the radio or TV was thorny. The most surefire method was sounding civil defense air-raid sirens designed to warn of impending nuclear attack, but the federal government balked at the APCD's desire about using them. Snubbed there, the district tinkered with substituting bells and horns. They noodled with deploying low-flying planes fitted with speakers until expenses and pilot-safety questions arose. There was brief discussion about turning on city streetlights. No-go there, either: flipping that switch, city officials said, would throw off their automatic, clock-adjusted timers. After considerable tail-chasing, the APCD backed a dedicated radio-teletype network with receivers at some 1,000 plants and contracts with the media. When an ominous forecast hit, district personnel would zip alert warnings to national wire services like the Associated Press and to their local counterparts. Using teletype machines, they'd transmit that information to area TV and radio stations for immediate broadcast on normal channels, and to the newspapers. Instead of taking fifteen minutes to order people to get inside, it would only require two. The speed was virtually "real-time" for the transistor era.

Industry was none too thrilled. A Richfield Oil Co. vice president named David Day questioned what a smog alert shutdown would cost the company's production ledger. He said the company would only close its refinery on a written order delivered to its corporate headquarters from the APCD control office. Furthermore, it expected the county to reimburse it for lost revenue if it were later determined that freezing its operations was inconsequential.[34] The Liquefied Petroleum Gas Association, edgy that a shutdown might drain its members of the ten-to-fifteen-days worth of gas they stocked, said serious shortages causing "undue hardship upon the general public" could ensue. "Our industry can be likened to the utilities," its West Coast secretary wrote in the summer of 1955. "The far-reaching effects of the proposed ordinance could . . . create a condition of distress among a greater number of people than are currently located in the smog [-affected] areas."[35] Whether philosophically resistant to summary orders or just playing it conservatively, many other firms were equally resistant or apathetic in their commitment. Of the 15,000 individual plants and factories in the basin, just twenty-seven sent the district a voluntary shutdown plan as mandated by the summer of 1956. Aside from plans submitted by steel and hot-asphalt sectors, whose willing compliance received scant publicity, most businesses were sitting on their hands.[36]

Crafting emergency logistics was like trying to buff a moving object. As the district itself came to acknowledge, its alert plan contained a structural deficiency indigenous to L.A.'s all-or-nothing commuter culture. In June 1957, after the region's twenty-fifth first-stage alert, the APCD's respected planning and evaluation boss, Robert Chass, admitted that the system was flawed because solo-driven vehicles were part of the work-evacuation sequence. Government couldn't snap its fingers and instantly transport a gigantic regional workforce from business to home, nor could it demand carpooling. "It's entirely possible," Chass acknowledged, "that the shutting down of industrial operations may only exaggerate the overall pollution program by having thousands of employees drive their automobiles in the worst possible time of the day." Stated another way, prodding people onto bumper-to-bumper freeways crusty with smog-belching tailpipes was no way to manage a crisis.[37] It was a way to proliferate it. Viewed from a Dr. Strangelove angle, the scenario resembled a theoretical nuclear accident, where events snowball exponentially and technology becomes a dagger. Everybody had merely figured it'd be radiation, not hydrocarbons, necessitating body bags.

Uneasiness about a smog cataclysm—the specter of people falling dead in their cars and homes—drenched L.A.'s politicians in a collective cold sweat during the three years officials wrestled with emergency plans. There certainly was no unity achieved from the proceedings. As the world mourned the death of James Dean, the pompadoured rebel who perished in an October 1955 central California car wreck, the dean of the UCLA Medical School, Dr. Stafford Warren, opined, "There is no medical evidence up to now of death by smog." Warren claimed this at about the same time that his very university sought millions of research dollars to study air pollution, because "death and illness from smog are sufficiently menacing." The next year, while Americans read about Grace Kelly's princess marriage and Jimmy Hoffa's union, county supervisors queried county lawyers again about preventative strategies that would be pivotal over the long haul to preempt the unthinkable. Might we, they wondered, forbid new pollution sources, whatever they might be, from entering the basin altogether? Yes, government attorneys told them, they had that power. "The time has come for this Board to take positive action on this matter," Hahn said. "While it may hurt some it must be done for the general good."[38]

*   *   *

The resolve of Griswold and the supervisors to end homeowners' do-it-yourself trash disposal during the 1950s had all the luster of a surprise property tax. The situation was richly illuminating, though, of the public psyche. Convincing millions of folks to halt their backyard trash burning, for only marginal clean-air gains, was asking a lot for layered, if maddening reasons. First, there was the difficulty of engaging individual sacrifice for a communal goal when citizens were still shaking off sacrifice-fatigue from the 1930s and 1940s. Never mind that L.A.'s infamous air slapped millions with allergy-like symptoms. People didn't want to accept that their lifestyles—their dual cars, their electricity-sucking kitchens—shared any blame. Off to the side was a quirkier component. Angelenos clung to old habits, and incinerating castoff egg cartons, magazines, and other dry waste in that fiery chamber was ritual. People didn't appreciate how much they treasured that routine until the beast endangered its existence. It was just that all that smoke contributed, by the district's math, about one hundred tons per day to the visibility-obliterating conditions.

Not surprisingly, the region sunk into another smog-blame brouhaha when the supervisors voted to outlaw all single-chamber incinerators. Air pollution, as it had with West Coast farmland, was influencing urban layout, social justice, industrial hungers, and the public's trust of authority. Fused together, these unintended consequences were reshaping—or warping—the fundamental Southern California experience. Yet waste disposal was unique, with many cherishing it as a right, and the confrontation reflected it. Citizen groups faulted the oil companies' purported refusal of bigger cutbacks for making this backyard intrusion against them necessary. L.A. City Hall requested a sixty-day tryout to observe the difference in air quality. Special interests banged for their own exemptions. The supervisors tried plugging their ears, realizing they had to either go through with their order or cave to public pressure. On June 9, 1955, in what historians described as one of the stormiest votes in county lore, the supervisors decreed that most rubbish burning would end by July 1 except in cities where trash pickup service could not be offered immediately. (Even in those cities people would have to burn their refuse at special times.) The audience erupted in protest and anger, as more than "500 shoving and shouting incinerator do-or-diers" rattled the hall. Bidding to temper emotions, the supervisors agreed to postpone the ban until October 1. The audience booed and interrupted the proceedings even more. Meeting again in August, the supervisors undertook about the only step they could, delaying the ban until October 1, 1957. For pollution-cops spun dizzy by their task, trash smoke was nearly as frustrating as ozone to deep-six.[39]

L.A. had been one of the last holdout regions in the United

States still relying on backyard disposal. The debris piled up: 6,000-plus tons of combustible rubbish daily. An estimated 1.5 million residential incinerators, plus another 17,500 at businesses and apartment houses, torched the sorts of refuse that residents in other cities left curbside for the garbage truck. Southland homeowners burned so much waste that a one-hundred-square-foot pile of one day's garbage would reach nearly eight miles into space.[40] On the West Coast, where personal choice and scrappy Libertarianism were political sacraments, the incinerator connoted self-sufficiency that air-quality regulators had trouble wrapping their minds around. Even residents who applauded when the APCD took on big business were stunned when the government moved to disrupt their backyard refuse habits. The combustion fumes rising out of them unfortunately weren't state colors. The charred gray-black smoke and cottony-white plumes melded with other contaminants in a hanging bouillabaisse that Griswold and his predecessors seethed about constantly. They wanted to attack every source, no matter how many citizens would be offended. From overhead, those incinerators looked like a sea of "open-mouth volcanoes" burning freely.[41]

It was just that imagining life without Old Faithful was a personal affront the public could not swallow. Back then, the stand-alone chambers resembled an outdoor fireplace or metal BBQ-smoker set on end. "Why don't you be adult about this and leave our incinerators alone," a Downey couple sniped to the supervisors. "You know where the smog comes from . . . your refineries and chemical plants."[42] Others fretted that leaving garbage out for municipal pick-up would attract armies of rodents and insects for all-you-can-eat trash buffets. After government-led extermination efforts going back decades, now the smog cops were inviting the critters back? people asked. Heaps of sanitary napkins and "five-day-old meat wrappings," they were sure, would be disease breeders for neighborhood kids and fire hazards for communities. Tack on the $1.25-per-month collection fee, and government might well precipitate a new "depression" for already-overtaxed California homeowners, some critics yelped. One woman questioned why the government would bother to organize such a "vicious attack" on an innocuous practice, while trucks, buses, boilers, and generators were stinking up the place. What would be the next small independence proscribed: the barbecue, dry cleaning? Even the *Times* expressed "mixed emotions" about the fiat, questioning its worth and the semi-McCarthyistic request for citizens to become "stool pigeons" by finking on trash-burning neighbors. The APCD had created a phone number for informers. "The psychology is bad," the paper editorialized. "A worthy civic improvement loses something by being associated with a practice so offensive to the free tradition."[43]

The demise of the backyard burner also equaled obsolescence for the companies selling and repairing them. Rushing to stave off irrelevancy, these trade groups accused the APCD of running a socialist-style witch-hunt. When Griswold's staff costumed an incinerator to resemble what one newspaper called a "Backyard Beelzebub" at a consumer home show, industry rhetoric escalated. A trade group spokesman raised the sensitive issue that smallish sectors like theirs lacked the political wallet of the big boys to buy their way out of crackdowns. "Unfortunately, this industry does not have the financial power to hire research institutes and foundations to run interference for us. . . . Besides we are not too sure that this [ban] is science at all. . . . Money can buy practically anything."[44] If authorities were genuine about capping every smog source, instead of merely fanning "hysteria" over trash fumes, anti-ban leaders recommended the APCD prohibit what people puffed as well, because that was a tiny source of air pollution itself. But why? As one anti-ban businessman snorted, "To date, no one has fallen over dead from the result of smoking three packs of cigarettes a day."[45]

The East Coast-based Mafia allegedly had an opposite reaction. The changeover from citizen trash torching to a publicly run curbside pickup system was its potential bonanza! Organized crime had run bookmaking rackets, prostitution rings, and offshore gambling ships in L.A.'s recent past, so it was no stretch it'd make smog its enterprise. Soon government grapevines shook with lurid rumors about mobsters in their midst. In June 1954, in a titillating development that had tongues flapping, the DA's office received a tip about this from a "mystery man." He claimed that shakedown artists were intimidating apartment-house owners confused about how to handle their waste now that they could no longer simply chuck it into their basement incinerator. Wiseguys supposedly were extorting the owners—"blackjacking" in 1950s lingo—to pay them off, purchase smoke-cutting equipment from them, or contract with corrupted waste-haulers. According to rumor, if they refused the mob would rat them out to the health department for violating the regulation.[46] There'd been a similar racket working L.A.'s water-softening and food-freezing businesses. Like other Smogtown urban myths, this one was bogus. There was no blackjacking, and prosecutors never filed a case. It turns out that the suspects actually were predatory incinerator salesmen—not stereotyped mobsters named Rocko and Vinny—tailing APCD inspectors to apartment houses to gin up sales leads.[47]

Anxieties about wiseguys plundering Southern California's new waste-collection districts, as they had on the Atlantic seaboard, would not fade away, and with good reason. "I even heard rumors that the Mafia was going to take over," Supervisor Hahn said in May 1955.[48] Grand juries and a state legislative committee investigated allegations about a "syndicate" operating monopolistically in concert with the Teamsters Union. This time, there was evidence of organized crime bullying legitimate dump owners with threats of pickets and bloodshed. A man who paid a $10,000 bribe to secure a trash-collection deal told officials from the postage-stamp cities of Maywood and Bell that they'd "eat their own garbage" unless they signed with him. LAPD Chief William Parker, in testimony to lawmakers, said that in one suburb, a union local had served as "an enforcer."[49] Paranoia so ricocheted that when the city of Los Angeles' new two-million-dollar public incinerator flunked APCD startup tests, there was scuttlebutt it had failed because the Mafia sabotaged it.[50] The heightened scrutiny had effect. The mob seemingly lost interest in Los Angeles, settling down instead in a town called Las Vegas.

Griswold tiptoed around the sore feelings, and called the end of the residential incinerator during the bickering proof of "wonderful public acceptance." After all, people must surrender something important to get back something grander. Positioning control of auto exhausts as his overriding objective, he gingerly began lecturing Angelenos about the challenges ahead. "One of our most distasteful tasks was to tell the unhappy citizenry that, in all probability, they can look to more smog attacks next year as bad, or possibly worse than those of this year," he said in December 1955. "Every resident, every industry, and every agency must pledge the fullest cooperation."[51] That adapt-or-perish message was a bitter pill for some politicians to ingest. Through a historical lens, the government garbage takeover jeopardized Southern California's "home rule" understanding—cities' pacts not to impinge on one another's authority. The hands-off policy, which outsiders compared to the principalities of Medieval Europe, had individualized the county's towns, unchaining them to cultivate their own identities in a loosely bound federation. Monterey Park, a hilly city of 32,000 northeast of downtown L.A., interpreted the trash-burning ban as such a risk to its future that it promised to take the issue to the U.S. Supreme Court. It and other recalcitrant suburban cities eventually dropped their reservations, however, partly because of the supervisors' lobbying. Soon, county-run landfills shuddered to life near population hotspots in Pomona, Monterey Park, Calabasas, and the Sunset Strip, alleviating the need for do-it-yourself incineration. In future decades, those trash hillocks fattened into virtual waste mountain ranges as the county population shot past ten million. Southern California today lives in a perpetual trash crisis—begun by the Smogtown crisis—where the incinerator is but a trivia answer.

*   *   *

Like atomic war, the fear of an L.A. smog disaster was never-ending, despite governmental head-patting that everything would be okay. Scientists tangled over it. Doctors squabbled about it. A Pittsburgh researcher said he detected "no significant relationship" between L.A. smog and sulfur dioxide, one of industry's most common gases, but he might as well have been mute. Comparisons showing that Meuse Valley, London, Donora, and other sulfur-smog abattoirs hadn't curbed usage of the chemical, as had the Southland, comforted few. Reports that workers exposed to normal concentrations of it were healthy, and that the chemical didn't appear to accumulate in the body as a cancer portent, was just more polarizing opinion for many. Technical misinterpretation and pandering by the area's elected leaders shoveled on additional confusion. In the worst moments, the dissenting voices reached such earsplitting crescendos that a sociologist might posit whether disaster was a self-fulfilling prophecy.

If there was any clarity around this juncture, it was that elected officials now were openly willing to politicize smog controversies. In prior local elections, they'd been backburner issues. After the incinerator prohibition enflamed populist feelings and the drumbeat of chilling stories about Los Angeles' susceptibility to a killer smog, air pollution policy became a campaign hot-button in the hardest-choked cities. Pasadena vice-mayor Warren Dorn was among the first to exploit the topic as a wedge issue. In his campaign for supervisor against incumbent Roger Jessup, Dorn accused Jessup of quashing an alarming report by the private L.A. County Medical Association about air pollution's effects on public health.[52] Jessup denounced the move as an obvious stunt, "an eleventh-hour trick." Accurate as his analysis was, Dorn had reasons any seasoned politician would've. An exhausted people needed hope. And if there wasn't a magic wand available, they needed a hero who'd bring one back. More often than not, they'd gotten runny noses from the air and excuses about why the gray tendrils remained. Other cities had already learned about the drawbacks of demagoguery to sensible policy. "It took thirty-five years to eliminate our smog," the head of Pittsburgh's air pollution agency joked in 1956. "Thirty years to get rid of the politicians and five years to get rid of the smog itself."[53]

Nobody fought harder against Griswold's sulfur blitzkrieg than the Western Oil & Gas Association in the late 1950s. More broadly, wrangling over changes to Rule 62 exposed the paradoxes of L.A. smog, revealing old vitriol over plant emissions, and cultural reluctance to question the American-made automobile. It all started when the APCD tried extending the existing fuel-oil rule year-round, a rule the district had enacted in November 1953 without much public emotion. That regulation disallowed steam power plants, oil refiners, and others from burning fuel oil with more than .5% sulfur content during the May-October "high-smog" months. Petroleum tradesmen quiet during the incinerator fracas lunged up in opposition with the district's push to make the fuel-oil rule apply every day. They espoused the macro view, saying oil—as state transit lifeblood and sub-economy—deserved special treatment. (Steam-powered electricity plants consumed about three quarters of local fuel-oil supplies.) What might happen, the Association asked, if oil-rich countries, presumably from the Middle East, cut off supplies in a national emergency and America was drooling for black gold any way it could get it?

The Association then argued that they were already in sorry shape. The existing seasonal ban on high-sulfur fuel, combined with the railroads' conversion to diesel, had dried up Southern California's fuel-oil production to a tune of $40-million to $45-million per year in lost sales to its members. If the district made Rule 62 apply year-round, the Association said nearly all its members would have to import 12.5-million barrels per year of heavy crude from out of state—at a $25-million yearly loss. Above all that, the law was only going to make the smallest of differences: 22,000 daily barrels of processed fuel oil would have almost no effect on the pollution needle. Consumers, in the meantime, would feel the pinch by paying higher bills, or scrambling to find energy in a crisis. "To insure the local availability of fuel oil when it is needed for emergency situations without resorting to costly purchases from other areas, the petroleum industry cannot be shut out of the market during a half of each year," the Association said.[54]

Prodded for his thoughts, Beckman, the Caltech professor and businessman considered one of Smogtown's shrewdest minds, agreed that sulfur dioxide concentrations were "negligible" in the basin. It wasn't part of the photochemical-smog mating dance, either. Nitrogen oxide, a byproduct of natural gas, was more hazardous, he believed. Nobody's position changed, and the standoff dragged on. Foreshadowing future air-quality skirmishes, where regulators' determination ran smack into industry's production realities, the Association summoned other allies: an economist, an environmental medicine expert, lawyers, an agricultural research chemist, and the slightly indignant L.A. Chamber of Commerce. When their arguments made no dent, the Association tried daring Griswold and the supervisors to say openly what they were implying—that refiners were coldhearted moneymen. They had to. The Los Angeles area, with its insatiable thirst for gasoline, fuel oil, diesel, and other petroleum products, was already the country's "largest single metropolitan market," by the Association's tally. As the group's smog-policy committee chief wrote in the summer of 1959:

> *The oil industry lives and works in Los Angeles. We each of us breathe approximately 50,000 cubic feet of Los Angeles air a day. If there is any danger of Los Angeles becoming a Donora or London, we propose everything we can do to prevent it. We have no desire to be an air pollution statistic. . . . Unfortunately, it is not that simple. Los Angeles already has cleaner air than almost any other big city in the world, yet we have smog. By now, we should know that it is not how much so-called 'contaminant' we remove from the air, but rather it is what specific 'contaminant' we remove from the air that counts. Counting the tons of so-called contaminants removed from the air gives an illusion of progress but makes no material contribution to the reduction of smog or the protection of the health of the community.*[55]

Griswold must've felt like Sisyphus, who spent eternity pushing a rock up a hill only to see it always tumble backwards. Every time he notified his bosses of headway, he had to calibrate how new residents and industry flocking to Southern California undermined what his people had just accomplished. For him, "growth" was becoming a dirty word. The original Rule 62, for instance, had slimmed sulfur dioxide emissions by two-thirds, down to 250 tons per day. Industrial expansion, partly spurred by rising consumer appetites, though, had jacked it back up to 500 tons per day. When Griswold thought sulfur, he thought mortalities. Plants burning fuel oil created "the grave potential of severely affecting the public health," he testified. Worse, there were no techniques for breaking up an inversion, and no barricades for the moving vans, either. Every year, no matter the statistical progress towards blue skies, one hundred polluting industries whose emissions equaled Salt Lake City's industrial base migrated to L.A.[56] For some residents living near sulfur-spewing power generators, this all spelled danger. They claimed gases floating around their homes had strangled their flowerbeds and surrounding vegetation.[57]

Southern Californians were jading by the minute. The community zeitgeist toward smog, which had always been uneven, was sharply dividing at the conclusion of the 1950s between hard-baked discontent and near-surrender. A proposed district rule had never made previously compliant residents agitate like wild-eyed loons as Rule 62 did, however. They wanted fuel oil outlawed and they wanted it now! "Between smog and the atomic fallout, we don't have very much to look forward to," one pro-ban North Hollywood woman wrote the supervisors.[58] In letters, phone calls, crude petitions, and public comments, people from all occupations and lifestyles stated doubts about their sturdiness to keep chugging forward. "Don't you think Los Angeles has been very patient regarding smog conditions?" asked the Rivers family of Van Nuys. "According to the rumblings heard everywhere, the breaking point is not far off. . . . Trucks, buses, etc. pouring out smoke and gasses can be stopped tomorrow, but they come under big business too, and we can't make big business angry or they'll leave. Never mind the people who are leaving by way of the undertaker."[58] Likeminded citizens tried anything to sway the decision. They threatened. They lashed out. They reminisced. They warned authorities would be shocked if they knew how many of their West Coast acquaintances planned a "general exodus." Vera Lehrer of Pacoima, concerned about the mental and physical strain that pollution thrust on her kids, admitted feeling overwrought. "I am right on the edge of hysteria, and if it went on a few more hours I would be down there after you with a hatchet."[59]

These exasperations reflected an alarming new skepticism, where Southern California's middle class saw politicians and regulators prioritizing corporate interests above its basic sur-vival. Nobody was humming patriotic ditties about unity any-more. "There is one choice between millions of dollars and millions of people," a worried citizen wrote in a Western Union telegram to Hahn. "Which will it be?"[60] Activists usurped some of this grassroots Establishment-bashing for their own message. The Anti-Smog Action Committee questioned which supervi-sors, if any, had the pluck to bring Big Oil to heel. When the supervisors finally approved making Rule 62 apply year-round in Fall 1958, there was community elation, but the Action Committee didn't waste time celebrating. It immediately went after another concession: "sealed automatic recorders" on refin-ery equipment to prevent the companies from secretly burning fuel oil at night.[61] Smogtown was concocting a new urban activism, where the noisiest voice often won.

*   *   *

To its credit, the L.A. business world recognized the sinking public outlook. Griswold and company, as a result, were able to extract concessions from entities previously hostile to granting them. In May 1955, for instance, a South Bay jury found behemoth power-maker Southern California Edison guilty of criminal violations of the region's clean air laws. A superior court upheld the conviction, and Edison's lawyers hauled their appeal to the U.S. Supreme Court. That fall, Griswold's troops began dropping the hammer on the utility despite its contentions of innocence. In a rulebook salvo, the APCD denied the company's operating permit for its $25-million El Segundo plant and refused to permit construction of three Edison facilities in the southerly beach communities of Alamitos, El Segundo, and Redondo Beach. Soon, the district attorney filed two more cases against the company, but shelved them while other legal issues were hashed out. Licking their wounds, a group of Edison suits, including its president, met privately with regulators and Supervisor Jessup in January 1956, where they received a good tongue-lashing. Edison, officials said, was doing "far less" than its competitors to roll back its emissions, and didn't even have a qualified chemical engineer on staff. "Approximately one month ago, there suddenly appeared to be a complete change of attitude on the part of the company and their top officials appeared at my office and suggested that they would like to go into a complete program of control for their various installations," Griswold wrote Jessup. Edison had budgeted $1.8 million for it. "By this action," Griswold continued, "they have in essence agreed that they have been violating air pollution laws and clearly indicated that they wish to take corrective action."

Did they ever! Following the district's recommendation, Edison hired Haagen-Smit as a consultant, dropped its appeal to the Supreme Court, kick-started efforts for control devices and prototype equipment, and filed lawsuits to secure its share of cleaner-burning natural gas. Commenting about whether prosecutors should pursue Edison on the postponed cases, Griswold said no. Edison's change of heart, he enthused, was one of his regimes' "greatest accomplishments." With Edison's promise to engineer the cleanest steam power plants in the country, "there was little to be gained in public 'crowing,'" Griswold said.[62] Nonetheless, Edison's transition from environmental slackard to industry leader, almost overnight, was real progress for the 1950s.

An urban canvas where the free market reigned, where real estate was more treasured than gold, was suddenly a more submissive, guarded metropolis. The railroad magnates, blueblood publishers, aviation executives, hoteliers, and their cigar-chomping cronies had ceded ground to stiff, erudite smog engineers. It was a choice borne from necessity. The old, popular conception of limitless commercial possibilities, of weather as exclusive advantage, had evaporated. No more was Los Angeles, as the *Examiner* phrased it, a "paradise of vigorous men in Hawaiian shirts or Spanish costumes riding bandwagons, with drums beating 'Come ye to California'—heaven on earth."[63] Even the boosters had to trim the welcome mat. The L.A. Chamber of Commerce, forecasting that auto-produced smog and regional growth would reverse the hard-won reductions in gross emissions, called in 1955 for rethinking Southern California's industrial landscape by being finicky about who could stay and who should leave. In sober utterances, they suggested that certain companies might just have to relocate outside the basin. It was fifteen years before

Earth Day, and the Southland's corporate cheerleaders were tooling a greener manufacturing base: electronic companies, instrument makers, research centers. They paired this unfamiliar language with another adaptive philosophy. "New industries to which smog-control devices cannot be applied shall not be permitted to locate here." It was a stunning acknowledgement, and the national media sensationalized it further by blaring specious headlines announcing that "LOS ANGELES WANTS NO MORE INDUSTRIES." Local officials puckered.[64] Even the Soviets had been able to do what L.A. hadn't so far. As they'd rebuilt Stalingrad after World War II, they had located industry downwind of the city to safeguard the population from fumes.[65] Beckman, visualizing the collision ahead between imperiled public health and a consumer economy feeding a burgeoning population, had urged that air pollution factor into zoning decisions as a "matter of the greatest urgency."[66] His idea never got the foothold he'd hoped.

By decade's end, the L.A. Chamber further equated industrial retrenchment with survival. So, rather than hosting 20,000 industrial operations, Southern California would have to settle for 16,000, it said. Rather than low-cost production abetted by spanking new infrastructure and talented manpower, the smog quagmire had cost polluting businesses twenty-five cents in smog prevention gear for every dollar invested in basic equipment; these combined expenditures totaled $76 million by 1959. Haagen-Smit, pitching mass transit and more parks as partial answers, believed the point for drastic action was fast approaching. He'd been a Chamber member before. "Even relocation of industry, plus other unpleasant measures, may be necessary," he said. The feisty *Examiner* offered its own prophecy about the consequences of unregulated tailpipe exhaust on the working man and his boss. "Only timely arrival of auto-smog controls will relieve the uncertainty of the future of the affected industries. This is unnerving, of course, for all concerned, including people who work in the industries."[67]

Embedding manufacturers downwind wouldn't protect developing places like Orange and San Bernardino counties for a simple reason—they already WERE downwind. In 1959, while the L.A. Chamber was sweating buckets about the county's image, these areas were complaining louder and wider about living downwind of big brother's aerosol barrage. The L.A. air district, as you might expect, disagreed. It couldn't just be L.A. smog strafing them—there were other sources too. APCD leaders cited immaculately drawn air-movement maps indicating that some of the jetsam originated from inland companies themselves. The backbiting continued. The perception was that L.A.'s ruthless manufacturing horde couldn't give a damn about the distant communities it affected. When L.A. officials suggested the massive Kaiser Steel Plant in Fontana—an industrial city just east of the county line—was responsible for the fouled climate there, the Fontana powers took it to new California Governor Edmund Brown. They lobbied for independent studies of where ozone originated. Brown treaded cautiously, saying he'd support further research and, eventually, creation of auto exhaust standards. Until then, everyone would have to deal with it.[68]

All told, the smog struggle felt less noble, more an unsatisfying draw. Both business and civilians believed that they were being unfairly burdened for the benefit of the other. People were sick of the slogan that "the greatest peril is relaxation of vigilance."[69] They had been vigilant. Now they expected unobstructed sunlight. While most industry and citizens had done what regulators had asked, the shiniest symbol of booming Southern California—the gasoline-swilling automobile—continued spewing veritable lakes of disagreeable matter. Ernest Branson, an Adventist pastor from El Monte, blamed air pollution, along with communism and over-population, for the worldwide spirituality crisis. He captured the mood of the moment: "Smog," he said, "is one of the manmade crises that caused us to realize that man is finding it increasingly hard to coexist with himself."

Still hot for the story, *The New York Times* and other major media continued sending their special correspondents for coverage of Los Angeles' woebegone state. For Angelenos, that outside attention mattered less than it had in the 1940s, because there was more permanency now. There was blind faith, then there was reality, and the reality was that air pollution, like so many of history's gauzy monsters, would only fade away after considerably more suffering.

The idea was almost outlandish—that the Land of Sunshine could be a place where the sun was a nostalic memory. A few enterprising cynics internalized the irony and packaged a symbol of how they felt. Soon arriving at retail shops around California were bright yellow containers for tourists to bring home. Priced at thirty-five cents each, the cans, which had authentic L.A. smog inside, had instructions that read:

> *When suffering from an over-abundance of happiness, puncture can and place directly under nose and get depressed.*

An alternative said:

> *Do you have enemies? If so, don't waste a bullet or dull a knife. Send any enemy a can of pure smog. Recommended by Jack the Ripper, Rasputin and Frankenstein. . . .*[71]

The community's patience was akin to a shortening fuse on an unmeasured bomb. Some small business owners and moms drove with their windows up rather than suck air that made their faces ache. Insiders and the affirmed occasionally walked the streets sniffing from oxygen canisters with the phrase "Pure Air" on them. All these victims of the severest, strangest crisis to wrack modern Los Angeles were less content to stew in the quiet majority.

Just at that moment, the beast started to evolve in its complexity. The APCD and other researchers noticed smog itself was mutating. The ground-hewing stuff wasn't solely monolithic gray anymore. It was often a surreal brownish-orange, reflecting the newly realized threat of nitrogen oxide: a threat that'd plague Southern California and its regulators in the 1960s. Again, the countryside reacted. A downtown department store propped up an asbestos fire-fighting getup and gas mask—the "smog suit," price unknown—as a sassy protest symbol. (A local dive shop offered one, too.) Even the animal world was revolting. Sometime in the late 1950s, legend had it that a hen laid an egg that L.A. pollution unaccountably turned green. What did the protective mother do? It kicked the shell out of its nest.[72]

CAMPUS LIFE AT
SMOG STATE U

Abrasive as it was on the lungs and lives of Southern Californians, smog was good for opportunists and even better for bureaucrats. Between the piling regulations and the unsolved aspects of air pollution behavior, APCD staffers nearly had themselves a lifetime employment act. A stranger touring district headquarters, where harried administrators oversaw beaker-pouring chemists and diagramming meteorologists, might've believed he'd mistakenly entered a technical university. In one sense, that wasn't far off. Call it Smog State U, home of the brown and the gray.

District technocrats focusing on industrial regulation from 1947 to 1957 had cross-sectioned every part of the beast they could haul back to the lab. But microscope slides weren't enough. They needed to furnish enlightened leadership for the cause, and Smog State U had a philosophy that modern-day pollution warriors still hold sacred: stay a step ahead of the next crisis with vanguard science. From the start, the APCD appreciated the benefits of never being satisfied with current methods, and therefore nudged, sweet-talked, encouraged, and otherwise coerced major companies under its regulatory thumb to innovate engineering solutions to shrink their emissions over time. The upshot was a shimmering array of private sector—developed gunk-stoppers—gadgets called "electric precipitators," "fume burners," "cyclone-separators," and "vapospheres"—and a resetting desire for the next anti-smog iteration.[1] From 1948 to 1958, the APCD boasted involvement with thirty-six of these engineering or mechanical "firsts," a record no other city could match. Complacency in an expanding metropolis, where every new car added to the burden, was tempting danger.

Just because they were trying to save the masses, however, didn't mean officials tailored their reports to the average high school graduate. If you weren't technically inclined, most of Smog State U's studies were unintended sleep aids: "the experimental program for the control of organic emissions from protective coating operations"; "airborne particulate lead measurements." Though written abstrusely, these reports signaled that in chaotic times, no source was too puny to inventory. The 64.8 million cigarettes puffed daily in the county were not exempt. All that smoke and ash slung 12 tons of contaminants into the atmosphere every day.[2] It was vital, if not bureaucracy-preserving, to mention such trivial sources even when cars were the predominant offenders. Angelenos needed to have faith that when Smog State U vowed to attack every source, the institution really meant it.

The APCD's technical wizardry, along with its research-and-experimentation credo, produced reams of top-notch science that went largely underappreciated during those days of burning eyes. Among other cutting-edge work, researchers synthesized wind patterns, traffic flow, geographical contour, photochemistry, and inversion-layer vagaries into ponderous studies read from West Covina to Berlin. They fussed over the inversion lid by measuring and shadowing it during the eighty-one smog alerts from 1955 to 1971. They could tell you with mathematical precision how seasonal weather subtleties could drive tailpipe smog into the Valleys, or describe with a mortician's detachment the solvent clouds released by paint-bake ovens, varnish cookers, and rotogravure. Automation futuristic by 1950s standards aided district scientists with the mathematical lifting. When the APCD established an air-analysis division, one of its marquis tasks was feeding monitoring data and trajectory computations into a mechanical brain called the "IBM 650."[3] Roughly the dimensions of an upright dresser, it was IBM's first commercial-business computer, and the maiden step in the digitalization of pollution numerology.

For Smog State U, it was not science fiction. Sometimes it just felt that way. From the late 1940s forward, the district leased mid-size Navy blimps to hang over downtown sampling contaminants and tracking their movement in the airshed. The data gained was valuable, the aftereffects something else. Pedestrians frequently mistook the gangly blimps and the smaller, unpiloted smog-research balloons the district released for UFOs observing Los Angeles life in a scene Orson Welles might have dreamt up for a screenplay. The dirigibles went up, and the district's phone lines would jam. Then again, L.A. smog itself had a spooky hand in propagating underground myths. One humdinger suggested that extraterrestrials hid their ships inside the fume-banks. Another condemned the ingredients in fresh-baked bread for generating ozone. Never mind the district's numerical, methodical bent. The rumors—sooty, light-blocking particles were solely responsible for turning boring sunsets into explosions of engrossing red—preoccupied whole bands of fringe-dwelling Angelenos. Unlike S. Smith Griswold's troupe, they were disinterested in environmental science or its budding tautology. They merely wanted the creepy side-stories.

Geography, latitude in particular, was not just a dry off-shoot topic at Smog State U. Southern California, district meteorologists learned, shared something pivotal with Casablanca, Cape Town, and Santiago. All four cities were "subtropical West Coasts" known for inversions and tepid winds. Each was roughly thirty-four degrees from the equator, and research determined that this made them ideal hosts for restricted air circulation. L.A., however, was the worst off of its latitudinal peers, because of the angles of its growing highway network. Freeways laid east-to-west were configured the same direction as the prevailing wind currents. On hot summer and fall days when the slight sea breeze rippled from the Pacific, traffic moving on these freeways concentrated the tailpipe exhaust over the cars along a naturally occurring duct. With mountains along one side, and the inversion layer above, there was no other place for the unburned matter to billow other than these "lines of source." Think of them as ultra-contaminated jet streams the color of brown sugar shadowing the cars from 1,000 feet above. When Southern California's colossal roadway network was completed in the 1970s, sections of four major freeways—the San Bernardino (10), the Ventura (101), the Foothill (210) and the Pomona (60)—pointed in a manner that fed and channeled that exhaust-rich air straight into the suburbs.[4] Since neither highway-planning officials nor zoning officers had employed smog-drift patterns into their plans, there was nothing dramatic anyone could do except not repeat the mistake.

While it was too late to pack up or reorganize whole cities, the time was right for embedded smog forecasts. They became an accepted blip of everyday life as shaded boxes in newspapers and the weather segments on TV news. "We can accurately predict, if it's smoggy in Los Angeles in the morning, what time it will be smoggy in Pasadena," one district honk proudly noted.[5] As they learned more, meteorologists revisiting old cause-and-effect assumptions presented Alice-in-Smogtown results. They determined, for instance, that an eye-weeping smog downtown could have relatively low ozone, though the conventional wisdom held that the two were synonymous. They also figured out that you didn't have to have scandalously brown skies to register high-pollutant readings. As one insider said, "it was the height of foolishness" to attempt smog forecasting when it was littered with variables, but somebody had to try.[6] The knowledge gap shrank with every fresh bundle of results.

The district's first forecasts tried to educate Angelenos that smog was more a function of meteorology than the specific contaminants that industry discharged from its towers and machinery. Using test balloons and airplanes in a widening, automated-monitoring network, the APCD's weather experts made 2,400 square miles of Southern California sub-atmosphere their permanent fixation. Given a blank check, they would've erected a mile-high instrument tower, literally, to size it all up.[7] Since they had finite cash, they did the best they could. In the mid-1950s, they strung together a skeletal, fifteen-station arrangement that grabbed and tested samples around the clock. When the number of stations later doubled, it created not only a more nimble alert system but also a rich database fine-tuned for daily forecasts, health advisories, long-term progress studies, and analytical modeling.[8] Smog Staters bragged that no other area analyzed its lower-atmosphere as intensely as did Southern California.[9] The peoples' priorities were more banal. As air quality predictions became a regular feature in the news cycle, often playing higher than sports scores, stock prices, and comics, folks lost their initial zeal for pollution science.

Doubtful there would ever be a cure, they just wanted their readings. Fatalism was like the common cold, infecting everyone in range. "Why wait till 1955? We might not even be alive," was the Optimist Club's banner for its smog-themed Fall 1954 meeting.[10] Club attire that day involved the gallows humor of gas masks.

Foreign engineers and scientists hoping to co-opt L.A.'s techniques and regulations streamed onto Smog State U's campus as it relocated over the years from Vernon to Skid Row to El Monte and, finally, to Diamond Bar. Camera-toting Japanese technicians toured plants. Mexican officials appeared with blank notepads, keen for L.A.'s expertise.[11] How much they benefited is a coin toss: years later, dense, gray air so engulfed Mexico City that the capital's government took the radical step of banning driving on certain workweek days. Russian and Chinese scientists arrived, too, and it quickly became apparent to dogged pollution officials that what they were witnessing were extensions of the Cold War as much as the smog wars. Besides elementary emission-control tips, the communist delegations thirsted for American industrial information for their spies. The CIA, likewise, wanted district greeters to prod their guests about Chinese economy cars, the country's fuel consumption, and so forth. During the 1960s and 1970s, the district's veteran public information chief, Jim Birakos, grew accustomed to the intrigue. Like others, he said that the FBI monitored some anti-smog protestors.[12]

*   *   *

As Smog State U's dean, S. Smith Griswold burst with the charisma that his wonkish predecessors lacked. In college, he'd been a take-charge fullback, and even into middle age, he was still fair-haired and buff, as well as avuncular. As boss, he displayed a no-nonsense tongue and holistic attitude aimed at checking off specific goals. Staffers pushed themselves for him, making headway that prior regimes had not. In the poorer, southeast cities of Huntington Park, Maywood, and Bell, for instance, homeowners for years had lived with "disagreeable odors" from the cooking and burning of animal byproducts at rendering plants. Residents phoned the APCD about their displeasure with these smells every other day in 1958. The industrial city of Vernon figured in, too, since almost all of the county's hog, cattle, and sheep slaughterhouses were there. Fuller and Griswold heard about all this, and about how the putrid aroma was affecting a "substantially" greater number of folks than the official complaint reports indicated. Staunch about bringing change, they successfully won board approval to tighten up an older rule governing the "extremely odorous emissions" from rendering operations. Until they acted, people downwind of processed animal carcasses had whiffed compounds hard to pronounce—cadaverine, putrescine, butyric acid—but virtually impossible for their nostrils to ignore.[13]

Just how different Griswold's approach was in jousting the beast was punctuated by a chancy personal decision that helped cement his environmental legacy. In July 1956, he volunteered to spend time in Haagy's smog-chamber to experience, under lab conditions, the psychological and physiological effects of what millions were weathering in their everyday lives. For two hours inside the Plexiglas booth heated to ninety degrees and outfitted with two chairs and a makeshift desk, Griswold inhaled ozone at twice the levels L.A. had ever logged. Inside, he hacked and sputtered, and had to read some material twice because of difficulty concentrating.[14] He exited the booth blinking and coughing, with a little tightness of the chest and dry mouth but his machismo unscarred. "I could have stayed in the chamber longer," he assured. By the next day, he wasn't feeling so hot: his lung capacity was down twenty-two percent. He'd developed bronchitis.[15] Months later, he realized he'd confused a euphoric feeling inside the chamber with mental impairment. "The gases made me high," he conceded. "I don't want to go back into that chamber again."[16]

Griswold repeatedly displayed this mettle under pressure. His charges were not as thick-skinned. Even as he batted down rumors that his best talent was deserting his agency, Griswold conceded the pressure of chasing rogue polluters and smog's biochemical perplexities had gotten to enough of them. Some of his scientists, he acknowledged, had grown "sensitive" with the public's "constant faultfinding" of district methods. "On some occasions, wives of our workers have been insulted because of the husband's connection" to the district, Griswold said in 1959. "Ridicule is commonly met, at social functions and elsewhere. Because of this, I have lost some good men. This public pressure is terrific."[17] Maybe that forklift operator or grandmother livid over weeklong smog assaults didn't appreciate what personal risks Griswold's men faced as they pulled over smoky big-rigs, investigated subterfuge emissions, tested explosive chemicals and ventured up dizzying ladders only an acrobat would savor climbing. APCD chemists regularly clambered up live, vibrating smokestacks "with the daring of a steeplejack," standing on three-foot-wide platforms to extract vapor samples or perform other tests. If there was no pre-cut opening, they might have to drill through the brick cylinder, bracing for a 1,000-degree vent of gas. "Me," one climber, said, "I don't look down."[18] Nor did they look for applause. NASA's astronauts were America's glory boys. Griswold's staff resembled sky janitors by comparison. They weren't the only ones winging it, either. Smog State U's noisy, refrigerator-sized testing equipment back then make today's laptops look like sorcerer's magic. The formative devices were so leak-prone that technicians arriving after the weekend frequently found that the caustic liquids dripping from the machinery had dissolved the walls or eaten into the the concrete floors. Even when it didn't leak, the equipment still demanded continual adjustment. "You'd sneeze and the darn thing would be out of adjustment," remembered one monitoring manager, William Bope.[19]

Southern California's smog czar appreciated that all of this heretofore-unsung bravery and innovation needed sympathetic exposure if his agency was to burnish—or salvage—its image. Among other assumptions, district brass, especially its authoritative engineering director, Robert Chass, believed the APCD's actions were a big reason Southern California had not frittered into a ghost town shorn of healthy air. To publicize the APCD's heady work, Griswold's staff organized its own mass production—of press releases, speeches, impressive-sounding statistics, and white papers. They placed slick opinion pieces, semi-disguised as news articles, in community newspapers in a series tabbed "Crossing the Smog Barrier." The Griswold-christened "Public Information and Education" division knocked out this material along with many more nuanced communications. Before long, year-end summaries portrayed the APCD like protagonists in a Hollywood underdog picture, where dashing engineers and hard-boiled smog cops spirited about rescuing a gagging paradise from diabolical sources. Rancor from ill-timed smog alerts periodically washed away his message, but Griswold knew the import of keeping the restless informed. By the mid-1950s, simplistically written "smog briefs"—No. 12 was entitled "RUBBISH BURNING: A PUBLIC ENEMY"—replete with cartoon-like diagrams and the district's hazy-sun logo made the rounds far and wide. Smog State U had its own story to tell.

One of the more uplifting communiqués involved the objectives the district had achieved in enacting recommendations from the Beckman-led blue-ribbon committee. The governor had commissioned it in October 1953, and five years later, there was traction. The residential incinerator had gone the way of the dodo (or, more appropriately, the kerosene lamp), and 53 out of 54 burning dumps had been extinguished forever. The pungent black smoke clouds once discharged by refineries' emergency flares to burn excess gas were now replaced with smokeless material. All but eighty of the Southland's open-hearth steel plants were under control.[20] These aggregate actions had thwarted 1,500-2,000 daily tons of contaminants from twirling into the inversion layer. All of this was neither cheap nor, as detractors shouted, for naught. Smog State U employed 444 people, 113 of them how out on the streets in enforcement patrol cars. They'd aided prosecutors' filing of almost 9,000 cases in just three years. Laudatory, too, was how former district executives—Louis McCabe, ex-research director Dr. Leslie Chamber—now held positions of federal responsibility on the subject.[21] Taken together, it was "striking proof of measurable improvement," the *Times* editorialized.

Dismally, for Griswold and the community psyche, the paper was one of the few large newspapers openly voicing that rosy picture. With new radio stations, TV outlets and newspapers adding their two cents, there was a new chamber to confront: the media's repetitive, bad news-oriented "echo chamber." It was for this reason that Griswold fattened his information apparatus with school appearances, pamphlets, speeches, and other PR activities that were sophisticated for the era. It was a versatile operation for the volatile times, serving as policy town crier one month and quasi-defense lawyer the next. A district-penned article for the *Montebello News* in November 1957 tried ascribing the blame where it belonged: on Detroit's carmakers. The headline: "APCD COMPLETES JOB—ALL EXCEPT AUTO EXHAUST."[22] Somebody once speculated that air pollution was the second most investigated subject in L.A.'s history behind communism, and the numbers were hard to argue. Griswold's Public Information and Education group in two years handled 23,000 phone calls and 6,000 letters. It typed 369 news releases and assembled a 7,000-person mailing list.[23] But wait—there's more! By 1957, it was forwarding whole stacks of news clippings to the supervisors, compiled by the American Society of Mechanical Engineers, spotlighting other cities' early toils with air pollution. In the misery-loves-company department, L.A.'s politicians learned that San Diego-area romaine lettuce crops were shriveling and Milwaukee's incinerator odors were nauseating. They read about how Cleveland politicians wanted polluters arrested and how Chicagoans pledged an all-out effort *not to be like L.A.* smog-wise.[24]

Unbeknownst to most was how competing Cold War demands from the Eisenhower administration were sidetracking Smog State U's cleanup drive. Instead of assisting with technical hiccups or danger alerts, the Feds were more interested in atomic national security, buffaloing the air district into monitoring airborne radiation levels caused by nuclear fallout. Aboveground hydrogen bomb tests in the Nevada desert, paranoia about communist intentions, and the conviction that nuclear power would someday be pervasive keyed the Feds' arguments for regular sampling. Above all was the fear that the Kremlin almost certainly would target Southern California's military-space operations in a full-scale atomic attack. There was no time for dillydallying. While they knew radioactive particles weren't something a population center like L.A. could disregard, district leaders still felt that Washington was ramming a job outside their bailiwick down their throats. They complied anyway, and in the process burst into another virgin eco-field: what kind of toxic air would result if Soviet ICBMs hammered the West Coast on a smoggy day? Because of the inversion-layer syndrome and the lethal effects of radiation contact, APCD scientists soon were sweating over how glowing dust, fumes, smoke, and whatnot might interact with air pollution's chemical traits. During a May 1958 weapons test that elevated radioactive levels in L.A. worrisomely, the question gathered fresh urgency. Experts from state government to the local universities concluded that the area's atomic monitoring was "inadequate" given the threat, and that more manpower was overdue.[25]

Soon, APCD officials underwent special training they had never expected. They added radioactive emissions to their chemical watch-list. They collected data on alpha and beta-gamma radiation samples in Burbank, Reseda, Azusa, Dominguez, and Vernon. They monitored space radiation from atop their headquarters and theorized about whether fallout particles would fuse with air contaminants into a pernicious aerosol never seen before.[26] Atomic physics, radiation-intensity calculations, medical triage, mobile labs—no, it wasn't just about the oxidant count in the troposphere anymore. District Engineer John Mills, designated as the agency's "Radiological Coordinator," received a crash course his APCD bosses weren't too thrilled about from state and federal civil-defense officers. Swapping, for the moment, his Ringelmann visibility chart for a Geiger counter, Mills attended classes, films, labs, and exercises designed to teach him what to do in the event of a nuclear attack. Like other civilians training for the unthinkable in the era before America's national security infrastructure was fully regimented, Mills ventured to the San Francisco Bay area to visit the Navy's Radiological Defense School on Treasure Island.[27] Based on news and archived material from the period, Southern Californians heard precious little about the smog-meets-radiation examinations or the bureaucratic chafing they provoked.

Maybe that was just as well. As one state health official predicted, "the smog of the future will probably include radioactive contaminants."[28] This was not an esoteric issue, nor, surprisingly, was it entirely gloom-and-doom. The U.S. Navy Radiological Lab indeed saw benefits in Southland air pollution. Navy scientists hypothesized that if there were a nuclear detonation in L.A. on a smoggy August night when the haze lingered, the ozone climate would block about 86 percent of the radiant heat, compared to on a clear evening, from as faraway as five miles.[29] Perhaps motivated by this cosmological providence, Lockheed Corp., maker of the Soviet-watching SR-71 Blackbird Reconnaissance Plane, improvised a more practical application for the inversion layer: as a natural filter to photograph radiation storms on the sun. Some compared it to the smoked glass kids used to watch solar eclipses.[30]

As much as L.A.'s pollutocrats wished other agencies were handling atomic monitoring, they also were up against the exuberance surrounding nuclear power, which proponents trumpeted as a fountainhead of emission-free, nearly inexhaustible energy. Los Angeles City in 1960 was so convinced it was the antidote for the region's surging population that it proposed erection of a 500,000-kilowatt atomic energy plant near the county's northern boundary. Asked for their expertise, APCD scientists said it might be a disaster in the making. They worried, in fact, that the chosen site had too much in common topographically with Donora. According to their analysis, an inadvertent release of substantial radioactive material in the canyon-fringed, low-inversion Santa Clara River Valley would burp a stagnant atomic thunderhead lashing Saugus, Newhall, and surrounding population centers as far as forty-five miles away from ground zero. No matter the elaborate safety precautions against a runaway reactor or coolant leak, it just was too much of a chance.[31] As events would have it, Los Angeles decided against assembling a reactor in that valley. Nonetheless, the incident underscored the potential of aerosolized toxic chemicals unrelated to Southern California's classic smog entering the picture.

Institutional memory about them kicked in during future years, none more than in 1987. It was then that the APCD's successor agency, the South Coast Air Quality Management District, began requiring large industrial companies to hold neighborhood meetings if they assessed their emissions exceeded state health thresholds. Though upbraided as too lax by environmentalists and too heavy-handed by businesses (sound familiar?), the Air Toxics Hot Spots Information and Assessment Act was essential in notifying the Burbank area about perils in its skies. The act forced defense giant Lockheed Martin Corp. in 1989 to disclose that its historic military-aircraft production plants were emitting 1,015 pounds of airborne toxins daily. Included in them were small amounts of so-called "hexavalent-chromium," the same carcinogenic compound that activist Erin Brockovich famously battled in several remote California cities. A $60-million settlement with about 1,300 Burbank-area residents who claimed health and property damage from those toxins, plus national exposure about the environmental baggage left by the Car War, resulted from the disclosure.[32] In Smogtown, the legacy of that 1950s radiation monitoring lives on today.

Jim Birakos was just twenty-five when he became the district's chief public information officer in 1966. While he hadn't gotten there in time for the atomic-smog conundrum, he'd navigate other weird, historic moments on the largest eco-stage of its time. He hailed from Greece and dreamt of being a writer. After college, he worked as a cub reporter, grabbed a good-paying job at the county parks and recreation department, and had no inkling of the wild ride ahead when career opportunity at the district bade him. His mandate: resuscitate the agency's tattered community reputation. Just like that, the young man had thirty-five people under him. The air district in those days was filled with USC-trained engineers and division chiefs regarded as "untouchables, cardinals. It took me a week to realize it was my dream job," he reminisced in 2007. "I was born for it." Through the years, he'd appear on national television with Walter Cronkite and Tom Brokaw, befriend Jerry Brown and L.A. mayor Tom Bradley. He'd try outwitting federal officials, who'd shrugged off district evidence about jet pollution at local airports and Navy-produced waste. He also learned smog whippings could be staged political theater. "Every Tuesday, I took a public beating from the L.A. Board of Supervisors. They told me in advance it was going to happen. Afterward we'd have coffee."[33]

Southern California's future was so indivisible from smog control that you could argue the agency responsible for it was a superpower unto its own. Birakos reveled in all its dimensions:

While I was shaving in the morning, I used to think about what I could do to forward our mission. By the evening, what I'd come up with often was the No. 1 story of the day, like saying there was no place in Los Angeles for diesel vehicles. The rest of the world was following what Los Angeles was doing. We'd adopt a rule and a foreign city copying it would call us to find out about enforcement. I remember canceling a trip to Rio because we were in the middle of a siege. You just were on a constant high. The smog was continuous, the politics were never-ending, the personal questions about it at parties never stopped, and we were all policymakers for an untried-agency responsible for the health of millions of people. One mistake with a smog forecast and the whole city could crash. There was no job like it in the world. It didn't end on the weekends.[34]

For Birakos, being the district's public face often meant thinking fast or shucking blarney for the media. When officials lost control of a smog-testing balloon that drifted over a freeway in the early 1980s, Birakos vamped it like the information-spinning veteran policy man he was by then. As the balloon headed dangerously toward Lion Country Safari near San Diego, rather than admit it was an experiment gone awry, he told inquisitive reporters the balloon was the first live test of exhaust pollution over an active roadway and they bought it. Before then, another test balloon went off course in Riverside. When somebody on the ground saw an object falling from it, it was mistaken for a body. Again, Birakos had an answer: he said it was a life jacket dumped overboard so the balloon could gain altitude. None of the reporters, Birakos added, knew another secret. LAPD vice officers frequently stationed themselves inside the district's San Pedro St. headquarters, where they'd use binoculars and cameras to watch prostitutes in the seedy hotels across the way.

*   *   *

Years before Birakos arrived, APCD pollutocrats had been scratching their heads about whether a potentially blockbuster smog remedy existed outside their ever-scrutinized walls.

Might there be an answer that imaginative engineers and government consultants had overlooked, because it was hidden in
plain sight? To squeeze out that answer, they gambled on an
untried strategy that pundits deemed novel, nutty, and
emblematic of Southern California's weary panting for clean
air. Put bluntly, regulators invited anyone in the world to float
ideas to them. You just needed creativity and a stamp. The
next sound Griswold and Co. heard was the mail truck backing
up with crates of dreams.

Almost overnight, the first batch of what would be thousands of schemes—submitted by a hodgepodge of engineers,
chemists, gadget-hatchers, basement inventors, wannabe mil-
lionaires, and middlemen—thudded into the APCD's mailroom
and other government offices. Some professionally sketched
and annotated their ideas. Others scribbled them on personal
stationary or notepaper. Chain-smoking Ph.D.s with mathematical aptitudes and faux-wood offices originated some of the
ideas. Coffee-gulping, high-strung dabblers typing madly into
the wee hour germinated others. Diverse in background, members of this brainstorming band all wanted to be the redeemer
who returned the blue skies—and more. They itched for fame,
scientific laurels, and yes, spectacular riches.[35] There was no
shortage of enterprise, and no shortage of vocal doubters rushing to predict futility from such a grassroots talent search.
None other than Governor Knight himself ridiculed the entice-
ment of amateurs. To him, the submitters were little more than
"crackpots, retired Navy chief petty officers from submarines,
engineers who have been fired from oil companies, a whole
army of Rube Goldbergs."[36] Regardless of the disparagement,
Griswold's agency combed through every submittal, every rendering, no matter how farfetched. It testified to the creative
spirit.[37] Griswold was so grateful for these submissions that he

wrote back personally to each inventor after the APCD had reviewed his or her idea. Usually it was to inform them the district had rejected their concept, but to keep swinging.

The outsiders' notions crystallized into three main categories: fanning or siphoning the smog out of the basin, rinsing it away with chemicals, or modifying the weather outright like a modern-day rainmaker. Early on, the most popular ideas involved boring smog-escape vents through the San Gabriel Mountains or deploying networks of giant fans stationed on building tops or foothills. The scorn shoveled onto these ideas by crusty politicians and others seemed only to inspire manifold variations of them. Concepts to rip open the inversion layer weren't far behind in volume. One inventor suggested sending up a one-thousand-helicopter armada to let the whirring blades puncture the fumebank; another envisioned setting fire to gas wells; yet another proposed releasing warehouses of dry ice into the troposphere. There was no stopping the smog-destruction derby. An enterprising German proposed deploying compressed-gas balloons to jostle cracks in the layer. Someone else hoped mothballed World War II bombers might wash away the lid by hosing salty seawater at it. Another person conceived of positioning solar-reflecting mirrors to heat the stagnant chemical sub-atmosphere up until it gave way.[38] Even the seasoned Citizen's Anti-Smog Action Committee dipped in their toe. It became the *de facto* agent for an un-named engineering firm, which warranted that it would end smog within three years with its muffler-like invention for Los Angeles' cars.[39] "EVERYBODY," declared a 1953 *Times* headline, "HAS A SMOG REMEDY."[40]

There was historical precedence for the layman taking up pen and paper against the beast. Some 300 years earlier, English writer John Evelyn outlined what likely rates as the first treatise on manmade haze with his publication of *Fumifugium*. Describing the scene in 1661, he said: "The pall of choking smoke was so bad men could hardly discern one or another." Evelyn's inspiration was to plant sweet, fragrant flowers to counteract the vaporous stink. It might've done noses some good had London not burned to the ground five years later.[41] Shakespeare's Macbeth also presciently referenced the city's sooty environs, snapping, "Hover through the fog and filthy air." (Weary APCD leaders probably longed for the powers of King Edward I. In 1272, acting on the smoky, offending skies, the king sentenced coal burners to torture or death.)

Back in L.A., inventors often wrote directly to L.A. politicians rather than submit ideas to the district. Numerous idea-meisters refused to divulge what they had unless the county showed up with a contract, or an independent panel of experts consented to evaluate its worth if APCD evaluators dismissed it.[42] Professional musician Tony Travers steadfastly kept quiet about his seawater-based panacea unless officials swore under oath that they wouldn't swipe it. The middle-aged, self-described "naturalist" had been tinkering with it for a decade, and didn't want to be lumped in with the hacks and snake-oil salesman deluging the APCD with untenable approaches. Since no one before had taken him up on his mystery solution, he was going to charge the government for it now. Travers actually turned so angry when reporters pressed him whether his secret involved excavating new lakes in the mountains north of Los Angeles that his attorney had to step forward. "My client is so convincing that I am inclined to believe that he has something," enthused Joseph Wapner. "I haven't the least notion as to what it is. I'm here only to protect his legal rights."[43]

Where Travers was tightlipped, others were fanatical, del-

uging the APCD with multiple or redundant proposals no matter the negative critiques their concepts had drawn previously.
A certain "Mr. Henry" was sure that smog came not from exhaust
pipes, or factories or photochemical reactions, but rather from a
methane-gas-belching ocean fissure sheared open hundreds of
years ago off the Southern California coast. Fireboats spraying
seawater on rising methane before it reached land, he believed,
were all that was needed.[44] Likewise, a geophysical engineer
intrigued about creating artificial thunderheads with rapidly
rising stream imagined nuclear reactors furnishing the power.
There was just one flaw in his blueprint: when district executives contacted him for further information, they were stu-
pefied to learn that the most rudimentary calculations were
missing.[45] A similar convention-defying scheme surfaced two
years later from a man who worked at New Mexico's Los
Alamos Scientific Lab. The air district, apparently swayed by
the man's pedigree, responded that the thunderheads had
potential.[46]

Just about the time Haagy was breaking down smog's DNA,
meteorologist Irving Krick became the first of many to hawk an
"aerial-sewage" system. Krick's grandiose contrivance melded
cutting-edge piping and propulsion around the old-fashioned
concept of marshalling the wind. His system would suck smog
fumes through intakes into sewer-based piping. From there,
electrical generators would pump the gases into venting stacks
so high they'd protrude 150 stories up, ending above the inversion layer. Krick's thinking had a mesmerizing appeal because
it seemed so plausible. Some asked whether it might also vacuum away atomic radiation. Still, no takers stepped forward. A
national waste company four years later, promoted a remark-
ably similar apparatus for $200 million to $300 million. In its
designs, pollution fumes would travel in leak-proof concrete

tubing that, at twenty feet wide, was larger than the pipe work bringing Colorado River water to Southern California. With a polished quality about it and the involvement of ex-APCD chief Louis McCabe, there was interest by local air regulators. Yet even with America's fixation on mechanical wonderments, the smog-sewer's price and complexity proved deal-killers.[47]

Day after day, the suggestions flooded into the APCD from almost every continent, until finally officials saw that the lion's share bore a depressing similarity. Had the sketches and renderings not been geared to sanitize the air, they might've fit better as a doomsday machine from a world-ending action picture or futuristic James Bond thriller. For these inventors, Morris Neiburger, the celebrated UCLA meteorologist and district consultant, became their "Dr. No." He was doing it on behalf of Smog State U, whose leaders must've asked themselves what they'd gotten into encouraging anybody with half a notion and an envelope to contact them. A widely referenced article that Neiburger wrote for the respected *Science* magazine in October 1957 was his bullhorn, and the APCD was quick to disseminate it.

Technical in tone, the *Science* piece was pedagogical in message: trying to manipulate the weather for smog relief was a fool's quest. Stationing enormous fans on buildings or mountains, Neiburger said, was as realistic as trying to drain the ocean. As he emphasized, a 500-foot-high inversion layer measuring 15 miles by 30 miles weighed 250 million tons and occupied 6.5 *trillion* cubic feet of space. Shoving out one day of smog from of the L.A. basin—an air mass twice as heavy as a year's worth of U.S. steel production—would deplete the power churned by a *dozen* Hoover Dams. Likewise, a 100-foot-wide smog smokestack discharging contaminants at 100 mph would accomplish almost nothing. All that force would pene-

trate just .2% of the inversion layer.[48] Now, Neiburger added, if
these whimsical inventors delivered something both technically sound and revolutionary, then maybe they wouldn't cop
such bad attitudes later:

> When it is suggested that the [inventors] should carry out
> some feasibility computations on their own to see whether
> their ideas deserve serious consideration, they frequently
> reply with the charge that the "vested interests" have "nega-
> tive attitudes. . . Having examined many proposals, one is nat-
> urally reluctant to spend time on detailed study of another
> variant. Only a completely new and unique approach to
> weather modification could have any hope of success. . . .[49]

Rejections notwithstanding, the schemers kept swinging.
District officials wrestled with the industriousness they incited
in the 1950s, not to mention the agency workload it generated,
for about five years. In 1955, they finally assigned a dedicated
five-member board to cherry-pick the best prospects. Sitting on
the APCD invention-evaluation panel were five scientists
expert in automobiles, chemical and mechanical engineering,
and meteorology. No longer would inventors whine about the
APCD's lack of objectivity, or rushed conclusions, nor would
the district hear public doubts about whether it was somehow
investigating "worthless" ideas. Besides, Griswold and his lieu-
tenants were fast tuckering out. Spurned inventors no longer
received a personal note from the big cheese. They received a
dry form letter categorizing their vision into the five most commonly rejected groupings. Just reviewing them munched time.
In 1960, the district conducted 249 interviews, studied 237
mailed proposals, launched 127 case studies, and expended
869 man-hours.[50] By 1978, the enthusiasm had waned, balanc-
ing out to about one unsolicited proposal daily. Most of them

were shades of the 1950s gigantism—cloud seeding, storm drains, mountain vents, solar-reflecting mirrors, tree-planting, and atmospheric "air conditioning." While these were precisely the non-starters that Neiburger had lectured about, someone had come up with a new slant: a time machine to leap backwards to the fresh-air past.[51]

Hard as it was to believe, from the farfetched arrived some sensible applications. Word that the APCD craved new, unorthodox gadgets stimulated the pros, in Wall Street terms, to "make the market" where one hadn't existed before. Technical firms of varying sizes were told they had a juicy customer base right here in L.A. They might also rope in new customers, now that air pollution had begun clamping over most of the world's manufacturing strongholds.[52] Griswold's invitation for proto-type-answers had another benefit: it was politically disarming. Cultivating what amounted to a science fair in the game-show milieu of the 1950s provided cover for embattled administra-tors. Moreover, it alerted local companies to the proposition that you didn't only have to be on the business end of fine-print regulation—you also just might discover the Mr. Ajax for smog. Griswold milked the discovery atmosphere like an impresario. Most humorously, he offered a one-million-dollar prize from the car companies—without asking them first—for a catalytic device or other fume-trapping equipment on auto-mobiles.[53] Griswold's enterprise telegraphed the point that Southern California was so tired of the aerial crud from its legion of cars that L.A.'s leadership would seek any cure, ply any avenue for relief. If General Motors, Ford, and Chrysler were really insulted, they could redouble their efforts to de-filth their products.

For non-automotive companies, Griswold's solicitiation was a way to get their nose under the tent. The Ramo-

Wooldridge Corp., best known in 1958 for its ICBMs, announced its engineers had successfully developed a "very promising" contraption. It distilled hydrocarbons into water and carbon dioxide by injecting air into a car's exhaust system with an auxiliary pump that increased engine temperatures. "We've tested it in the laboratory and it works," said company vice president, Gen. Harold George.[54] It's difficult to know what happened next, except that Ramo-Wooldridge's "smog muffler" was similar to the equipment that California air regulators in the 1960s implored U.S. carmakers to install on their models. (As was typical in the fifties, the Stanford Research Institute and the private Air Pollution Foundation furnished the company with technical counsel.) Why the diversion from Cold War missile research? Because, Ramo-Woolridge announced, its research was a "public service to the Southern California community" and a shot at commercializing a now-proven technology.[55]

Morris Deodorizers from Tennessee had a fume-burner it declared was adaptable to any engine type. The company's ad claimed the electrostatic system stopped the "majority of smoke output and purified exhaust," and with a quick installation.[56] After 1961, the Smogtown archives don't chronicle much about the gadget. There always was another lined up. Romancing the APCD, while auguring petroleum's future, the Tidewater Oil Co. announced at a Hilton Hotel news conference that it had formulated a new "clean-burning gasoline with significantly less smog" by scouring away sulfur and nitrogen. A rival independent refiner mocked it as a "sales gimmick," and truth was that cleaner-burning, re-engineered gasoline was still years away from widespread consumer use.[57] Tidewater executives, nonetheless, said their gas could bring five to ten percent reductions in hydrocarbons. Griswold, whose own agency was researching low-smog fuel, withheld comment about the Tidewater gas pending tests. Inside, however, he must been delighted at the creativity his call for inventions had provoked.

Of course, a few eager-beaver companies couldn't wait to grab a market share. Car dealerships were among the first, offering customers free exhaust-inspections. As one solicitation teased: "San Gabriel Valley Motors' skilled operators will demonstrate to *your* satisfaction the causes and cures of automobile air pollution."[58] Off the beaten path were at-home products for the Leave It To Beaver set. Puriton's "Electronic Miracle" air-purifier was a stove-size machine engineered to keep pollen, smoke, and odor out of the lungs so you might "work better—all day."[59] Occasionally a pitch over-promised. When the firm behind the "Solar Volt All-Electronic Super-Charger" published a brochure saying the City of L.A. vouched for its hydrocarbon-killing properties, Griswold scolded them to halt that promotion or he'd sic his lawyers on them for false advertising.[60] Smog State U did have standards.

ROADTRAP

ON DECEMBER 13, 1913, IN AN AMERICA ENTHRALLED BY MECHANICAL innovation, 3,000 spectators gathered over Pasadena's treacherous Arroyo Seco ravine to celebrate the opening of a concrete deck. Marveled at as an engineering first for its curvy, unorthodox design, the $200,000 Colorado Street Bridge was both tribute and concession to the onrushing automobile age. When the marching bands stopped and the applause tapered off, the crowd buzzed in excitement upon hearing a local politician predict that every one of the county's 40,000 thin-tired cars and trucks would traverse this eleven-span jewel. Soon, there would be signs, sponsored by the Automobile Club of Southern California, pointing motorists toward New York City or downtown L.A., because now you *could* get there from here.[1]

The car bug never had a more receptive host than burgeoning Los Angeles. Barely two years after Henry Ford's revolutionary assembly line pumped out its first Model T in 1915, there was one car in the county for every eight residents, a gaudy ratio at a time when the national average was one vehicle per forty-three people. L.A. County boasted a landmass bigger than that of some small nations and a population, at five million in the mid-1950s, greater than all but eight states in the Union.[2]

The West Coast's auto addiction deepened in the flush post-war years, though proportionally more of the country was driving. "The place of the automobile in the transportation problem of Los Angeles is far more important than in cities of the East," said well-known urban planner Frederick Law Olmstead, Jr.[3] Whether through popular culture or blockbuster sales, California and cars went together like celebrities and sunglasses. In 1956, there were about 7.1 million cars in state (eleven percent of the nation's total), and nearly 2.9 million just in L.A. County.[4] All told, it was the "greatest concentration of motor vehicles in the world," with ownership rates topping those of any foreign country except Britain, Canada, and France.[5] Motoring clubs. Sunday drives up Mulholland or Pacific Coast Highway. Utopian freeways. Gas-station giveaways. Blondes in convertibles. Car-hop restaurants. Yes, the versatile automobile might've been more beloved than the Pacific Ocean. Yet even in L.A., the ocean lover can change.

*   *   *

Mrs. Alexandra Abrams of Allenwood Street resented her tailpipe. Correct that: she detested it, and that's why she drove her new 1969-model station wagon to a demonstration with her opinion affixed in the window. "THIS LOVELY GM," her sign read, "is a SMOG MACHINE." Abrams and other mothers were picketing outside GM's Van Nuys plant to announce that they would no longer tolerate "stalling" by some of the world's wealthiest corporations. Southern California, any literate person knew by now, was the pollution capitol of the world *because* it was the car magnet of the world. If the oil and auto companies kept excusing the linkage, the women in their miniskirts and Audrey Hepburn hairdos pledged support for a Sword-of-Damocles bill by state senator Nicholas Petris (D-Oakland). It would outlaw the internal combustion engine by 1975.[6]

The next large anti-car protest, this one at a local Chevrolet dealership, was considerably tenser. The banners were the same as before—"YOUR KIDS' NEW PLAYMATE—SMOG BY GM"— but the participants were more eclectic. Salted in the crowd of chanting moms were conservationists, bothered hangers-on, a scene-setting columnist, and a tort-minded attorney. At first, the gum-snapping car salesmen watched the sidewalk spectacle with amusement. Once the crowd's vibe pierced them, though, they squirmed like besieged middlemen. "Don't attack us," one salesman whined. "Attack the factory."[7] Barring an industry U-turn on smog, the middle-class militants said they'd deliver pickets all over town. About 1,500 of them already had torched the credit cards they held with an oil company fined for air quality violations.[8]

Around this same time in the late-1960s, a legal secretary appearing before a state assembly hearing told the carmakers what they probably never expected to hear from the stereotypical materialistic Californian: "Our message is very clear," she said. "Substitute a strong smog control system for the expensive gadgetry; give us a car without power steering, without power windows, with a minimum of chrome and frills. We'll call this new car Mr. Clean."[9]

*   *   *

U.S. carmakers as early as January 1954 recognized the value of resolute promises. For years, those promises were their kryptonite from harsh scrutiny. On a trip from Michigan to carsodden Los Angeles back then, ten visiting auto engineers stressed how motivated they were to pin down the exact contribution of each smog source. "We are dead serious," said the association's technical group. "We mean business. We didn't come here to fool around."[10] To demonstrate it, they formed two committees comprised of the Big Four automakers (General Motors, Ford, Chrysler, and American Motors), some independents, and the American Manufacturers Association. On the surface, the panels' goals were straightforward stuff: coordinating joint studies into cars' air pollution role, and formation of customer programs to install future emission-capping gadgets. Behind this outward decisivness, Detroit's motives were not as transparent, a district automotive consultant suggested in November 1954 after returning from a visit there. "The real activity," he observed, was refinement of exhaust-gas analysis equipment, not some astonishing smog-stopping hardware. Ford, Chrysler, and General Motors, he believed, were focusing on engine modifications as a double-barrel solution that'd cut hydrocarbons and improve mileage.[11] Whatever their tactic, the APCD trusted them initially.

The automakers institutionalized their endeavor with a cross-licensing agreement that would become one of the most provocative in U.S. corporate history. They budgeted $1 million per year for research and development. Should one of them break through, they'd all break through, and in theory so would L.A.'s sunshine. Soothing in tone, the plan was divisive in practice. Ask Ford. It received an icy reception from its competitors when, in 1957, it released publicity about its awkwardly named "vanadium pentoxide" gunk-trapping device. The other automakers grumbled that Ford had breached the licensing deal, and the grumbling led to muzzling. Committees working on vehicle combustion and engineering subsequently blocked press releases, speeches and anything else seen as disloyalty about the carmakers' supposedly heady work on pollution.[12]

Detroit was determined to speak with one voice on more than just that. For the Big Four automakers, L.A. smog was nature's doing, not theirs. Their self-exonerating defense blaming the region's moribund air movement had been the doctrine of the Stanford Research Institute, and where that proposition was exploited before, it was handy again. Eventually, Detroit conceded vehicles were the largest burners of hydrocarbons, that auto exhaust was probably Southern California's "major source of air pollution," but even these allowances were qualified. They said they needed "confirmatory work" to tie the exhaust to eye irritation, plant damage, etc. As late as 1960, the manufacturers held firm that Southern California's atmosphere was a "special case" too "peculiar" to attribute solely to vehicles. "As you know, scientists and engineers explain that the California problem results from an unusual combination of persistent blanket temperature inversion, encircling mountains, very light wind movements and intensive sunlight," an official from the carmakers' association explained. "The popular term 'Los Angeles smog' has a sound origin."[13] Detroit stuck to this mentality until overwhelming evidence stacked up in affidavits and labs.

Southern Californians' transformation from wide-eyed believers to cynics about the automakers' honesty was already under way, though. Griswold, in a 1957 opinion piece, revealed his bitterness that "the world's most complete air pollution program" still left his jurisdiction with the world's most notorious "smog headache. We have reached the practical limit of what we can do for ourselves—the hope for future improvement rests squarely with . . . Detroit. Until a cure is found for the auto exhaust we can look for little reduction" of contaminant levels.[14] Just a few years later, in the time leading up to the state's takeover on auto emissions, Griswold seemed to be bracing for Smogtown's biggest squall yet. APCD scientists, after all, had discovered the photochemical reactions damaging to people, plants, property, and visibility. Its engineers ran a machine-lined lab humming with experimental exhaust catchers.

Tailpipe regulations that the automakers couldn't dodge were needed to complete the job. In one of his periodic reports to the people, Griswold reminded them why: "The more than three million motor vehicles of Los Angeles County would extend in a double line from here to London." Curb their exhaust fumes, he said, and "smog no longer will be a problem."[15]

Hearing this assessment, Hahn tried thumping the automakers where they'd feel it most: their future sales. The bespectacled populist had been the first county supervisor dubious of Detroit's promises, and he realized he needed legal flypaper to hold them to their word. Seizing his chance with a headline-grabbing act, Hahn in 1956 asked the county's legal team whether the supervisors had the authority to initiate a remarkable step: ordering *every* car operating in the region to have pollution-filtering equipment or essentially banning them from the road. Theoretically, the attorneys told him, the proposed mandate held water. In practice, however, the law would be "capricious and void" because no working devices existed commercially. It was always the same answer. Since at least a hardware breakthrough was possible, Hahn made sure the carmakers knew the legal underpinnings were there to try bullying them into submission. (Borrowing from Hahn's playbook, the Los Angeles City Council later explored the same question.)

Despite that threat, the automakers offered few new improvements. The APCD, hoping to stoke competitive fires, held a conference of leading firms and figures to brainstorm ways to improve cars' leaky vapors. Only everything depended on those vapors. Where car emissions once produced two-thirds of Southern California's murk, studies said they now represented eighty-five to ninety percent.[16] How boxed in were Griswold and his men? Boxed in enough to appeal for mass transit construction, an idea with tepid political and public luster in the era of happy motoring. By August 1958, the obvious was undeniable: Detroit's efforts to de-smog their showroom beauties, the district summarized, had "fallen short" of L.A.'s expectations.[17]

No longer, either, were officials buying the automakers' scientific explanation of Los Angeles as a meterological freak. To punctuate this, the district published an authoritative report entitled "The Automobile and Smog" that sharply connected ozone-forming gases with the area's car culture. "Other areas have inversions, topographic traps, and even sunshine, to retain and energize locally produced pollutants," the report said. "Within the past few months adverse concentrations of ozone, eye irritants and phytotoxicants have been reported within, and near, numerous other metropolitan centers. In only one important sense does the Los Angeles situation remain unique: its use of motor vehicles exceeds that of any other city in the world by a large margin."[18]

When the automakers continued refusing to quicken their research, Griswold, Fuller, Hahn, Dorn, and a posse of other stanch L.A. officials detoured around them. After considerable badgering and cajoling, they finally found a way to jostle the car-building industrial complex into taking the West Coast's eye-tearing predicament seriously. They convinced state government to take the job. In 1959, the legislature ordered the California Department of Public Health to develop statewide air quality standards, including maximum-allowable levels for hydrocarbons and carbon monoxide. A year later, the district celebrated again when lawmakers fashioned the first-ever state authority to certify automobile smog-control equipment. The thirteen-member "California Motor Vehicle Pollution Control Board" was a mouthful, yet sweet words nonetheless for worn-out L.A. smog cops. In 1960, in a moment of uncharacteristic optimism, Griswold predicted that by mid-decade smog might be in its "final chapter"—provided Detroit was sincere and California motorists accepted the money they'd have to fork out. A used-car owner might have to pay forty to fifty dollars per car for a retrofit.[19] Somebody buying a new vehicle would also spend slightly above the sticker price. For blue skies, it was a bargain

It was a new day, or so went the fantasy. Convincing Detroit to switch priorities from flashy design accoutrements to unglamorous pollution re-engineering was too big a task for a new, unproven organization. There was simply insufficient manpower, money, scientific experience, and political backbone. Not surprisingly, the vehicle control board had trouble establishing its footing out of the gate, as auto clubs and rural counties torpedoed one of the board's earliest gambits: legislation for the California Department of Motor Vehicles to handle the arduous task of licensing and inspecting device installation. Next, the board proposed requiring that used cars have a crankcase-gas collection system on them, since older vehicles disgorged at least two-thirds of L.A.'s smog.[20] (The crankcase is the engine compartment beneath the combustion chamber, where firing pistons turn the shaft that supplies driving power.) The state, anxious about the "psychological problem" of slapping nitpicky rules on individual, money-conscious drivers, spent $24,000 on billboards, brochures, and announcements to educate these motorists about their responsibilities. All the so-called "pink-slip controversy" did was confound the bejesus out of drivers, so the legislature in 1965 abolished mandatory installation and inspections of crankcase gear.[21] During this timeframe, California's used-car drivers were required to sign pledges that they'd obeyed the device-retrofit rules. Nobody understood them, either. Governor Brown blasted the idea as a "fiasco," partly because so few mechanics knew how to install the equipment. Once more, officials took the embarrassing step of abolishing the mandate they'd previously hailed as a lifesaver.

Out of public view, the auto trade-group committees scavenged for reasons *not* to embrace another innovation—a "blowby device"—even though some automakers told officials they could have them on 1962 models.[22] (The blowby redirected unburned hydrocarbons back into the combustion chamber through tubes, with the aim of burning off a quarter of the fumes.) The knottier problem was automobile exhaust, from which roughly two-thirds of the hydrocarbons and all of the carbon monoxide originated. In a bold step later seen as seminal the green-world over, the control board mandated that *all* 1966 models have anti-exhaust equipment. One known remedy was the catalytic converter, which the French invented in 1898. It reduced fumes in an undercarriage-attached compartment by introducing chemical reagents—usually light metals—able to break down the compounds into harmless substances like water. The carmakers' trade group, generally hostile to anything raising sticker prices, wanted that converter kept out of sight and off the repair-shop shelves. When California certified an independently made converter, the industry's old delay tactic was too transparent. Rather, manufacturer-association insiders recommended a change of subject: "It would very much be to our advantage to avoid this topic."[23] This time, however, there *was* no avoiding it.

Gov. Brown hissed that somebody had better do something. He had no intention of shelving freeway construction because of the exhaust plume over Los Angeles. He intended to make California the ecological gold standard for other cities roiled by air, sewage, and trash crises. "Our problems," Brown said, "apply to every state in the country . . . California is a good place for these problems to be studied and their solutions found."[24] That last bit might've seemed delusional considering ozone's toehold. Even so, in 1966 Brown signed a viable law requiring smog devices on used car tailpipes. With all the comparisons to the space programs, carmakers probably grunteded upon hearing NASA's name uttered with theirs. "American industry has produced equipment to hit the moon with a rocket and take close-up photos of Mars," Brown said. "Certainly [Detroit] can produce a device that will mean cleaner air for California." His words highlighted the disadvantage to freewheeling economic growth: an environment stretched so beyond its saturation point that it reacts in unanticipated manners. Every year the state's population mushroomed by 600,000 people, and each year there were 830,000 new vehicles. What did this ratio mean in L.A.? Fuller saw that without wholesale slashing of automobile emissions under the state's jurisdiction, area smog could be *double* 1940 levels by 1975.[25] The internecine wrangling between cautious Sacramento and agitated L.A. over what to do next was so distracting that the grand opening of the world's first auto-smog training center, at a West L.A. Midas Muffler shop, felt like much ado over a losing proposition.[26]

From the community's perspective, California's bureaucratic tiger had barely gotten off its haunches. A year after establishing tailpipe-exhaust standards, the state vehicle control board had certified only a single catalytic muffler. The dribble was not lost on local authorities, either, who lambasted the board for "snail-slow" progress. They spoke with a trembling urgency bordering on alarmism. Griswold, playing up worst-case scenarios, in 1964 said that foot-dragging might result in gasoline rationing to preserve "breathable air" for people suffering with asthma, bronchitis, emphysema, and similar respiratory maladies. "The millions of people in Los Angeles County," Griswold told reporters, "are actually competing for air with the millions of automobiles." Lack of healthy air, he believed, was a more pressing shortage than the drought-shrinking drinking water supplies.[27] Normally subdued County Supervisor Frank Bonelli voiced his fear, too. Maintaining the status quo could lead to the general issuance of gas masks.[28]

Luckily, a controversy that reconfigured California's entire attack on automobile smog reared its head quickly. It began with the board's policy assumption that the best way to test the effectiveness of tailpipe controls was to measure their cumulative average emissions after 12,000 miles, "with a hope for more perfection later." It was stopgap regulation.[29] On hearing those modest goals, though, Hahn flipped out. He suggested that the county withdraw from the state control board's jurisdiction, as was its prerogative under the chartering legislation. If Hahn was piqued, Fuller, in turn, must've wondered in 1967 why he ever left the LAPD. After a year of highly awaited testing, thirty-seven percent of cars failed the new standards after just 2,000 miles. Eighty-five percent flunked after 20,000 miles. To Fuller, the averaging method exemplified another misguided state policy. The pilloried state board, conversely, insisted that a weak rule was better than no rule. It'd kept 100,000 gallons of unburned gas out of the L.A. skies every day. This half-loaf logic satisfied few, and the next year the state control board nixed the hated averaging method.[30]

There were no two ways around it: the state's takeover was a mess. The APCD's vision of triumphant engineering fostered by California's hard stance had not produced a tabletop of exhilarating hardware for the environment's betterment. It had produced more stalemate.

Whatever sore feelings existed between Los Angeles and Sacramento, both concurred that the heart of the problem lay with the automakers' profit mindset, which held that smog-cutting gadgets on new cars would nudge them out of consumers' price range in an uber-competitive marketplace. "I have the feeling," said control-board member W.W. Nissen, "the industry has several devices ready to go but that some strong triggering action is needed to get them out of the lab and into production."[31] The carmakers stuck to their guns, emphasizing, among other things, that it'd be impossible for them to equip their vehicles with exhaust filters until the '67 models were ready. The state board, chafing at the delay, approved three catalytic mufflers and a direct-flame afterburner manufactured by independents. Those approvals led to the predictably *abracadabra* results. In August 1964, the carmakers announced that they had ingeniously pioneered new methods—primarily engine modifications—so their '66 cars *would* meet California's standards.

Trouble was, every time a technological development hinted that a rollback to clean, pre-1940s air was possible, the law of unintended consequences ruined the moment. In Smogtown, little ever came easy. In 1966, for instance, scientists were learning that car engines tweaked to burn off un-combusted vapors ran at higher temperatures than older models, and that kicked out more nitrogen oxide than anticipated. According to Fuller's dramatic interpretation, the state's efforts to curb hydrocarbons and carbon monoxide had resulted in a fifty percent spike in the toxic substance. The possibility of a nitrogen-oxide poison cloud drifting over Southern California was not an abstraction.[32] Autos at that time produced about half of the substance; industry, especially fossil-burning power plants, coughed out the rest. Oxides of nitrogen gave smog its brown tint. People who inhaled excessive amounts received something worse: lung irritations, and possibly pneumonia or bronchitis.

Los Angeles would regularly stumble through side-effect causeways like this, as the state tried purifying its millions of cars with iffy, incremental technology. In this way, Southern

California simultaneously was a working metropolis and cleanup test case. The *Times'* auto editor, Bill Dredge, cautioned consumers that even the best pollution-capping concepts were captive to the unknown since they were reactive, not preventative. No company was assembling an emissions-free car from the ground up. They merely were retrofitting ecologically damaging merchandise. "The state of today's smog battle," Dredge explained, "is much like the fight against polio when the symptoms were treated with hot packs, massage and swimming pool exercise. Iron lungs became the hardware which kept victims alive. But they did nothing to end the problem."[33] As terrifying as polio was, the virus's source was biological. Los Angeles air pollution, on the other hand, spewed mainly from automobiles. Worsening it, not creating it, was the region's inhospitably sunny meteorology, urban sprawl, and an evergreen faith in American science. So, blame the state control board for dithering or industry chumminess. Berate L.A.'s politicians for allowing its old rail system to vanish without as much as a referendum. The truly culpable remained half a continent away, in the midwestern town that controlled much about what Angelenos inhaled and nearly everything they drove.

*   *   *

LA's summons for federal help with car-generated air pollution only was half-heard. Why? Because America was a nation still trying to organize itself about smog. Barely half of U.S. cities had air pollution districts in the 1950s, despite the lethal episodes that walloped Donora, London, and New York, and even though some experts believed worse was possible. President John Kennedy, eager to uncork activity, supported the Clean Air Act of 1963, because that's all there was. While supposedly intended to jumpstart federal research and environmental technology, the law really was but a supplemental $25-million program to encourage industry. Washington still left pollution management to local governments. Even if they'd had the money, Uncle Sam's anti-smog regimen still would be lagged two years behind California's.[34]

After hearings in Southern California, though, that gap began to narrow. Senator Edmund Muskie, a Maine Democrat, lit the path, introducing a national vehicle-emissions standards law that kindled hopes for spirited federal activism. Then came Kennedy's 1963 assassination. The succeeding Lyndon Johnson administration opposed across-the-board standards, more focused on Johnson's "Great Society" social policies. Detroit, meantime, tried inoculating itself from criticism about its ties to the new president, a Texan from an oil-rich state, by agreeing to equip its cars with smog controls, given the proper lead-time.[35] Many on Capitol Hill interpreted that concession as a half-measure rather corporate commitment. Congress consequently forged a harder line with passage of the Motor Vehicle Air Pollution Control Act. It mandated emission standards, provided the technology and economics were feasible.[36]

Washington's entrance into the smog world, torpid as it was, also showed just how flawed the California control board had been chasing results. As one observer framed it, "The agency's political credibility and popular reputation had been seriously eroded by the pink-slip and averaging controversies, making it difficult to command compliance from the auto industry or cooperation from the public. There had been too many fiascos and too much fighting with Los Angeles County."[37] Even some control board members acknowledged that a stronger, better-organized agency should replace it. The legislature and a new governor—former actor and corporate pitchman Ronald Reagan—both weighed in with a plan, and, in 1967, the California Air Resources Board came into being. The new board could research air pollution damage, inventory sources, review local districts, and be an emissions taskmaster. It divided the state into air basins and adopted standards customized to each. After a brief stint by Fuller as its inaugural chairman, the board picked another "name" as boss: Arie Haagen-Smit.

Sadly, even the professor was out of bravura ideas. Airborne contamination from L.A.-area industry, small business, and residences had been aggressively curbed. Engine and tailpipe pollution, in Fuller's description, had "scarcely been touched." On the worst days, the beast overhung a 250-square-mile swath from Santa Barbara to the Mexican border. While APCD regulations prevented 5,000 tons of contaminants from entering the atmosphere, almost triple that amount still escaped. Whatever gains there actually had been carried a momentous price tag, too. In late 1966, citizens learned that the county's blue-sky campaign had cost $11 *billion* since 1946, when industry expenditures, regulatory expenses, crop damage, smokeless garbage-collection systems, destruction to building exteriors, tire replacements, and other damaged consumer goods were totaled. "The figure is so staggering we feel inclined to discount it," Fuller said. "But . . . we cannot help but conclude the loss has been tremendous."[38]

Not long afterwards, they reached a more productive con-clusion: the Golden State's air pollution situation could not wait for the Feds or automotive executives to make amends. Like the patriots who dumped tea into Boston Harbor, county leaders, and state officials to a lesser degree, decided to take matters into their own hands. If California was going to tackle automotive smog head on, it needed a loophole in the form of a waiver granting state government the right to set standards stricter than federal thresholds. It was an original tactic, precedent shattering and risky, and the carmakers immediately snarled it would be an untenable policy. They wanted uniform national rules for all fifty states, and were prepared to ensure they had them. A version of the Air Quality Act of 1967 that included the California-waiver provision romped in the Senate, passing 88-0. A competing House version, though, included an amendment deleting that provision. Representative John Dingell, a Democrat whose Detroit-area district was home to Ford, had inserted the waiver-killer without even discussing its significance with his California colleagues or L.A. officials. Equally dismaying was that the carmakers' association had written the amendment.[39] It was a brute reminder of the power wielded by America's industrial heartland.

L.A. County had weathered snubs before, but this was a double-crossing. A Congress that had first ignored the West Coast's plight, then raced to catch up, was now too headstrong—or bought off—to permit aggressive local oversight? The state's normally fractious congressional delegation united behind reinserting the waiver in a second bid. "Air pollution," one said, "is a bigger issue than Vietnam in California." Dingell, still in Congress to this day (and with similar positions) responded that fair was fair. "If we give special treatment to California," he said, "I see no reason why we shouldn't give special treatment to Nebraska, Kansas, or Detroit, or New York, or any of the other states that might have to have them"[40] His opponents on the House floor deciphered that argument as a smokescreen for guarding his home district and an industry with its own army of flesh-pressers. San Diego-area congressman Lionel Van Deerlin had tired of their lot, excoriating automakers for "swaggering through our House office buildings with high-handed lobbyists."[41] Could anything stop them?

As it turned out, the airwaves could. An enterprising young reporter named Al Wiman aired a multi-part series on the Los Angeles radio station KLAC entitled "A Breath of Death: the Fatality Factor of Smog." Though there'd been dozens of newspaper installments about the issue, few packed the pop of Wiman's October 1967 series. It shook Congress and inspired journalists. It aroused bourgeois anger and scared car-industry apologists. Just as importantly, it ran with impeccable timing. "Southern California is on a collision course with disaster," Wiman began. He interviewed Fuller, who agreed with the introductory statement, and Hahn, who was gleeful that reporters and the public were finally on to the carmakers' denial-and-delay strategy. "Just whose interests are being served?" Wiman asked of Dingell.

Whatever its data-leaden, repetitive content, "A Breath of Death" articulated points worth reviewing. In the decade prior to the series' broadcast, the L.A. basin existed in unhealthful conditions roughly nine days out of ten as measured by state oxidant standards. Denizens of central L.A., the San Gabriel Valley, the eastern San Fernando Valley, and the Pomona-Walnut Valley lived under substantial peril. Wiman demonstrated that the auto companies knew plenty about alternatives to the internal combustion engine yet had sunk too much money and pride into that power source to consider abandoning it.

"A Breath of Death" infused the public soul into the waiver discussion. District spokesman Birakos, known to millions as "Mr. Smog," was a point man on the issue. For him, Wiman's series was a rainmaker. It generated 500,000 anti-amendment letters and postcards from across the state, which Bekins' moving service flew to Washington and dumped on the Capitol Hill steps. "We set up shots of Los Angeles in the rotunda area where you couldn't see anything," Birakos recalled. "They accused us of using shots of forest fires." As L.A. officials searched out legislative allies, Birakos set up his base camp in then-Senator Robert Kennedy's office. He recalled the senator's advice as instrumental. Kennedy suggested they invoke states' rights as the overarching theme, and this brought Louisiana, Mississippi, and Texas into the anti-Dingell camp. New York's delegation then joined California's side of the floor fight—a fight that neither Gov. Reagan nor Louis Fuller expected the state to win. (Fuller, in fact, was so pessimistic about the waiver's chances in Congress that he largely stayed put in his Washington hotel watching old Westerns on TV.) Nevertheless, on November 2, 1967, the bill passed with California's exemption in the fine print.   The state-rights' tactic had been the winning argument. "We were jubilant and tried not to dance in the streets," Birakos said. "The waiver was going to change the face of air pollution in the United States, it was that historic."[42]

*   *   *

The collusion among carmakers was now the nation's worst-kept secret. Some, like Hahn, repeatedly framed it a "conspiracy." County supervisor Dorn viewed it as an epic bamboozling.[43] One state control board member griped that had Detroit devoted as much effort to anti-smog controls as it did to cosmetic changes for its vehicles, the whole subject would be moot. "The only reason we have made any progress at all is that California buys so many cars."[44] As you're seeing, Smogtown of the 1960s had more than disappointment with Washington to exorcise. The realization that Michigan had openly duped the county with promises and PR for going on ten choking years made Angelenos feel like rubes tricked by fast talking con men. Soon, that sense of exploitation set the civic mass in motion. Griswold, in a defining 1964 speech in Houston, spit bullets at Detroit's shenanigans over catalytic

converters, blowby tubes, and other fume-stopping doohick-
eys. "What has the industry accomplished in the last ten
years?" Griswold thundered. "How has this worked out?
Apparently it has served to guarantee that no manufacturer
would break ranks and bring into the field of air pollution control the same kind of competitive stimulus that spokesman for
the industry frequently pay homage to."[45] Translation: even leg-
endarily laid-back people have their limits.

Of course, Southern California had heard its share of car-
conspiracy theories before. Wasn't it beyond coincidental, historians and observers marveled, that when Haagy incriminated
the American automobile, the region no longer had those clang-
ing downtown streetcars or interurban "Red Car" lines to offer
as low-polluting commuter alternatives? Didn't ripping out that
track coincide with the ascension of the U.S. automobile-high-
way-industrial complex, which eventually gave Californians
hundreds of miles of concrete-ribboned freeways and archipel-
agos of car dealerships, gas stations, repair garages, tire shops,
and regional auto clubs? In other words, didn't the railway's
systematic dismantling ensure smog's permanency?[46]

Horses notwithstanding, travel in early twentieth-century
Los Angeles involved steel track and ticket fares. The Pacific
Electric Railway, then part of the Huntington family's
Southern Pacific Railroad empire, operated an interurban trolley system called the Red Cars. They stretched over 1,200
miles through four Southland counties at their peak. The Los
Angeles Railway Company, which controlled most of downtown's streetcars, wound through the inner city. For years, the
two systems ferried the city's masses while propelling commerce downtown and real estate sales in the outskirts.
Sustaining efficiencies was profoundly harder. Once comfortable, the trolleys and streetcars grew jam-packed and creaky

during the Roaring Twenties, as a spurt of Model Ts and other automobiles flooded the streets. Even rich Southern Pacific couldn't lay tracks fast enough to keep pace with frenetic suburban home construction. Downtown, progressive-era leaders trying to halt rail's decline demanded better service for the commoner on the grounds that it was a public utility. City merchants, for their part, whimpered that motorists were bypassing their storefronts. Neither of these would matter: both groups were on the wrong side of history.[47]

In a land of transplants, the car signified freedom from dehumanizing existence in the concrete canyons and slaughterhouse-districts of the eastern cities. Drawn-out controversies over a central rail terminus and possible Chicago-style, elevated trains further persuaded Angelenos that bankrolling a modern rapid-transit system was not a prudent idea. During the 1930s, Pacific Electric Railway and Los Angeles Railway hemorrhaged money, and ticket sales plummeted. Besides the usual criticism about smelly, sardine-can cars, there were complaints about irregular fares and poor routing. The private automobile, on the other hand, was convenient, and surprisingly affordable, if not fabulously suited for the West Coast idyll. "We in Los Angeles," said one resident, "realize the value of sunshine, of space and of individual homes as against the crowded housing conditions and tenements without proper provision for light, air, yards, lawns, trees, shrubs, flowers. . . ."[48]

Car-entranced as Los Angeles was becoming, there still were a million rail and bus passengers per day in 1939. The war years, with gas and rubber rationing, saw boardings increase. When the Allies won, suburbanization and personal choice once more trumped public transit. As its ridership drooped again in the late 1940s, Pacific Electric Railway sought fare increases that California officials rejected until the company upgraded its equipment. Watching LA's growth spring outward from the old downtown powerbase, Pacific Electric Railway executives gave up. They sold the Red Car system to a firm that mainly operated electric buses. Five more years of red ink, and the sentimental train car of the city's bygone era ceased operations. Owners of the downtown trolley system, now mired themselves in car-spawned traffic, reckoned that buses would work better than expensive fixed lines. Two deals later and the buses belonged to National City Lines, which operated transit systems throughout America.

It was not a peaceful transition. The U.S. Justice Department objected to the consolidation, and filed a news-making antitrust case against National. The main charge in the so-called "Great American Streetcar Scandal" involved the company's policy of exclusively buying equipment and parts from corporate stockholders, primarily General Motors. (Also associated were Standard Oil of California, Firestone Tires, and Mack Truck.) It was *not* a bid, the judge stressed, to monopolize a whole industry, or bulldoze transit options so car sales would reach the moon.[49] Years later, the belief that GM and others colluded to destroy urban rail as a way to fatten their corporate coffers made a comeback. In 1974, an antitrust lawyer testified to Congress that the Big Four automakers had "used their vast economic power to restructure America into a land of big cars and diesel trucks."[50] Fourteen years later, in 1988, the hit movie *Who Framed Roger Rabbit?* introduced the conspiracy theory to a new generation of cynics. Had they dug into the subject, they'd have found hard evidence of premeditated manipulation wanting. Thus, the Great American Streetcar Scandal became the equivalent of tales of mass alien-abductions: pure fiction that made for juicy conversation.

The Automobile Club of Southern California in 1937 believed it could solve downtown's bumper-nicking gridlock with a quilt of dedicated highways. With greenbelts in the median, they'd be "magic motorways." It was a futuristic, appealing concept, and, sure enough, the state broke ground on what is now the Pasadena Freeway in the early 1930s. Also known as the Arroyo Seco Parkway, it was California's first freeway, and the tip of what became a $400-million, 211-mile state-highway web known the world over. Mass transit seemed outdated, wasteful even. A proposal to erect a downtown-San Fernando Valley monorail died over sticker shock. It wasn't until decades later that the enormity of L.A.'s rail abandonment came full circle, with sales-tax proposals to finance a new subway-commuter rail grid. Widespread citizen disgust with freeway bottlenecks and associated problems scuttled almost forty percent of the local projects in the state's 1954 freeway blueprint, including roadways planned for Laurel Canyon, Beverly Hills, and several gap closures in the Pasadena area.[51] For all their annoyances with traffic, though, the masses adored their cars.

It seems appropriate that LA's foremost science fiction writer was the loudest early critic of autopia, to whom nobody listened. Ray Bradbury, who in 1964 was writing the screenplay for his novel *The Martian Chronicles,* never learned to drive and wished others hadn't either. Without rail, Bradbury predicted, "We can look forward to 30 or 40 years of hosing off our highways, burying our dead, and wondering why the world thinks we are some kind of Southern California nut or something."[52] Mistrustful as he was about the auto-industrial complex, the nub of the problem might have been leaders' attention spans. L.A. mayors who could've dedicated themselves to rejuvenating mass transit in the peoples' hearts were too preoccupied trying to keep their juggernaut from toppling sideways. Fletcher Bowron, who served four terms from 1938 to 1953, had to be a wartime mayor managing air-raid blackouts and Japanese-interment camps. He wrestled with violent, anti-Hispanic xenophobia that culminated in the beatings of young Mexican-American zoot suiters. In 1949, a police-run prostitution and extortion ring, with mob figures Mickey Cohen and Bugsy Siegel in the center of it, rocked City Hall. Opponents instigated recall efforts against Bowron, and the mayor confronted those alongside anti-communist security, redevelopment fights, sewer repairs, and street traffic improvements.[53] Neither Bowron nor his successor, Norris Poulson, foresaw the petrifying scenario that too many cars and plants in exactly the wrong place might dangerously overwhelm the local airshed. There were no memorable soapbox speeches or righteous editorials demanding fewer freeways and more express buses. Instead, Poulson believed that people should buy smaller vehicles, not boat-sized sedans, and that the city cars, taxis, and ambulances should boycott purchasing any vehicle not equipped with smog-trapping gadgets.[54]

Political wariness about taxes also figured in. When the county's Metropolitan Transit Authority sought legislative permission to impose a rail-building, bus-line-expanding property tax increase without a direct vote in 1963, the supervisors and Mayor Sam Yorty resisted it in a welter of Sacramento-L.A. name-calling.[55] For Supervisor Dorn, levying a tax, no matter how miniscule the amount, in such a manner was a "flagrant violation" of the home-rule principle that Californians expected.[56] Governor Brown, as usual, saw regional myopia, if not cowardice. "You have an abdication in leadership here," he said. "If [county] residents are not willing to pay twenty cents a month to get rid of smog, and at the same time build a good transit system, then I despair of Los Angeles' future."[57] The legislature squashed a similar mass transit tax levy two years later, despite highway engineers' plea for it. Plans for a fivefold increase in local freeways, the engineers cautioned in Summer 1965, would bring unimaginable congestion and sullied air.[58]

Consequently, smog transformed from the episodic to the systemic with the rise of the automobile culture. Southern California's planners, unable to trench a network of commuter light rails, subways, and fast buses next to the freeways, had but one impassioned, tacit hope. They gambled that techno-engineering would zap the smog out of cars, and then people's lives. Had their bosses reintroduced rail in the name of sun and public health, who knows how long Angelenos' notorious gridlock would've lasted?

*   *   *

Ralph Nader, just beginning his career as America's legendary consumer-advocate and public-interest lawyer, detected Sherman Antitrust violation when he heard Griswold's Texas speech. Soon he laid it out to Justice Department officials while Griswold won a Board of Supervisors resolution seeking a formal federal probe. For once, Washington did as the Southland sought without officials begging or groveling for it. A federal grand jury impaneled in Los Angeles heard evidence for eighteen months in 1967 and 1968. It gathered so much information, in fact, that prosecutors purportedly hungered for a criminal indictment. Higher-ups favoring a civil case overruled them. At least Washington wasn't letting the carmakers wiggle out, and California hoped for vindicating, white-collar charges the industry would not soon forget.

Against this backdrop, LBJ's lame duck administration in January 1969 brought antitrust conspiracy charges against GM, Ford, Chrysler, American Motors Corp., and the automaker's trade group. Justice officials alleged that the carmakers had lied to California about the availability of crankcase ventilation gear back in 1962. Likewise, tailpipe-exhaust controls were available in '66 when the industry stated that they were technologically infeasible. Motor City wasn't swaggering anymore. GM called the spectacular charges "unwarranted." The carmaker's association said the Justice Department's evaluation was based on the "profound misunderstanding" of the joint venture.[59] Why, auto executives asked, was everybody so incredulous of their motives?

They would rather have faced the Red Army than watch Nader link arms with L.A. officials. Nader's strident activism, encapsulated in his muckraking book *Unsafe at Any Speed,* had stimulated federal auto-safety reforms. Part of the book was devoted to Southern California air pollution, and local officials capitalized on it. Dorn presented Nader with a commendation for it in 1966 in sincere respect and official buttering-up. Nader, in his acceptance remarks, was an iconoclast who wanted to see electric cars or steam engines become king, not continued genuflections to the fossil-fueled engine. He interpreted automakers' suggestion that erratic "nuts behind the wheel" deserved blame for the brown air as a "contemptuous joke."[60] You could almost feel those Michigan skyscrapers tremble in anger toward the funereal contrarian.

If Nader was Detroit's archenemy, then County Supervisor Hahn was The People's heel-nipping Agitant. He'd bird-dogged the smog issue before it was fashionable and after it was declared hopeless. Of all the supervisors, he was the most vociferous, the most consistent, at once civic-minded and charmingly buffoonish. (His stated dislike of women's cleavage-revealing attire was pig heaven for columnists.)[61] An old-style, pothole-fixing Democrat, whose son would become L.A. mayor and whose daughter would be a San Pedro councilwoman, he cemented his legacy as the man who challenged everybody's favorite machine.

In what would become a time-capsule record of carmaker's intransigence and deviousness, Hahn began writing to the auto company chiefs in 1953, respectfully asking them about their smog-device intentions. To Henry Ford II, he posed fundamental questions about them: are they effective, affordable, replicable, or just first generation? (A Ford PR man answered that the company believed exhaust waste gases dissipate in the atmosphere.) His letter to Chrysler's president cited Haagy's research that Los Angeles' cars produced Los Angeles' smog, and said it'd be a "great public service" if the ingenious auto industry stepped up. (A Chrysler vice president referenced the trans-company R&D as proof of its commitment.) All that polite discourse heated into a respectful harangue by the late 1960s. Hahn had been the sole supervisor to meet Martin Luther King, Jr. He'd championed an inner-city hospital after the 1965-Watts Riots, and coaxed the Dodgers out of Brooklyn. He may have seemed dorky with his big dark glasses and monotone drone, but he was accustomed to results. "For over sixteen years I have urged (the) leading manufacturers of automobiles to equip the cars . . . with smog control equipment. . . . As each year's model rolls off the assembly line, I am extremely disappointed that the automobile industry has not accepted its rightful obligation to preserve the health of the citizens."[62] Nobody told it like him.

Hahn, believing a well-connected adversary held the county hostage, tried leveling the odds with a parallel letter campaign seeking federal intervention. "It seems to me there has been some kind of agreement between the major automobile manufacturers not to put forth full effort," he told LBJ's attorney general Nicholas Katzenbach in Jan. 1966. He articulated similar beliefs to the next two top Justice officials. Months earlier, he'd told GM, in an unappreciated letter, about his fact-finding trip to Detroit in 1955. It was there, he claimed, that a company engineer acknowledged that GM could absorb the cost of anti-smog research if it put as much into it as its subsidy for *Motorama* TV shows promoting new models.[63]

Hahn's persuasion offensive still was no match for Beltway power circles. Consummate Washington insider/lawyer Lloyd Cutler represented Detroit and its trade group. Cutler, a gravely voiced Yale man who would counsel two Democratic presidents and lend a hand to Republicans, too, had represented the carmakers on auto safety.[64] To nobody's shock, he recommended that the Justice Department forego criminal charges on the smog allegations. County officials who dreaded facing Cutler—one congressman called him one of D.C.'s "smoothest operators"—organized a preventive strike back home. They filed a $100-million lawsuit against the carmakers, citing the "large sums" government spent treating indigents with respiratory problems, a somewhat novel angle. The suit's other objective was to keep the Feds from sweeping their antitrust case "under the rug."[65] More than fifteen years had flown since the carmakers expressed how "dead serious" they were about pollution relief.

Los Angeles experienced its own awful September 11 with the stroke of a pen. It was on that day in 1969 that the Justice Department agreed to a consent decree sparing the automakers from admitting guilt or paying major fines. The Nixon administration had been in office less than a year, and Attorney General John Mitchell tried to slab gloss on the settlement. He said the decree would "spur aggressive and competitive research and development efforts" that would benefit the health and welfare of millions of city dwellers more than a punitive stoning of an entire industry. President Nixon's science advisor, former Caltech majordomo Lee A. DuBridge, added that it was an "important step" in fighting air pollution.[66] That was about the nicest thing anybody said. What Nader had described as the "antitrust case of the century" felt like the smog war's biggest bust.

California congressman George Brown, practically apoplectic over what had happened, cast the settlement as a "sellout" to campaign contributors at the expense of Americans' right to "clean and healthy air." He immediately hollered for a full trial to present the incriminating evidence.[67] Hahn, speaking for the county, demanded the unsealing of the "roomful" of grand jury evidence. "This is the most important legal battle in the history of the air pollution fight," he said. "If we lose it, we will go back twenty years."[68] He ached for local justice, where the heads of GM, Ford, and Chrysler were dragged to a Los Angeles witness stand for a courtroom cross-examination.[69] Resorting to habit, he wrote to New York mayor John Lindsay, senators Edward Kennedy and Muskie, assorted mayors and politicians he'd probably never met for support to reverse the agreement. Many, including twenty-nine different congressmen, agreed with Los Angeles' position it'd been stabbed in the back. Amid this fury, Nixon aides repeated the decision had been "apolitical."[70]

Frantic, the supervisors turned to Nader, their designated pot-stirrer, for interpretation. He told them the decree was "not worth the paper it was written on," because of limp policing and requirements on the carmakers. "The whole enforcement process is so mythological as to be the subject of supreme satire," he said.[71] Equally perturbed was county grand jury foreman Martin Walshbren. Asked by a reporter if there was more to the case than embodied in the consent decree, he answered "a great deal more." Asked if he could elaborate or help, he answered, "Not unless I wish to risk going to jail."

Even California's attorney general jumped into the harried campaign by trying to file a separate antitrust case. It was not to be. On October 8, 1969, unaffected by the protestors outside his window, U.S. District Court judge Jesse Curtis approved the settlement. "Smog," he opined, "is not a legal matter."

Two years later, California representative Phil Burton got hold of a sixty-four-page Justice Department memo he said proved the federal government had shielded "previously undisclosed evidence" about the antitrust action. This memo, which Burton submitted to the *Congressional Record*, confirmed that prosecutors had recommended a criminal case rather than the corporate equivalent of a traffic ticket carrying no ironclad stipulations or restitution for damages. The document, drawing from exhibits and earlier grand jury testimony, indicated that prosecutors believed they could "prove beyond a reasonable doubt" about the existence of an industry-wide compact "not to compete in research, development, manufacture and installation of motor vehicle air pollution control devices for the purpose of achieving interminable delays." Despite that bombshell document, the courts, including the Supreme Court in a subsequent filing by eighteen states against the automakers, serially rebuffed local governments concerned about exhaust-laced air pollution.[72] The ledger didn't lie. In 1969, GM's budget for anti-smog R&D was $24 million, a surprisingly robust number until one considers it represented about one-tenth of one-percent of what the industry giant made off gross sales for that year.[73]

Like the iconic sixties' song says, however, the times were a changin'. The American car industry, once lauded for its lightning-fast transition from car manufacturing to the production of tanks and warplanes as part of America's World War II "Arsenal of Democracy," no longer was a sacred cow in the aftermath of the waiver and conspiracy imbroglios. In March

1967, Petris, the liberal state senator, introduced a bill you might've expected in China. It would have limited one gas-powered car per family, citing the "poisons" out of the tailpipe. "We can't sit back and leave it entirely to industry," he proclaimed.[74] After the waiver victory in 1968, Petris withdrew his bill. Imposition of austere new state regulations that Detroit had resisted so long was one of his reasons. Those protesting moms would accept nothing less.

California had bled for the right to set its own automotive emission standards and it was hellbent to exert it. So in 1970, the still-fledgling California Air Resources Board set binding regulations that effectively forced the automakers to begin installing catalytic converters on all vehicles sold in state. At first, the converters attacked hydrocarbons and carbon monoxide, but manufacturers later enhanced them to shrink plumes of nitrogen oxides as well—an irresistible innovation that regulators soon seized upon in future rules. These changes, bound later with engine improvements and development of cleaner-burning gasoline, set the stage for mammoth reductions in unhealthy air as new vehicles slowly replaced dirtier older models. The emboldened Air Resources Board had other arrows in its quiver. A week after the Justice Department announced the consent decree, the board cranked down the health-protective levels for oxidants and carbon monoxide.[75]

Feisty Ken Hahn continued his Detroit-dialogue in the same relentless, "do-something!" tenor. Now with the waiver and grand jury findings, he had unprecedented bargaining power and it showed. GM notified him that among other concessions, it was expanding its two Southern California smog-research centers. Henry Ford II thanked him for the letters he'd written over the years as "an instructive record of too slow a response" to a national problem. Chrysler said it was anxious to learn why its 1971 Plymouth station wagon flunked California emission standards. But American Motors went one better. To finance its emission-capping work, the company announced it would shave expenditures in other areas. These cutbacks included, drum roll please . . . vehicle styling.[76]

California, at last, was imposing its will over the carmakers, whose sexy, vapory products had shaped Los Angeles the way the tides mold the shoreline. The state's assumption of control over its millions of cars, ponderous and hair pulling as it was, marked as epic an achievement as Haagy's discovery of smog's photochemical genesis. It gave other states ideas, introduced new minds to the issue, outed the internal combustion engine as villain, and all these years later remains proof of what is possible. One writer expressed it this way:

> Los Angeles and California had accomplished much to control automotive air pollution by the early 1970s during their period of national leadership on the issue. Primarily through the efforts of Angelenos, vehicular exhaust had been identified as the major source of pollution it was and had gradually been elevated to the level of . . . federal regulatory efforts.[77]

The enduring results speak for themselves. Today's automobiles emit just *one percent* of the noxious fumes they did back in the 1960s. With apologies to Ralph Nader and Congress, it was a four-eyed Don Quixote named Ken who first saw through the haze.

7
BOUFFANTS &
STETHOSCOPES

THE LOS ANGELES SMOG BEAST WAS UNACCUSTOMED TO RETREAT. Truth was, nobody had come close to staunching the atmospheric backlash to the West Coast's languid, suburban lifestyle in all the years since that downtown siege of July '43. The clingy wisps, in fact, mocked government assurances that resurrecting the crystal-clean airshed merely required completion of a list of action points. Ever since the early 1950s, authorities had repeated this list like Maoist propaganda: blanket regulation over all emissions, industries forever pushing the engineering limits of technology, and a robust emergency plan, all with only minor sacrifice asked of the guy down the block. Yet, an entire generation of Southern Californians had watched those assurances come to naught—and felt the consequences in their bodies, at their jobs. Gloriously, the 1960s would see the tables turned, the beast bested in ways unrelated to chemicals under the car hood. What made this reversal more delicious was that the upstarts propelling it were neither the longhaired psychedelic specimens of the counterculture, nor government men with tongue-twisting titles. Instead, one was a headstrong physician with a dangerous pen. A gaggle of socialites with gumption in their pricey heels sashayed in from the other direction. Together they would rouse the real champion: a beaten-down middle class with fighting vinegar still in it.

The self-described "amateurs in floral skirts" were socialites from a pressure group that cleverly tabbed itself after the international-distress signal: "SOS," an acronym for "Stamp Out Smog." Occupying its core membership, which coalesced in 1958, were wealthy, middle-aged women from the city's upscale Westside. Marjorie Levee of Beverly Hills, the wife of a Hollywood producer, was one of their first directors, as was the mellifluously named Afton Slade. Many other SOS founders had husbands in the entertainment world, as well. They included Mrs. Art Linkletter, comedian Robert Cummings' wife, along with the spouses of a Warner Bros. producer and a Music Corp. of America executive. Several young actresses, and even the wife of USC doctor, later joined them. As these rookies would learn, navel-gazing and movie-star gossip was not the older ladies' bag: kinetic activism was.

They dove right in, ready to hurl dismissive portrayals of them as mascara-primping "female warriors" against their male labelers. In no time, they aligned themselves with county supervisor Dorn, a loose-cannon conservative who recognized what a sparkplug the group could be. Dorn counseled the ladies to make themselves heard, and they heeded his words. They debuted noisily, chanting for the sulfur-fuel-prohibition with hooting enthusiasm. They appreciated "strength-in-numbers" as organizational philosophy, and hustled to enlist twenty volunteer organizations—groups like "United Hostesses," "Helping Hand," and several garden clubs—into their protest-network pyramid.[1] Most admirable was the seven-point prescription that SOS distributed in its early phase. It seamed together in one common-sense manifesto what it had taken experts years to assemble, encouraging, among other goals, basin-wide rapid transit, state exhaust standards, fuel-composition laws, and better-coordinated research. The housewives had done their home-work. And, they could run a mean organization. SOS bore alliances with so many women's clubs statewide a decade after its formation that it could legitimately request Governor Brown's ear as it dominated the 1960s smog-protest movement. Levee, who some remember for having a haughty, socialite-like air, even found herself on the Air Resources Board.[2]

In the late 1950s, though, sulfur-laced smog, real or imag-ined, from South Bay-area refineries was SOS's adversary. The Western Oil & Gas Association, which had wheeled out scien-tists and economists to defeat the proposed fuel-oil ban, dis-liked the ladies for what it saw as their pitiful ignorance. "The group," Association vice president Felix Chappellet summa-rized, "simply does not understand the real causes of smog or the economics that make our Southland thrive."[3] That was a sizable underestimation, but not the last. Before key votes or meetings, the ladies brandished the telephone like a commu-nity bullhorn and coupled it with old-fashioned chain letters. Each member would write a letter to a decision-maker. Then they'd dial ten other members, asking that they duplicate the effort. The result usually was a "landslide of anti-smog mail" that effected policy.[4] SOS' leaders also reinvented themselves as issue provocateurs with their own stable of experts. In their push for the fuel ban, they not only zeroed in on the Western Oil & Gas's conflicting arguments but also quoted an American Cancer Society prediction that "more than one mil-lion American school children are doomed to eventual death

from lung cancer if present trends [in air pollution] continue."[5] Never mind that the region's oil industry by then had
achieved radical cuts in smokestack waste. SOS appeared the
well-informed crusade, the industrialists surly and defensive.
Soon, political aides, county lawyers, and other smognoscenti were angling to pose for photographs with those same
"female warriors."

Notoriety was hardly enough for them. SOS's troops, starting in the early 1960s, regularly dragged their bored-stiff kids
to marathon rulemaking sessions, appreciating what good
imagery it made in an increasingly telegenic world. Using humor,
they then wittily commemorated air pollution lowlights. The
apex was the "Unhappy 21st Birthday Party" SOS threw for
smog in 1964 at the Ambassador Hotel, the centerpiece of
which was a skull-and-crossbones cake rich in sugar and
symbolism.[5] (A few years later presidential candidate Robert
Kennedy was assassinated not far from where that un-celebra-
tion had occurred.) All these tactics originated from a
pigeonhole office on the Sunset Strip, in a group where many
members were dues-deadbeats. For $85, you did get the organ-
ization newsletter.

Earning credibility as more than dabbling Good Samaritan
Suzies with the patronizing, male-dominated media was
sometimes as daunting as operating off a shoestring budget.
Women at that time typically were outsiders in public affairs,
and uncomfortable in the spotlight. Then SOS president,
Afton Slade, upset about the *Times* characterization of her as
the "smog lady," said in 1965 that rethinking was overdue.
"The picture of a little old lady draped in gray veils whisking
in and out of the hearing room" is "misleading," she said.
"There are plenty of crackpots involved in the smog battle,
but we beg to protest we are not one of them."[6] Group reputa-

tion notwithstanding, practicing early environmentalism when the traditional role of women in American society was just breaking the membrane of domesticity did spark its frictions—inside personal relationships. An Orange County SOS member and housewife named Jean Somers had witnessed it. She confided that husbands and boyfriends of fellow members sometimes became upset, if not jealous, about how much time their honeys devoted to the cause. One husband purportedly delivered an ultimatum, telling his better half: "It's either me or smog, baby!" It was not clear whom she picked. Few of the SOS rank-and-file, meanwhile, had experience appearing in front of big, emotionally charged crowds. Every time Somers spoke up publicly, she was certain that people could hear her knees knocking. Assigning her three young sons, ages five to twelve, to photograph gunk-emitting planes and cars was a cakewalk by comparison.[7]

*   *   *

Dr. Peter Veger was not budging, not one iota. On the death certificate of his patient Nathan Gordon, a seventy-three-year-old store clerk whose heart gave out in November 1963, Veger simply and sensationally wrote that "Los Angeles smog" was a contributing factor.[8] The county health department, unable to find air pollution listed as an internationally registered disease, dissented. It flatly rejected Gordon's death certificate. "We could be opening up the gates to speculative certification" if the department accepted Veger's post-mortem, explained county coroner Theodore Curphey. Unhinging those gates, he realized, invited turmoil, and maybe legal payouts beyond the wildest dreams of an office full of ambulance-chasing lawyers. A month earlier, county supervisors had been so apprehensive about such a prospect that they asked their lawyers to guarantee they were not liable. After looking into it, the county counsel's office informed the board they were immune from litigation provided there was no malice, graft, or sinister motives in their rule adoptions. The politicians stayed jumpy, anyway. They knew other local physicians had reportedly deleted smog as a cause of death after calls from the coroner, no matter Curphey's denials.

The burden of proof stuck on the physicians, and many non-MDs viewed the paperwork rebuttal as a clash of egos. Not Veger. "I am a bona fide doctor," he said, "and a free citizen can express (his) opinion." Veger had already done this once before, when he cited air pollution as a factor in the death of an eighty-year-old man whose aorta had burst while coughing. Veger believed that something in smog's composition over-stimulated the heart, putting undue strain on it, especially among folks with coronary troubles.[9] His colleagues' case files would back him up. So would the past.

In the late 1920s, well before smog was synonymous with health crisis, a local doctor had listed it as one reason for the death of a sixty-nine-year-old female patient. Dr. John V. Barrow was no dime-a-dozen sawbones, either. He was president of the esteemed Los Angeles County Medical Association.[10] "Other doctors," a peer later reminisced, "haven't had the intestinal fortitude to list smog as one of the death causes."[11] Thirty years later, that same medical association's pollution committee was nearing consensus that inhaling Los Angeles' exhaust-imbued air was shortening lives. "I know that individuals suffering from pulmonary trouble and congestion leave here and seem to get better elsewhere," Dr. Francis Pottenger, Jr., the association's smog-panel chairman, said in 1953.[12] Given other physicians' views about smog as a pathogen, he was not speaking recklessly. A USC surgery professor at about the same time testified to Congress that air pollution might be inducing *more* lung cancer than cigarette smoking.[13]

Chilling theories like this, as well as contradictory ones suggesting air pollution wasn't harmful at all, came and went through the zeitgeist. Hampering across-the-board acceptance about the long-terms effects of smog was the absence of proof—statistically fortified, replicable proof. That's because smog's effect on the human anatomy long had been a goblin in the lab and a red flag in the doctor's office. It would be this way for years after Veger's courageous words. As a result, L.A. physicians frequently were unpopular messengers relaying their observations of the environmentally sick. Matched up against them was a "prove it" business establishment incredulous about air contaminants' capacity to trigger disease. It wanted stone-cold evidence, especially since it had felt unjustly scapegoated before. Hence, for some physicians, anecdotes were all they had. Working without the benefit of MRI machines, deep-panel blood tests, or hard drives full of topic literature, they extrapolated upon what *they* saw in their patients and heard through their stethoscopes. And, based on what they observed, many hypothesized that Los Angeles' compromised air probably killed and definitely injured. The medical association, in a 1952 open letter to the mayor recommending a major health study, reported its compelling statistics. A poll of its membership determined that ninety-one percent believed smog was damaging their patients, from their noses to their internal organs.[14]

Fatefully, that's about as specific as it got. If you compared early 1950s reports about smog's health detriments to those of the early 1960s, you might think you were reading Xeroxes. In 1955, Dr. Paul Kotin, a temperamental, harried USC pathologist spearheaded much of the research. He suspected smog in the rising tide of throat and lung cancers, but was unsure about what role increasing cigarette smoking played. Kotin, in a landmark 1955 journal article he coauthored, likened the quest for answers to medical stumpers over microorganisms. In both, unknown variables—exposure duration and intensity, genetic differences, living conditions, etc.—muddied cause-and-effect conclusions. Later, he noticed that tumors in mice exposed to air contaminants jumped "enormously." He was positive airborne toxins were an agent in cancer production, too. Calibrating exact probabilities was something else altogether.[15] As studies lumbered forward, the assistant dean of the respected University of California San Francisco medical school said in 1961 that his studies corroborated Kotin's findings, to the extent that number crunching could. "The connection between air pollution and cancer of the respiratory system is as sure as statistical studies can make it," said Dr. Seymour Farber. Also disturbing, though less definitive, he added, was its inflammatory effect on people with bronchitis, asthma, and emphysema.[16] On heavy smog days, male cigarette smokers were unable to walk a half block.[17]

For 1960s officialdom, the smog-cancer linkage was alternately circumstantial and troubling. Eisenhower's surgeon general declared the government dared not wait for triple confirmation before responding. This is what a battered environment does: it leaves officials hanging in a Hamlet-like pickle, pitting preemptive action against coolheaded, gradual change. Griswold's chamber stunt crisply, albeit unintentionally, exemplified government's no-win situation regarding public health. L.A.'s smog czar couldn't shake off what he'd inhaled, just as hundreds of thousands of smog-belt citizens couldn't shake off their pains. If air pollution just caused temporary irritation and visual blemish, why act rashly at the risk of alienating local industries that employed millions? On the other hand, if pollution was slowly strangling the whole basin, perhaps even threatening its extinction, shouldn't treatment commence?

Science and medicine had no absolute answer because hard data was only beginning to filter in. Authorities hand-cuffed by this dilemma frequently only had sympathy to offer. An early APCD report stated it was understandable that people were distraught. It recommended medical studies that future district officials eschewed as beyond their forte (and possibly lawsuit encouraging). "Their pleas for help," the report said, "should not be taken lightly."[18] A draft of a follow-up study, likely published in the late 1950s, beaded with nervousness. It referred to the County Medical Association's 1956 question-naire, in which ninety-five percent of responding physicians outlined a "smog syndrome" that included the usual respira-tory and neurological symptoms. Researchers already knew about the existence of pollutants capable of inflicting lung damage *without* the victim's detection. Similar alarm existed about carbon monoxide buildups for residents living adjacent to freeways and power plants. In spite of all this, there was no commanding evidence between inhaling smog wisps and dropping dead. For Dr. Leslie Chamber, the district's research director, narrowing that chasm between observation and scien-tific confirmation was urgent. Or, as he put it, in his Mr. Spock-like way, "From the viewpoint of an air pollution control agency, the long range importance of established knowledge as to the kinds and quantities of materials capable of producing ill-nesses or death cannot be overstated."[19]

A movie buff might suggest the risk-reward subplot in Steven Spielberg's 1975 blockbuster *Jaws*, about a preternaturally hungry great white shark inhabiting the waters off an East Coast resort town, as instructive. In the film, the unctuous mayor must choose between his town's summer tourist season and closing the beach to protect swimmers from becoming shark bait. In Southern California, the most aggressive response to smog would've been partial evacuation, the least disruptive doing nothing regulatory until the data was in. When that notorious October 1954 smog wrapped its blue-gray mitts around the area, Governor Knight had to muster all his persuasive powers in telling jittery Angelenos that air pollution did not pose a dire health threat to them. He based his assertion on "hastily called" consultations with twenty local scientists and doctors. The experts summarized for him what Fletcher Bowron was told a decade earlier. They said smog was an "annoying inconvenience" incapable of unleashing lasting damage on *most* people—a noticeably more optimistic conclusion than colleagues who still saw patients. In an insidious flagging that nobody yet had the answers, a news brief about a Boy Scout whose eyes had swollen shut from smog appeared alongside the story about the governor's reassurance that "all is well." A month later, a ten-year-old Alhambra girl apparently susceptible to aerosol toxins died mysteriously.[20] Whether these were anomalies or harbingers would take years to ascertain. Until then, Kotin surmised, "neither an emergency nor imminent disaster was at hand." UCLA School of Medicine dean Stafford Warren said he had yet to see hard evidence of "death by smog," either.[21] Using our *Jaws* metaphor, Knight after the October 1954 attack stationed lifeguards at an open beach.

Recommendations sailed afterwards to stop toxic buildups before they accumulated, as the state set maximum contaminant levels based on animal-tissue tests and carmakers' exhaust research.[22] It was another of California's environmental novelties, another chance to beam light where there'd been shadows before. Lab animal gave their lives for it. Six thousand carefully selected mice, rats, and guinea pigs, imported from around the nation, including the Army's Maryland bio-research center, anchored a USC/Hancock Foundation experiment on lung damage. At exposure sites in Burbank, Azusa, East L.A., and near the Hollywood Freeway, one set of critters inhaled contaminated supplies while the control group ingested purified air. Experts framed it as the largest animal study ever devoted to a single medical question.[23] Parched for human data, state health officials began tracking 140,000 American Legion members in California, forty percent of whom lived in the L.A. area.[24] Four years later, doctors at County General Hospital solicited volunteers with chronic lung problems to breathe the junk in lab settings.[25] Everywhere, it seemed, brainy technicians were running pollution tests. They left the conclusions to someone else.

Until scientifically unassailable evidence fluttered in, it was up to the County Medical Association, as the APCD's health advisors, to voice their discomfiting beliefs. They condemned sulfur dioxide as a public-health time bomb. They shot down fringe theories that smog caused malaria or cirrhosis. Most daringly, the association surveyed 2,803 member doctors about their patients. The vast majority responded about how destructive inhaled chemicals were. "Air Pollution Can Kill" titled its 1955 report.[26] The association strengthened its findings with an unnerving 1957 study that questioned whether air toxins associated with freshly minted plants were billowing new or mutated pathogens over the heads of Californians. Still, it was the association's oncologists, pathologists, and X-ray therapists—doctors who saw

lesions firsthand—who were most convinced that ozone, per-
oxides, aldehydes, and related effluents were disease-causing
agents.[27] A Caltech chemical warfare expert advanced the
same theme about the same time after experimenting with
microbes. Invisible particles of dust, sulfur, salt, and metals,
he said, can heighten toxicity levels of smog by as much as
2500 percent![28] It wasn't as flabbergasting as it seemed. A
1961 survey by The County Medical Association and the
local Tuberculosis and Health Association revealed that doctors had advised 10,000 residents to leave Southern
California to safeguard their health. Amend that—they had
been urging 9,000-10,000 people *a year* to go![29]

Leap ahead two smog seasons to 1963. California's emphysema rate was four times what it had been a decade earlier, and
noticeably higher than in industrial, blue-collar bastions such
as Pennsylvania and Illinois.[30] While no smoking gun had surfaced to incriminate smog for poor health—one doctor said the
needed diagnostics still were in the horse-and-buggy era—
patient files suggested it be hauled in for questioning. Downtown
exceeded the state's new oxidant standard during more than
half of 1963. The smog-belt cities of Burbank, Pasadena,
Azusa, and Pomona surpassed it on more than 200 days. (By
contrast, San Francisco crossed the line only twelve days out
of the year, San Diego, 35.)[31] Dr. Sanford Bloom, president of
the L.A. chapter of the American Academy of General
Physicians, put it as well as anyone:

> We cannot prove that Los Angeles smog is a killer but we
> assume it's dangerous because of what we see in our
> offices every day. . . . There are orderly scientific experi-
> ments being conducted to learn of objective answers but we
> cannot afford to wait. . . . All of us who live in this urban

*area are part of a huge cancer experiment. . . . This experi-
ment must not be permitted to proceed because it is our
necks on the line.*[32]

It was more than their necks giving leaders insomnia. The
air district's two maximum leaders, S. Smith Griswold and
Louis Fuller, refused pulling their punches about the scenario
that frightened people the most: a toxic air slaughterhouse
developing in spite of intense precautions to preempt it.
Southern California, the district's medical experts believed, so
far had lucked out that the conditions for a mass calamity—
mainly a prolonged temperature inversion combined with an
acute smog buildup—had not gelled. As of October 1967,
alerts had grown steadily the previous five years.[33] One subset
of doctors estimated that of Southern California's ten million
residents, sixteen percent would be at risk in a two-week emergency, partly because they lived in inland valleys where ozone
and its sister contaminants agglomerated most. Among that
susceptible subpopulation were 160,000 people with respiratory issues.[34]

Lynn Atkinson, Jr., who had been under a doctor's care for
emphysema for fifteen years, could not hide his dejection.
Atkinson had been a prominent contractor whose company
had erected massive public works projects that included the
Coolidge Dam in Arizona and an Oakland reservoir. Then his
lungs turned diseased, apparently from exposure to L.A. air,
sidelining him permanently. In July 1961, he asked the nurse
with him at his West L.A. apartment for some apple juice.
When she went to fetch it, Atkinson locked the door to the
bedroom and opened up a window, leaping to his death from
twelve stories up. The LAPD found his suicide note: "I have
lived here for almost fifty years in perfect physical condition

except for smog. . . . But it may be my passing shall accent the need for change [and] it will serve a good purpose."[35] It wouldn't be until much later, well into the 1980s and 1990s, after thousands more succumbed, that the epidemiology was sophisticated enough to corroborate what Atkinson had sensed. The average person breathes 15,000 times per day, and what they don't exhale immediately, especially from air smudged with civilization's ash, can shorten their lifespan.

Smog researchers' exploration of the human body, nonetheless, was an exciting and frightening frontier where epidemiology, genetics, and public health interwove. Why, they wondered, did hydrocarbons and nitrogen oxide, diesel and other floating matter, leave some deathly ill, some moderately sick, while the rest just felt lousy temporarily? Specialists who'd been preoccupied in the early years examining organ damage started thinking smaller, directing their attention to alveolis, the hundreds of millions of microscopic air sacs in the lungs. Air pollution seemed to trigger the mechanism for their cellular collapse, which shrunk lung capacity, especially in people with pulmonary defects. During autopsies, pathologists observed that the lungs of the smog-afflicted were not the normal pink. They were a gray-yellow, or streaked with rib-shaped black bands, many riddled with holes.[36]

Gulping Southern California's smoggiest air, some doctors were convinced by 1970, was tantamount to puffing a pack or two of cigarettes a day.[37] A County-USC study of the effects of ozone and nitrogen oxide underscored the presence of free-traveling pathogens. Long-term exposure to them might well weaken the walls of red blood cells, and maybe even allow those pathogens to penetrate the brain and muscles. The state health bureaucracy found its own linkage: fatal heart attacks spiked when smog was at its worst.

Atkinson's widow would add that it fueled hopelessness, too.

*   *   *

L.A.'s mind-rattling skies also fanned health and policy
effects like a crop duster, as questions of physiology segued
to misgivings about geography. Downwind position, another
Smogtown hallmark, was economic malignancy for one desert
resort city about one hundred miles east of downtown. In the
1950s and 1960s, Palm Springs and the surrounding scrub-
brush communities were playgrounds for suntan junkies and
the reclusively rich. Like prewar L.A., Palm Springs' fortunes
rested on its bankable sunshine and therapeutic heat. Old
Blue Eyes himself, Frank Sinatra, reinforced that cachet by
moving there in 1967—specifically to escape his hometown's
lung-burning air. Bob Hope, Red Skelton, Debbie Reynolds,
and Chuck Connors maintained vacation homes in the area,
as well. Even so, getaway homes can disappoint if they are
not distant enough from a source of misery, and that was the
rub in Palm Springs. Though separated from it by a vast
desert, it still was too close to the L.A. smog machine. Hence,
the migrating fumes made it feel more like clobbered
Pasadena, where auto exhausts and plant gases amassed from
cities miles away, than a getaway, white-shoes oasis packed
with celebrities.

The people of Riverside County, on whose western edge
Palm Springs sits, breathed adverse levels of L.A.-pumped
pollution for more than half of 1962, a doubling of the previous year's levels.[38] It got worse for the region long belittled,
Palm Springs the exception, as a barren, poor-man's Los
Angeles. (Today it's reshaped itself into a growing, cheaper
alternative thick with tract-home developments and wide-

open recreation.) The San Gorgonio Pass back then streamed the clotted air into Palm Springs like a funnel. The city attorney snatched a different metaphor, comparing the fumebank to a "gun pointed right at the heart" of the city. Too many whiffs of it and there goes tourism bucks, the town's lifeblood. One resident, chastening authorities as a radicalized professor might, said continued inaction by Palm Springs City Hall made it "accessories to murder." Why wasn't it bird-dogging its L.A. counterparts for relief? If that wasn't bad enough, one scientist pointed out that Southland air pollution was creeping into Arizona almost daily now.[39] San Diego city leaders asked not to be ignored, either. Forty percent of the aerial jetsam its citizens were inhaling was "made-in L.A."[40]

Other out-of-towners needed no warnings. Athletes visiting Southern California during the worst months always were seemingly eager to leave, clutching their return tickets in amazement of how anybody could live in L.A. full time. The University of Illinois football team, out for the 1963 Rose Bowl in Pasadena, sucked tanked oxygen.[41] When Hollywood smog clocked the Detroit Lions, they scampered to a practice field in breezy Santa Monica. The Minnesota Vikings, in California for a 1965 game against the L.A. Rams, wished they'd stayed cloistered inside their hotel. "Everyone was gagging," Vikings coach Norm Van Brocklin said of his team's workout. "Just look at my eyes." The headline was raw: "L.A. Too Smoggy, Vikes Too Groggy."[42] And so it went, Southern California's infamous air reducing burly men of the gridiron into doubled-over wrecks longing for the frozen tundra of icy Midwest stadiums.

Municipalities competing against Southern California for marquis sporting events invariably dramatized athletes' pain in their presentations. The Motor City cynically expressed revulsion at L.A.'s "wily tactics" to reopen the bidding for the 1968 Summer Olympics. Visualize, they said, the world's greatest athletes competing in *that* air.[43] (Mexico City eventually landed the games.) Knowing pollution would hurt its bid against cutthroat competitors like Moscow, L.A.'s promotion for the 1976 Summer Olympics included a twenty-one-minute video of a crystal-sky horizon. When the Olympic Committee in 1969 awarded the games to Montreal as an apolitical choice, West Coast ecologists skipped deliriously about the selection. So did a snarky columnist. "Nice as it would be for the merchants and airlines to have the Olympics here, it could wreck U.S. foreign relations if we invite other countries to run their youngsters through our ozone curtain," quipped *Times* columnist Art Seidenbaum. "We might have the Wheezo-American war on our hands. . . ."[44] L.A. mayor Sam Yorty was unamused.

New York had been the first major city to harp on Southern California's environment when a historic athletic deal was at stake. Just as the then-Brooklyn Dodgers were on the verge of relocating to Los Angeles in the late 1950s, New York governor Averill Harriman tried squashing the transcontinental relocation by predicting the area's manmade haze would torpedo its new franchise. Recurring air pollution, Harriman said, would prevent so many fans from arriving at the stadium on time that the new owners would literally have to wipe night games off the schedule.[45] The Dodgers moved anyway, Jackie Robinson and his teammates adapting to the 3-D air.

Members of the Soviet Olympic team were not as fortunate. Soviet track coach Gavriil Korobkov, in fact, intuited something researchers still were learning when he brought his squad here in July 1964. "Our athletes couldn't get used to the climate in Los Angeles even by the seventh day of their stay in California, and suffered from languor, headaches, and drowsiness," he said.[46] Other teams would contract similar symptoms in the years to come in the L.A. dichotomy: there was the Los Angeles of starlets and convertibles, and then there was the starless city that took your inflamed lungs days to forget. For the home team, it was a sweet advantage. Researchers unable to explain this phenomenon in the 1960s kept slogging at it as medical testing improved by midpoint the next decade. What they hit on was a spin-off of Charles Darwin's tenets about species' capacity for indigenous adaptation. In tests at Rancho Los Amigos hospital in Downey, a group of predominantly white, middle-class Canadians exhibited *twice* the sensitivity to ozone as lifetime Angelenos. Southern Californians, so it seemed, had developed a tolerance for toxins. Did this mean that evolution encompassed smog, or that immune systems could arm themselves from environmental perils within a couple generations? "We just don't know whether the adaptation is a good or bad thing," said Dr. Jack Hackney, the chief of Rancho's environmental health lab. "It may have hidden costs" if it camouflaged disease.[47] Notice researcher's favorite qualifier about smog as carcinogen—"may."

Pro and semi-pro athletes needed watching. Younger competitors required caretaking, and once again California pickaxed a trail out of necessity. Even in the late 1960s, it was "about the kids." Alert-level smog was draining student athletes of breath, endurance, and spirit. There was nothing subtle about it. High school football coaches who had previously lived for win-loss records now had to think more like school nurses. Summer football practice and fall games on school fields in the San Gabriel-Pomona valleys, where ozone concentrations resistered three times higher than the rest of the county, often could resemble an asthma clinic, with young players bent over, bloodshot-eyed and wheezing. There were 200 schools situated in this attack zone. Sometimes, the cumulative effects made kids lose focus as their bodies searched for invigorating oxygen during a violent game. "On bad days, you can hear [students] with a shallow, rasping cough," said Monrovia High School's P.E. coach. "The smog inhibits their movements. It's bad."[48]

The kids' vulnerability weighed heavily on the conscience of the County Medical Association. It said a special alert for student athletes might be a lifesaver, because researchers believed that children's physiology could not take the same beating as adults. The supervisors embraced the recommendation and codified it for the rulebook. When the localized oxidant level reached .35 ppm, the schools canceled strenuous outdoor activity. The California Interscholastic Federation Southern Section convened over it. Might smog cancel all football games, traditionally played in any weather, from August through October? Yes, it might. In 1969, there'd been a dozen alerts. Soon, coaches and administrators were shifting practices and game times to minimize exposure, or bringing their helmeted boys into the gym. It was dreadful publicity for teen sports, another demonstration of the beast's influence, but ignoring it could mean teenage-sized toe-tags. "We'd be playing with fire if we it didn't comply," Claremont High's football coach acknowledged. "We'd feel pretty bad if a boy keeled over."[49] The games went on as smog anxieties stayed in the huddle.

Arguably, the best tiding Southern Californians received about this time was the confirmation that they no longer were alone inhaling what the medical world knew was unhealthy at some level. Just about the point *Sgt. Pepper* debuted and the

Vietnam War started going south, scientists recognized air pollution as a global occurrence of low-dose, self-inflicted chemical bombardment. Sure, *Time* magazine in January 1967 featured a nauseatingly obscured L.A. freeway, where drivers flicked on their headlights at mid-afternoon. Shock value notwithstanding, a photographer might've captured those tell-tale plumes in any big manufacturing town. Ashen, hideous air clutched Baltimore, Chicago, Detroit, Houston, and Washington, D.C. It reemerged where civic campaigns had beaten it back before and introduced itself in German and French manufacturing cities, the Far East and the old Roman Empire.

You practically needed a grease board to keep up with the results of this worldwide epidemic. In New York City, stripping away soot, grime, and airborne acids cost each resident $200 a year. Nationally, air pollution damaged or destroyed in excess of $10 billion of property a year, with fallout that dissolved stone, destabilized steel, and blocked panoramas.[50] Skyline views weren't what they used to be in the Big Apple, nor were they in the nation's capital, where tourists some days couldn't spot the building-dwarfing Washington Monument. Then there was the incalculable sledgehammer to public health, the lives cut short, the human impulse for air and sun thwarted. Experts needed look no further than industrialized Japan for a glimpse of people capitulating. In the port city of Yokaichi about 230 miles southwest of Tokyo, school kids routinely played outside wearing yellow, surgical-like masks over their faces to protect them from petrochemical plants' fumes. The animal kingdom was ailing with the humans. At the Chicago zoo, the polar bears now had lung cancer and emphysema.[51]

As air pollution went global, a dovetailing interest in the wider atmosphere followed it. Where hydrocarbons and sulfur compounds once dominated catastrophe scenarios in localized areas, there now surfaced a more apocalyptic possibility from a rapidly industrializing planet. So-called "greenhouse gases," in fact, gave scientists bug-eyes forty years or so before Al Gore's *An Inconvenient Truth* confirmed their anxieties about global warming. These scientists speculated that atmospheric carbon dioxide from the burning and processing of coal, oil, and other fossil fuel-based products essentially could fry the Earth. If their equations proved correct, world temperatures would rise nine degrees by 2020. Even an immediate phasing out of fossil fuels for cleaner types of energy would not completely reverse the havoc already visited upon coastal areas, drinking-water reserves, and endangered species. The trend, the head of the U.S. Department of the Interior explained, was "unprecedented in rapidity in known geologic history."[52] The magazine popularized the scenario to its readers in 1967, as the nation's ecological movements became more than a twitch:

> Because it is being produced faster than it can be absorbed by the ocean or converted into carbon and oxygen by plants, some scientists think that the carbon dioxide in the atmosphere has increased by about 10 percent since the turn of the century. The gas produces a "greenhouse" effect in the atmosphere: it allows sunlight to penetrate it, but effectively blocks the heat generated on earth by the sun's rays from escaping back into space. There has already been a noticeable effect on earth—a gradual warming trend. . . . Scientists fear that average temperatures may, in the course of decades, rise enough to melt the polar ice caps. Since this would raise ocean levels more than 100 feet, it would effectively drown the smog problems of the world's coastal cities.[53]

Steamier global temperatures foreshadowed an especially glum tomorrow for Californians, where future doomsday movies by Irwin Allen and his acolytes were supposed to be escapism, not potential documentary. Geologists and others scientists, going where smog research never led, hypothesized that the melting of the snowfields and ice caps might send some continents into tectonic seizures. According to this theory, the shifting of incomprehensible amounts of raw weight from landmasses to the oceans would release correspondingly gargantuan levels of energy. Geologically active areas such as L.A. would be most vulnerable, exposed to a possible fusillade of volcanoes, earthquakes, and other natural convulsions.[54] For the hundreds of thousands of Southland residents living near the San Andreas Fault, which experts had long predicted was primed for a devastating "Big One," neither the air nor the land seemed especially hospitable.

Disneyland's "It's A Small World" ride, though about humanity's smallness, also was applicable to contaminant linkages between distant coasts. Someday, star meteorologist Morris Neiburger predicted in the *Time* story, that fresh air wafting over the Pacific Ocean on the jet stream from Asia might not be so benign. Everybody knew diluted L.A. smog spread as far eastward as the Rocky Mountains. Now imagine, Neiburger said, if 800 million Chinese residents owned cars. A globe-encircling smog girdle could develop, and civilization would perish, not in an instantaneous cataclysm but in a prolonged suffocation, like dying in a caved-in coalmine.[55] Neiburger's vision was eerily prescient. Today, Asia's galloping economies and motorizing societies regularly kick up an ungodly "layer cake" of atmospheric pollution filming over the Pacific. The temperature-affecting band, baked with smog, sulfates, carbon grit, factory fumes, and nitrates, can account for *one-third* of

L.A.'s air on certain days. Dust particles yanked into this ring as the result of global deforestation and drought has worsened it. "There are times," remarked one atmospheric physicist, "when it covers the entire Pacific Ocean like a ribbon bent back and forth."[56]

*   *   *

Up until the end of the Establishment-hewing 1950s, Southern California's conservation groups had a reputation for jerky, sputtering activism. Measured against the bread-winning family man or combat veteran, society wrote off the bulk of protestors as kooks or misanthropes. Recognition, though, by the late 1960s that big cities no longer could take the earth's climate and ecosystems for granted gave activists a second shot at relevancy. On a seeming dime, local groups retooled and refocused themselves onto specific fights: a controversial new road in hippie-Hollywoodish Topanga Canyon; bacteria-strewn water at L.A. Harbor. These activists, most of them "believers" with day jobs, were not all alone. They had a lodestar to emulate in SOS, which mobilized its volunteer forces with telephone trees and mass mailers, recruiting fresh blood and data where it could.[57] Louise Duemler, the homemaker-wife of a USC medical school faculty member, snagged a dozen SOS members for her San Gabriel Valley chapter with her fervor. Duemler could spit out statistics like a CPA, describing how Pasadena failed to meet health standards on 299 days one year, more than any other U.S. city. She could show you the pictures inside her home of diseased lungs. "Our very survival depends on our becoming concerned and applying pressure," she said. If official inaction persisted, her family would vacate the area.[57]

SOS's pyramid-building, awareness-raising actions turned so many heads that when the flower power era petered out and the age of Pet Rocks and Earth Shoes glided in, the organization had formal ties with nearly 600 citizen groups, not to mention enviable name recognition.[58] Perhaps one of its most unheralded legacies was inspiring other crusaders. One may have been Pacific Palisades attorney Roger Diamond, who believed it was up to citizens to punish smog emitters since politicians, from the White House to California's gubernatorial mansion, had blown the job. Diamond, as such, concocted a piece of devilish agitation that full-time environmentalists later copied. In 1969, as the city lay traumatized by the Manson family murder spree, Diamond filed a $500 *billion* class-action lawsuit against 291 smog-producing companies, including automakers, oil companies, airlines, and big factories. Importantly, he registered his action on behalf of local residents whose "health, comfort, and welfare" L.A. air pollution had compromised.[59] A judge dismissed the case as too complex and amorphous, but the upshot for activists was profound. The courts, they were appreciating, could be fertile grounds for forcing corporate powers to take responsibility for the ecological harm they wrought. Right after the judge tossed Diamond's case, in fact, a similar action pressed by a pair of Angelenos—one an investment banker, the other a law student—further married air quality with jurisprudence. The two asked for $15 billion from the same sources as Diamond had, as well as governors and two members of the Nixon administration cabinet, for damages and "impinging on" Southern Californians' right to clean air. While nothing came of the suit statute-wise, even distant observers like the *New York Times* rejoiced that disillusioned Californians at least had one forum to hear their grievances.[60]

Against all this, mainstream attitudes also were shifting. There was no better example than the insistence by one organization that California's lawmakers relaunch an "all-out" onslaught on vehicle air pollution to make it disappear by 1975. The rantings of a precocious, save-the-world organization? No: it was the most impassioned appeal for smog abatement the L.A. Chamber of Commerce ever voiced.[61]

As the state and federal government squabbled over regulatory underpinnings in the aftermath of carmakers' concessions, SOS did what it did best: it incited another hullabaloo with the powers-that-be. In 1969, in a verbal blast the media amplified, the women charged that smokestacks were "mushrooming all over the county" as part of a broader indictment of the APCD's supposed regulatory slippage on big industry. SOS members hoisted signs that read, "THE MONSTER'S COME OF AGE." They complained that Southern California's smog generals had lost their chutzpah. They charged that district hearing boards granted permit exemptions "wholesale." They and other conservationists then swore their undying opposition to construction of new or expanded power plants that consumed sulfur-rich fuel when natural-gas shortages struck. Louis Fuller, now head of the district after year serving as Smith Griswold's no-nonsense enforcement chief, went bonkers over the ladies' accusations. He asked the grand jury to investigate the "irrational, unsubstantiated, and rabble-rousing statements" flaying his office. There was a human cost; Fuller said SOS's agitation had recently driven him into the hospital, and his doctor warned him to lessen the strain. Fuller, sixty-two, disliked marches or profane placards, and the activists knew it. He saw conspiracies behind the women's antipathy toward him. With a Nixon-like paranoia, Fuller questioned whether SOS might've been a stalking horse for members of the old state vehicle control board, who he believed held a vendetta against him for his earlier criticism of their missteps. As he explained, "We have put our foot down on industry and enforced rules to the point where they are almost too severe to operate. . . So [SOS], quit beating us up."[62]

Griswold, before he departed for a federal air pollution post later in the decade, had been more prone to look outward than inward. There was a professorial aura about him. He regarded his jurisdiction as a singular field test, and continually sought reinforcements, particularly social scientists, to observe L.A.'s populace as one of America's most contaminated generations. Now that chemical sheens were blanketing 6,000 other cities, what better time, he asked, for a multi-disciplinary study of smog's original flashpoint. Griswold craved understanding into how the West Coast culture was adapting itself to breathing minute amounts of poison daily. He also sensed that the state's inability to pry changes from Detroit presented itself, in pop-psychology terms, as "transferred anger." L.A.'s traditional industry had received roughshod treatment in direct proportion to rules and restrictions the more politically influential carmakers had eluded. It made for bushels of secondhand angst. After those gleaming power plants and corporate manufacturers had cut their emissions to the bone, regulators had to extract more concessions from firms least able to meet them— small metal finishers, the family-run steakhouse. The resentment was widespread, and Griswold reckoned the best way to slug the rich and responsible was with consumer choices. Speaking evangelistically, he reminded the nameless masses, in a reflective 1963 speech, that they had to draw the line:

> "We know that air pollution is no more an evil necessity of
> urban existence than smallpox. . . . What makes the difference

of these states of public health is not superior knowledge,
for the information is available to all; what makes the dif-
ference is attitudes, and value judgments. . . A community
that is willing to tolerate typhoid and cholera, does not
purify its water supply.[62]

SOS applauded this philosophy of citizen engagement.[63] Perhaps it's the reason they rarely feuded publicly with Griswold, unlike the more irascible Fuller.

To the establishment's consternation, however, even Arie Haagen-Smit, the man who discovered the roots of photochemical smog, shared SOS's distrust of the local power companies. Their multimillion-dollar intentions provided them both lots to pick apart. Near decade's end, the Los Angeles Department of Water & Power was constructing its Scattergood plant at Playa del Rey while Edison sought expansion of its Huntington Beach operations. "Unless the community is pretty alert," Haagy warned, "it will wake up with other plants in the area [and the] smog pattern will repeat itself."[64] The oil companies had been activists' preferred target in the fifties. Power plants integral to Southern California's growth-gene had replaced them. Nuclear-fueled generators, trumpeted as cost-efficient and "smog-free," appeared a better alternative than conventional electricity-makers studded along the coastline. Los Angeles city officials, determined to keep pace with bulging demand, had earlier proposed a $92-million atomic energy plant in Malibu. Critics and residents railed against such a facility, worrying it would be vulnerable to accidents and earthquakes, to say nothing of its ungodly eyesore status. As a result, the concept faded, just like the proposed nuclear generator in the northern county. As such, that "not-in-my-back-yard" mentality, which leaches into every Los Angeles infra-

structure fight today, defeated SOS's quest for clean electricity.[65] L.A.'s murk, nevertheless, had thrust energy policy into
the public conversation. With it came ahead-of-their-time
questions about constitutional rights to healthy breathing that
world health organizations eventually co-opted

When America marked its first Earth Day in April 1970,
SOS was a 5,000-member citizen's army with a few last gasps
in it. The women had spent years hellraising inside sterile government meeting halls. Now the people even critics conceded
were Southern California's most dedicated smog fighters tried
their hand at advocating lifestyle changes. Instead of bad
mouthing district policy, SOS decided to illustrate what a
"pleasant place" LA could be by co-sponsoring a "Share-A-
Ride Day," the first organized demonstration of carpooling and
bus riding. Like the future bumper sticker, SOS was thinking
globally but acting locally, and that included trying to talk
motorists out of their solo-driven sedans and station wagons.
A group called "Operation Oxygen" joined the ladies, using
early computers to pair up carpoolers. The transit agency
arranged express buses. The studios hopped aboard, too,
shooting promotional commercials featuring "The Brady
Bunch," Lucille Ball, and other celebrities. SOS member and
actress Sabrina Schiller, later a divisive liberal member of the
Air Resources Board and her local pollution district, publicly
scolded those commuters disinclined to participate. People
needed to offer some ecological penitence—and what better
way to stick it to Detroit than by economizing. Asked about her
personal motivation, Schiller maintained she had a good one.
Her husband was a TV writer who worked in the Valley for
The Flip Wilson Show, and she admitted her trepidation that
one day he would drop dead from a toxic-air-induced coronary. "I guess you could say my motivation is selfish."[66]

"Selfish" also described Angelenos' loyalty to driving big cars with big engines well before sports utility vehicles started road-hogging L.A.'s freeways in the 1990s. SOS's Share-A-Ride Day was a spectacular flop, entrenched commuting habits not crumbling overnight. Just six people boarded the three "Ecology Special" buses. Operation Oxygen's director, whose car broke down that day, rationalized the paltry turnout by saying the masses had yet to "appreciate the seriousness of the situation."[67] Others had, though. New entities such as the Coalition for Clean Air borrowed the fight-to-breath baton. Older groups, such as the American Lung Association, refocused their energies. As they did, the organization that Levee and Slade had nurtured from their fancy living rooms was yellowing. Environment activism was no longer a fringe movement: it was a sizzling discipline. "For a while, SOS was *the* group," Schiller reminisced in 1980. "But it just got plain tired. There's only so much you can do for so long when no one gets paid. There's sort of a life cycle to these groups."[68]

Similarly, there was a hard ceiling to how much Southern Californians were pliable to change for the common good. Nevermind timid endorsement by mayors and other local politicians of lifestyle reforms to blunt smog's ascension. During SOS's reign, Californians twice defeated, in 1968 and 1970, two mass-transit-funding initiatives in spite of polls indicating strong county support for them. The community's schizophrenic attitudes—banish the fumebank, not the mechanical contraption that prodigiously coughs it out—rightfully locked in the image of the two-faced Angeleno. It also helped bleed the public kitty of billions of dollars. People's obsession with what they drove made them susceptible to self-serving proposals by freeway/highway interests in business, labor, and government, if not gooey PR from the auto clubs. For this lobby, it was about *keeping* Californians in their cars, and drooled to pave roadways or erect new ones on the public dime regardless of the exhausts kicked up. From this vantage, SOS had as hard a sell with the "suburbs to city"-driving small businessman or errand-hopping mom as it did with the arrogant power plant executive. Point is, California earned its green credentials one commuter at a time. One writer framed it brutally.

> *Californians . . . took for granted their lavish chariots to carry them on any number of essential or frivolous trips of any length at any time of the day or night, but wanted these to be emission-free. They also did not think they should have to pay much or suffer any minor reduction in range or performance to reduce air pollution, and when called upon to do so, many Californians . . . could get very childish. Rather than considering their own behavior and possible changes to it, Californians and Angelenos have railed unreflectively at others as the entire source of their problems: politicians, regulatory agency officials, the auto industry. . . As one early student of the subject observed, "Whatever the public's distaste for air pollution, its attachment to the automobile is probably greater.*[69]

Hollywood and the TV networks, once content to wise-crack about these realities, were establishing their own environmental bona fides. CBS, in 1966, broadcast a critical documentary, co-written by Daniel Schorr, called (big surprise) *The Poisoned Air*. The program argued that government could prescribe the harsh medicine needed to dispatch air pollution by shaking voter apathy and its own business-cozy outlook. Just airing this supposition was a sea change for the media. Ten years earlier, the writer of a CBS TV movie about an imaginary Illinois town overcome by a deadly fog was arm-twisted to change the ending so that the source of the mist was not industrial waste, à la Donora, but an abandoned mine.[70] (Chrysler had been the show's sponsor.) Three years later, a locally produced KNBC-TV documentary, *The Slow Guillotine*, stood out not so much for its content as its inspired stroke of employing left-tilting actor Jack Lemmon as narrator. "In heavy smog conditions," the two-time Oscar winner told viewers, "I don't know what it's like to breathe out of my nose. My eyes practically bleed. God knows what it's doing to the rest of my body." Despite critical acclaim, *The Slow Guillotine* aired only locally, and on a $30,000 budget, not the usual quarter-million.[71] Undeniably, however, Hollywood was emerging from its cocoon. America's caped crusader himself, Batman, announced in 1969 that he could stand idle no longer. He was abandoning his Bat Cave and sprinting off to nasty Gotham, where he planned to finger polluting companies who hid behind "phony respectability" in their "fortress towers."[72]

Visions of a libertarian, self-policing environmental community blossomed alongside the new spirit of accountability. President Johnson's Science Advisory Commission and scattered editorial writers recommended serious consideration of a tax on everyone who polluted, individual drivers included. Connecting the gas pedal to the wallet, they said, would finance research on unleaded gasoline and alternative power sources, removing smoky jalopies from the roads—and monitoring atmospheric greenhouse gases.[73] Today, with the Artic glaciers melting and the Middle East in perpetual bloody conflict, visualize what this might have accomplished. Yet when asked their opinion at the time, most Americans disliked the idea of digging into their own pockets when they already felt over-taxed. Joe Sixpack was regularly hearing that a technology-addicted, consumption-driven society might be civilization's noose. Still, a nation of doodad-lovers and bill-payers can only adapt so quickly.

Ambivalent as many Californians were about embracing ecology, there was no shortage of people aching to convert as many as they could. They'd tap into the state's storied history of rangy populism and zany causes because this was *their* time. New organizations popped up like dandelion, the majority clustering their headquarters in the Bay Area. For these groups, their pursuit was in their names: "Friends of the Earth," "DDT Commandos," "Zero Population," "Green Panthers." Labeling themselves "eco-activists" and "eco-freaks," they moved to a new frequency that much of post-World War II America weren't ready to tune in. Regardless, the activists wanted you to know that besides ozone and carbon monoxide, a sub-roster of heavy metals, like cadmium and lead, was spreading silent death. To them, the automobile was no longer a symbol of prosperity; it was a materialistic scarlet letter. People were beginning to sit in front of bulldozers to block developments. A Berkeley man refashioned his old car into a sculpture. In an early act of eco-terrorism, vandals in Riverside struck four gas stations, scrawling, "CLOSE DOWN— CUT SMOG" on the pumps. Somewhere between LBJ's Great Society and the moon landing, America had uncovered its next urgent crusade, and it was ardent, unsettling, and due in no small measure to Southern California's inversion-layer battle scars.

A clique of local doctors and university professors later united with these ecologists, giving them legitimacy they'd sometimes lacked. Few of them believed Angelenos appreciated the threat from above, and commissioned themselves to try scaring the community into action. A Nobel Prize-winning scientist named Willard Libby was one of the premier sensationalists. He stirred up old trepidations with a hotly circulated, co-written magazine piece depicting the carnage from a stage-three smog alert, where the hospitals overflowed and city dwellers fled a "sickly yellow curtain" that snuffed out 50,000 innocents. "The scene I have just described is theoretical. But it so plausible." Libby noted that citrus farmers once able to harvest 500 oranges per acre could now only squeeze 300 from the same area. A doctor quoted in the piece said it was deeply troubling, because "what is happening to your plants could eventually happen to you. Protoplasm is protoplasm."[74]

SOS and its allied groups were listening. In their final critiques of the air district, they honed in on public health. Where the women once obsessed over regulatory minutiae, they now screeched about the district's refusal to acknowledge or consider the possibility that Los Angeles existed in the perpetual state of a "low-level health emergency." District veteran Robert Chass, who replaced the retiring Fuller in 1970, interpreted the dissenters as Fuller had viewed many SOS members: they were idiots jumping onto the green bandwagon when there was no concrete evidence indicting smog as a disease-maker.

A collection of Caltech students in 1968 nonetheless burrowed into the movement with a feather-ruffling campus initiative for the atmosphere. The students coveted harmony between Mother Earth and the mothers of invention, between vehicle propulsion and low oxidant levels. To make headway, they tested gasoline alternatives and offered classes to teach the "jobless poor" to be skilled environmentalists. Some stodgy faculty members rebuked the "misfit" students for raising "a big cloud of intellectual dust" by trying to do too much, ecologically, too soon. (Haagen-Smit, having become more skeptical about the adults around him in the pollution tableau, thought the Caltech kids were all right.)[75] It was only a matter of time, too, before the seedlings spread. The Sierra

Club, the nation's most respected parks-and-preserves conservation group, began devoting resources to the issues of air, water, and alternative energy. SOS had done as much as it could.

Naturally, pop culture interpreted the thrashing for change in verse, poems, campy products, op-eds, stand-up routines, and just any other platform you can imagine. The Doors' song *Ship of Fools* mirrored fears about spaceship Earth: *"The human race was dying out/no one left to scream and shout/people walking on the moon/smog gonna get you pretty soon. . . ."* San Bernardino newspaper satirist John Weeks suggested black humor as motivation to remember what's important. He campaigned for a regionally observed "Smog Day" with all the trimmings: greeting cards with chest X-rays on them, youth groups caroling, "Hark the High-Level Ozone Stings."[76] All that was missing was an Andy Warhol interpretation of the patented "Smog in a can."

What wasn't missing was opportunity to reconsider the beast that had shanghaied Los Angeles' sunny culture. Besides what it *inflicted*, experts in the early 1970s seized on what it *revealed*—the fragility of a shrinking, flattening planet. Workers motoring to their downtown jobs from San Pedro heaped smog into the eyes of Pasadenans, just as Soviet nuclear weapons testing in the Barents Sea rained radioactive dust on produce sold by Winnipeg grocers.[77] People once unsure about why the Earth's bill of health mattered to them started re-examining America's nearly spiritual belief in science and consumerism as conveyor belts to the good life. Was it worth ingesting toxins from cheaper, insecticide-sprayed fruit, or blue-collar job loss from factory automation?[78] Southern Californians already had plenty of views about smog from millions of charred lungs.

Whatever those lessons learned, the question remained whether a technology-dependent people could adapt themselves, even force-feed themselves, to preserve nature alongside modernity.[79] The consensus derived from the agitating 1960s was that you had better try or own up to the truth. The individual mattered. Ask Marjorie Levee. Quiz Dr. Veger.

To a large degree, people breathed the air they deserved.

THE PEOPLE'S REVOLT

MOVING AMONG THE FLANNEL-CLAD BANKERS AND ATTORNEYS, WHO were cutting a brisk pace through the downtown Los Angeles financial district, was a foppish figure with muttonchop side-burns and a shock of white hair. Barrel-chested, wearing a rumpled polyester suit and white socks, the middle-aged man gyrated wildly. He pretended to bump his crotch into parking meters and then bellowed out in mock pain. Stumbling and staggering along the curbs like a drunk, he drew suspicious glances from office workers in the crowded streets of lunch hour. The wild man had fun with his antics for a few blocks before turning to enter the building housing KGO radio. Within a few minutes, the voice of the irreverent, wisecracking Ed Koupal, a talk-show guest that day, was booming across the Southern California airwaves with nutty relevancy. Once an obscure businessman leading a quiet life, Koupal was now a boisterous and colorful fighter, working against smog and for the public interest. He left his mark on California by engaging the citizenry in the environmental movement with his People's Lobby.[1] At the time, a filthy cloud of brownish haze hung over that area of California on almost any day when it was not stormy, even during the winter. It was more than twenty years after the politicians had taken up the fight against smog and begun making promises that pollution soon would be ended.

Koupal, who came to be lionized as "one of God's angry men," was not somebody you'd expect to be leading a citizen movement.[2] "I didn't register to vote until I was thirty-five years old," he said. "I came out of the World War II syndrome of 'Let George do it.'" Rather than engaging in civic affairs, like many of his generation had done, Koupal had been content to focus on home and family and rely on the government to handle the bigger problems of society. But when Governor Ronald Reagan began closing down public health care centers for the poor—as he and his wife once had been—public life suddenly mattered to him. Koupal became so incensed at Reagan that he started a recall movement against him. The B-grade movie star, who walked and spoke with a healthy swagger, was everything Koupal detested. Unlike the governor, who had his fancy mansion and weekend dude ranch, the unpretentious Koupal had spent most of his life broke, struggling as a chicken rancher, a bartender, a musician, and a door-to-door salesman, until he found modest success as a used-car lot sales manager.[3]

Once bitten by the political bug, Koupal couldn't stop. It so energized him that he upended his old life, leaving his suburban house with a pool and $30,000-a-year job near Sacramento to move his family to a gritty urban L.A. neighborhood. There, Koupal committed himself to fighting what he saw as a multitude of injustices and social ills: key among these was the air pollution that hung so thick over the city that you could cut it with a knife. With his wife Joyce, he founded the People's Lobby in 1968 and used the populist ballot initiative process to press for political reform in California. If environmental historians went searching for the foundations of the Green movement in the United States, they would invariably land at Koupal's clamorous house. Inside, the crowded living quarters shared space with the office and a printing press. Koupal recruited students and volunteers in his bid to qualify two anti-air-pollution initiatives for the California ballot in 1970. As the Vietnam War raged and Reagan ordered the National Guard to quell Berkeley student protesters, this small band of volunteers crashed on the floor of the couple's house after fanning out all day, under smog-streaked skies, at supermarkets, strip malls, and discount stores. Amid the stench of hydrocarbons and acidic particles dubbed "L.A. perfume" by *Tonight Show* host Johnny Carson, they gathered signatures from Democrats and Republicans, the rich and the middle class alike. Everyone in L.A. was fed up with the smog, the traffic, and the seemingly endless sea of housing tracts springing up like tumbleweeds across hillsides and valleys that had been unpopulated just a decade or two earlier. "I like to talk about smog because it's a non sequitur," Koupal said. "Smog's in the middle of the road. Smog's a four-letter word. It's nonpartisan."[4] But the People's Lobby failed to gather enough votes to qualify its initiatives for the ballot just as it had failed to force a recall election to be held regarding Reagan. Koupal was resilient, though. He wrote off his defeat to store proprietors who blocked his volunteers from gathering signatures. He also realized that people were confused by the Lobby's strategy to place two air pollution measures on the ballot: one to amend the state constitution so that it would require smog controls; one to establish a detailed anti-pollution law. To cure the property access problem, he convinced Attorney Roger Diamond, who was active in SOS (Stamp Out Smog), to sue for the right to gather signatures outside stores. The Los Angeles attorney fought the matter all the way to the California Supreme Court, using the reasoning that shopping plazas had become the modern-day equivalent of town squares, where the people could reimagine their republic.[5] The unflappable Diamond won his case in a hastily borrowed suit after United Airlines lost his luggage when he flew to Sacramento to appear before the justices.[6] This 1970 victory cleared the way for the People's Lobby to regroup and qualify a rewritten Clean Environment Act for the California ballot in 1972. That initiative—promoted under the slogan "Smash Smog"—sought to require pollution monitors and controls on smokestacks, make it more difficult for companies to obtain "variances" from the APCD, require cleaner fuels, and end conflict of interest among air pollution regulators. It's popularity rested on the increasingly shared perception that the APCD was failing to do its job and kowtowing to major and powerful industries.[7] By 1972, the U.S. Surgeon General had said there was "compelling evidence" that pollution was killing and disabling Americans.[8] Dr. Sanford Bloom, president of the L.A. chapter of the American Academy of General Practice, also had urged immediate action[9] and USC researchers had by 1970 documented "smog syndrome," in which children suffered tearing, coughing, sneezing, chest pain, and an increase in respiratory viral infections within the four days following a smog alert.[10] Ironically, during stage-two smog alerts—when the Air Pollution Control District would order major industries to close down and people to refrain from driving—the only cars on the road in Los Angeles were those taking sick people to emergency rooms full of patients with breathing difficulties, observed Nobel Laureate chemist Willard Libby, a UCLA professor, who pushed for restricting the number of cars on the road in the polluted Southern California region.[11]

As they had been for years, members of Air Pollution Control District brass still were reluctant to admit that smog posed any imminent health hazard. They'd debated it internally, considered it with the Board of Supervisors, heard horror stories from local doctors, and read some of the accumulating scientific literature, but invariably left it to the state and the Feds to sort out. The APCD was having enough trouble fulfilling its chartered mission: bringing back prewar air. The closest it had come to health statutes were the contaminant levels enshrined around its tiered smog-alert system, which triggered varying levels of restrictions on industries and drivers based on the severity of pollution. "I don't think there is any emergency—because of the work that has been accomplished," summarized Robert Chass, APCD control officer at the time. "Our whole approach to the problem has been on the basis of nuisance. Nuisance may cover the appearance of unsightly plumes of smoke emitting from stacks or the fact that visibility is obscured or that one's eyes may begin to sting and tear, or that one's property may be damaged by fallout from certain contaminants. We are not a medical organization and we do not have medical doctors on our staff."[12]

For some, the APCD officer's words were proof of blatant dereliction of duty by a bureaucracy that had become too cozy with the very polluters it was supposed to be controlling. By 1972, the district was notorious for filling advisory panels with scientists and managers employed by regulated industries.[13] In the early 1970s, the district's Hearing Board viewed its main mission as granting exemptions to industry rather than seeking the advice of medical professionals on the health implications of allowing companies to emit more pollution than allowed by law. "No, we never have doctors here," said Delmas Richmond, Hearing Board chair. "We don't have to. Of course we've had these ecology groups coming in the past. Usually they take the attitude that there shouldn't be variances at all. If that were so, there wouldn't be any need for a Hearing Board. We are set up to give variances and most people coming in here are entitled to one—it's a matter of their proving it."[14]

Not surprisingly, this attitude fanned the ire of activists, and even that of the general public, as people wheezed on scorching smoggy days. APCD officials themselves were dismayed at the outcry. After all, were they not the good guys? Recalling a typical district board meeting, Jim Birakos, the agency's deputy executive officer, explained how members of SOS came into the hearing room with a banner that read "Smog is a four-letter word: Shit." The vulgarity offended the APCD executives and the board. They voiced disgust and disregard for the brash activists in private; in public, the staff simply did not acknowledge them. The antipathy between the two sides was so charged that Birakos refused to debate Koupal during the initiative campaign. "He would just yell," Birakos recalled. However, this strategy backfired on Birakos when debate organizers went ahead and placed an empty chair on the stage with his name on it.[15] It was just another ding in the agency's credibility.

The People's Lobby arose against this backdrop of official apathy and growing public concern about pollution. That concern was stoked by the silent pesticide springs chronicled by Rachel Carson, the burning-water pollution on the Cuyahoga River memorialized in the Randy Newman song "Burn On," and, of course, the lung-burning, eye-tearing smog in Los Angeles. Armed with a growing body of scientific studies and computer models predicting the human misery that had resulted from a barrage of toxins, overpopulation, and indiscriminate use of finite resources, long-haired environmentalists, mainstream engineers, and irate mothers converged on the mall at the foot of the nation's capitol on April 22, 1970. It was the first Earth Day. While the action in Washington drew most of the national media attention, more than twenty million Americans participated in smaller protests held in polluted cities across the nation, including Los Angeles.[16] "We were just ordinary people," recalled Joyce Koupal, looking back on her days with the People's Lobby. Despite their activism, the Koupals shared a simple philosophy of life with which most Americans would agree. In 1970, it just so happened that ordinary people like the Koupals had been turned into an angry mass, pressed by smog, war, growing economic problems, and racial strife.[17] In a 1983 letter to her children, Joyce Koupal wrote that to be successful in life, they should develop enthusiasm, tolerance, a habit of doing more than they were paid for, a habit of saving, and a pleasing personality. The rising tide of citizen outrage over pollution was not lost on politicians. In Washington, lawmakers responded with an outpouring of new laws that lead to the formation of the federal Environmental Protection Agency under President Richard Nixon, a native Southern Californian. The president escaped the smog in Los Angeles by spending time at his Western White House by the seashore of San Clemente. In Sacramento, Ronald Reagan, who also had inhaled his share of sour air during his acting days, signed a law to create the California Air Resources Board. He also actively supported what L.A. smog fighters coveted most: federal legislation to let the state board set its own auto emissions standards tighter than any federal standards.

Yet even as the political establishment basked in the glow of their new ecological accomplishments, air pollution seemed to be worsening in Los Angeles. A fall smog episode in which ozone levels climbed above .50 parts per million for the ninth day that year—forcing schools to keep students indoors at recess and cancel sporting events—represented the highest contaminant levels seen in more than a decade. After twenty-three years of institutionalized war on smog, the air hovering over Los Angeles on October 1, 1970, appeared to be as brutish as it was during the 1950s. While it was merely suspected then, today it has been scientifically documented that the ozone levels seen on that day would have sent thousands of asthmatics and respiratory disease sufferers to hospitals gasping for air. Many would have never come home. L.A. County Air Pollution Control Officer Chass blamed the spike in pollution on an anomaly created by emissions standards for cars that reduced one type of pollution, but increased another. He also blamed that favorite scapegoat—weather conditions—which he claimed had created a particularly intense inversion layer.[18]

*   *   *

Deep within Disneyland in Anaheim, California, stands Tomorrowland. In 1970, at this spot was the General Electric Carousel of Progress. Ronald Reagan was perhaps best known to Americans as the host for the television series the *General Electric Theater* on CBS from 1954 to 1962. There, he delivered homilies to America about the promise of technology developed by the show's sponsor to create never-ending technological advancement. Repeating the company's motto, "Progress is our most important product," Reagan plugged the virtues of jet engines, turbosuperchargers, sonar, atomic safety devices, and the kitchen of the future.[19] It was no accident that the steady advance of technology was the vision of Tomorrowland. That area of the Magic Kingdom featured the Autopia ride, in which children could drive miniature cars that sputtered and belched authentic hydrocarbons from their engines under the orange-colored air. Inside the GE carousel stood a mock suburban-style city with wide streets full of model cars and a nuclear reactor in the middle. Despite its futuristic theme, Tomorrowland looked and smelled a lot like the megalopolis just outside the gates of the theme park, smog and all.

While Reagan may have believed in Tomorrowland's vision of progress, his efforts to eradicate smog as governor were half-hearted at best. His administration did score some early victories against smog—like the formation of the California Air Resources Board and the right to set automotive emissions standards. Reagan appointed Sierra Club member John B. Livermore as his secretary of natural resources, and he remained attentive to smog throughout his governorship. In 1970, Reagan wrote that "the smog problem in Los Angeles and in other cities was something comedians would joke about. No one is laughing about smog today."[20]

However, Reagan—who once said, "I was the Errol Flynn of B movies"—did not approach the environment as swashbuckling crusader.[21] Rather, he campaigned for limited government involvement and stated that the primary role for government was to help "develop the technology and realistic controls." In Reagan's mind, the principle of individual liberty always trumped a communitarian approach to air pollution. His Secretary of Natural Resources claimed that Reagan felt too much government regulation to solve smog in the name of public health and the common good would limit lifestyles. Reagan's key question when it came to regulating air pollution, Livermore recalled, was always: "Is it public good versus private rights?"[22]

The governor's skepticism about a massive, New Deal-like offensive against smog became clear as the state worked to regulate standards for the auto. Unlike his L.A. constituency, Reagan was largely content to wait until automakers developed emission-control systems on their own schedule, rather than forcing their hand. "Our problem is simply to be realistic in imposing controls on the makers of fuel and the makers of automobiles that meet that tenuous line where we force them into creating what they have to create and yet not be so unrealistic as some of the things that have been proposed, like saying that if they can't do it by x number of years, throw them off the road," said Reagan in a December 1970 interview.[23] In a 1973 letter to Ford president Lee Iacocca, Reagan invited the auto giant to tell California whether the state's plans to require catalysts—devices that remove harmful gases from car exhaust— were reasonable. His request for Iacocca's assessment came even though his own smog cops and rival General Motors felt the devices were ready to play a major role in reducing automotive emissions.[24] Reagan still was not quite satisfied that requiring catalysts was reasonable for automakers.

His ambivalence was reflected by the aging Haagy, whom the governor had appointed as the first chair of the state's new Air Resources Board. Legislators who had once praised the Dutchman's groundbreaking science now accused him of failing to look beyond existing automotive pollution control technologies to cut tailpipe exhaust. Why, lawmakers asked, was he relying on the auto industry to develop and install control devices? "The board started with tremendous goodwill, especially with Dr. Haagen-Smit at the head," Senator Nicholas Petris said in October of 1973. "Now we're very discouraged." Under Haagen-Smit, the ARB had even fought a bill that would have given prize money to inventors of automotive pollution controls. "They're in the same intellectual box as the auto industry," Petris said.[25]

Haagen-Smit, the discoverer of photochemical smog, had taken worse beatings, and he dismissed this last salvo by saying that market economics, not state assistance, would bring clean technologies. "A guy with a good idea will be picked up by the auto industry," he said. "They're not stupid."[26]

The state's inaction inflamed the so-called "downwinders" in Riverside County, an area east of Los Angeles still dotted by farms. Air quality there had decayed so much that the city of Riverside's mayor, Ben Lewis, petitioned Reagan to declare a state of emergency in the South Coast Air Basin. "A disaster is imminent, Governor Reagan," he wrote in a 1972 letter. "Medical evidence of pollution's truly lethal effect upon all living things is growing as exposure to pollution is prolonged." The mayor said that "even if the 1975 emission standards [requiring catalysts] were met, the increase in number of vehicles in the South Coast Air Basin according to authoritative studies . . . will cause the oxidant level to exceed the currently established acceptable health standards." In addition to the auto standard, Lewis argued that the state must impose an "emergency plan" on the greater Los Angeles area that would convert all autos to cleaner fuels.[27]

Lewis's Draconian suggestion was not original, but it was emblematic of the brake pads beginning to slow California's growth wheel. Two years earlier, an inland group known as the Environmental Quality Study Council asked the governor to declare not only a state of emergency, but to demand cleaner vehicles, limit traffic, and restrict the operations of heavily-polluting industries.[28] Not surprisingly, the Reagan administration rebuffed these suggestions, explaining that the state had "turned the corner" on motor-vehicle pollution and that other sources of chemical destruction were the responsibility of local government.[29] Likewise, Reagan claimed that agreeing to the Riverside mayor's request would exceed his authority as governor. Instead of taking the earth-shattering steps Lewis sought, the governor took less drastic ones, ordering his crack team at the ARB to study what more could be done to clean up car exhaust and to set up air monitors in the Riverside area to measure the exposure of its residents.[30] At the air board, Haagy praised Reagan's measured response and scoffed that Riverside's mayor was behaving "wild-eyed," knowing "damned well" that smog did not pose a health crisis. "The Riverside Chamber of Commerce shut him up. He was hurting business," the revered scientist said. "We got the show on the road. Now we have the exhaust devices. Now you will see this working in a few years. The air is already getting better."[31]

Though it went nowhere, Lewis's petition paved the way for major movement on the smog front by pinpointing two key issues that could not be ignored: the lack of political representation of residents downwind of L.A.'s emissions and the role of population growth in perpetuating air pollution. Two activists, who would later become major establishment figures on the issue, took up where he left off. Gladys Meade, a Republican housewife with a Massachusetts accent and an expansive mind, would become instrumental in helping outlying counties achieve political clout on the environment. Mary Nichols, a young attorney who had only recently moved to Southern California, would bring pressure on the region to deal with growth.

Meade became active in the battle when she moved with her husband to West Hollywood. Seeking to develop social ties and always interested in politics, she became active in the League of Women Voters. Initially, she had no particular concern about smog as it rarely engulfed West Hollywood, which was closer to the sea.[32] Balmy ocean breezes blew pollution east soon after it was emitted.

Then one day the smog settled in at her home and her children began sneezing and coughing, a special worry as one of her sons was an asthmatic. The New Englander's other primer on smog occurred when she took a trip to Pasadena, where hills form the western end of the sweeping San Gabriel Valley. That valley had lived through Riverside's nightmare long before: it was so directly downwind of L.A. that it was almost intolerable in the hot months. "When I went to Pasadena, you couldn't see one block away," Meade recalled of her trip to the Huntington Museum and Gardens there. "I didn't realize how bad smog was until I went to Pasadena."[33]

As her children grew older, Meade enrolled at UCLA to finish her college degree in history, graduating in 1966. "I was one of the first recycled housewives to arrive back on the campus," she joked. By the time she graduated, mounting traffic seemingly had worsened pollution in West Hollywood and West Los Angeles despite their proximity to the sea. So Meade again became active in the League of Women Voters and took on the task of studying what might be needed to clean up Southern California's smog. To start, she interviewed the state's air pollution leaders, including Haagy, who puffed his cigar and expressed his trademark optimism that pollution soon would be conquered.[34]

Meade and the League of Women Voters concluded that the political apparatus needed to be shaken up and remade. Repeated studies, and the daily sufferings of inland residents, showed that most of the smog choking them came from L.A. County. But the suffering of the three neighboring counties—Orange, Riverside, and San Bernardino—had little say in how giant industries blowing noxious contaminants out of their stacks should be regulated. Even within Los Angeles County itself, Pasadena and the other small cities in San Gabriel Valley had only limited representation on the Los Angeles County Board of Supervisors, which set the standards for major industries.

As an outsider jumping into an entrenched battle, Meade decided in 1969 that the solution was to create a regional agency covering the multi-county area that would merge each county's APCD under one board. The idea, however, went nowhere under Reagan and a legislature packed with L.A. County representatives.[35] Former L.A. APCD executive Birakos recalls that his agency opposed consolidation because the other county districts had done comparatively little to control air pollution within their own boundaries.[36] However, justice eventually would triumph: the aggrieved in Orange, Riverside, and San Bernardino counties got a fighting chance to catch a breath of fresh air after a new super-regional agency was formed in the mid-1970s under a change in state leadership.

Meanwhile, two new laws—and lawyers who knew how to use them—put the kibosh on business and residential growth in Southern California even as Governor Reagan chanted the mantra of perpetual progress and personal liberty. One was the federal Clean Air Act. The other was the California Environmental Quality Act, a state version of the National Environmental Policy Act.

On its face, the federal Clean Air Act of 1970 required states to develop plans showing how they would clean up air pollution within their borders by 1975; however, due to its severe pollution, Congress gave the Los Angeles area until 1977 to accomplish the task. The state dutifully prepared and submitted its plan to the federal EPA, but the agency rejected it. The problem, the EPA found, was that California's strategy for the spread out and car-dependent Los Angeles area had ignored the law's requirement that the state control land development and transportation in order to help clean the air. Under the federal law, the EPA had a duty to write its own blueprint for enforcing clean air health standards whenever a state failed to develop an adequate plan.[37] At the time, EPA administrator William Ruckelshaus faced the problem of constructing such blueprints because smog had a chokehold on most large metropolises, so he balked at writing federal enforcement documents for all of them. Adding to his consternation, in Los Angeles he faced legal trouble from a young attorney named Mary Nichols. She was fresh out of Yale Law School and had little idea that in twenty years, she'd be running the EPA's air pollution control program under President Bill Clinton.[38]

Nichols used the "citizen suit" provisions of the new federal Clean Air Act to press the EPA chief for remedial action. While laboring as an attorney at the new Center for Law in the Public Interest, the confident young woman sued Ruckelshaus, who was the first head of this newly formed agency. She told a federal judge that Ruckelshaus was failing to enforce the clean air law in Southern California in a timely way. "It was exhilarating," recalled Nichols about winning her case.[39] The suit, along with others filed under another new environmental statute, set the stage for a major clash of worldviews that played out under the whisky-tinged skies of the not-so-Golden State.

*   *   *

In the early 1970s, Ronald Reagan was caught between a Republican White House and his own business constituents. While acknowledging the need to address sprawl and transportation as key sources of air pollution, he was reluctant to impose any state control over land use. After all, building had long been one of the main engines of economic growth in California, especially in Los Angeles. His bottom line was that local politicians—"the level of government closest to and most responsible to the people"—should retain the ultimate authority over where and how projects would be built. "Unfortunately, there are those who do not share those views. They would have the state or federal government take over all land-use decisions and, in the name of the environment, tell all landowners what they can or cannot do with their own property. That kind of philosophy is totally inconsistent with every concept of home rule and the best interests of a free society."[40]

After Nichols had won her suit, however, the EPA had little choice. It moved to limit auto use by cutting the amount of gasoline that could be sold in the Los Angeles area by twenty-five percent beginning in 1977 unless the state devised its own plan to control the effects of growth on air quality.[41] Ruckelshaus pressured the state to pass laws that would limit driving to and from shopping centers, recreational centers, and even on highways in general.[42]

Reagan turned to Democratic California senator Alan Cranston, imploring him to get Congress to amend the Clean Air Act. "No effort to clean up the air should cause unreasonable economic or social hardship," Reagan wrote in the summer of 1974. "We must do everything reasonable to clean up the air, but not in such a way that causes significant unemployment or unacceptable personal sacrifices."[43] The California Manufacturers Association and other business groups were quick to back the governor.[44] He even found support in a new group that former Democratic governor Edmund Brown, Sr., formed, the California Council for Environmental and Economic Balance. "Having lived through the Depression when a halving of the gross national product was an all too tragic and painful reality," said Brown, it was clear to him that limiting growth "was the hard way to purify the atmosphere."[45] At the heart of Brown's new council were businesses and labor unions, which had profited mightily from the construction boom that had swept the state almost unabated for three decades.

Ironically, Reagan wrote to Cranston seeking relaxation of the Clean Air Act only days after a smog emergency struck Southern California. It hit on June 27th, right after school had adjourned for summer. As children and teenagers ran in parks and splashed in public pools in the bedroom community of Upland about forty miles east of downtown Los Angeles, panicked officials at the San Bernardino County APCD resorted to flying a helicopter overhead to bark evacuation orders through a loudspeaker. Pollution had reached the hazardous level in the 100-degree heat, recalled Mel Zeldin, a meteorologist for the agency at the time.[46] The quiet suburb, where families hoped to provide a safe and pleasant environment for their children, had been besieged by a stage-three smog episode, the highest level known. Ozone had reached .51 parts per million, enough to make eyes run, chests sting, and heads ache. That evening, Reagan went on television and urged people to "limit all but absolutely necessary travel" by carpooling and using public transit.[47] The only problem with the second part of the request was that General Motors had dismantled most of the public transit system in the 1950s. With people and jobs scattered widely, carpooling was difficult and there was no organized system to match drivers and riders.

Reagan's insistence on dodging EPA rules in the face of such as crisis was astutely explained in a report on land use by a young Ralph Nader. In his study, Nader found that most of California's undeveloped private land was held by a small number of corporations. Together with banks, builders, developers, insurance companies, and an "army of 235 lobbyists in Sacramento," what he called a "land interest complex" had firm control over the political establishment—including the governor. Large landholders, like the Irvine Company in

Orange County, were busy paving over farmlands to build suburban developments with no public transit and far from most
places of employment as new freeways opened. Politicians
were always happy to smile for the camera and preside over
the ribbon-cutting ceremonies for these new developments,
even though the result of building them was increased auto
dependence and air pollution. After examining the impact of
land-use decision-making in California, Nader observed that "in
a society that must increasingly pay attention to future impacts
and longer range costs, the legal permissiveness surrounding
and shaping the corporate structure . . . allows the seizure of
public resources with an immediacy comparable to a croup-
ier's grasp."[48]

His observation struck a chord within a growing new
American subculture: environmentalists. This group used the
newly enacted California Environmental Quality Act to get a
handle on the unprecedented growth that was over burden-
ing the Los Angeles area's air and roads. The law, passed in
1970, was a backlash against smog, water pollution, and traffic. It required government agencies to assess the environmental impacts of projects and do their best to mitigate any
problems. For instance, building a new freeway would open
new land to development, which would bring more cars into
an area, thus more air pollution. One way to lessen the added
pollution would be to build a carpool lane or set up a public
transit system.

At first, builders interpreted that law to apply only to government projects, like new freeways or airports. But an ambitious attorney representing a group of ski buffs at California's
towering Mammoth Mountain used a private plan to build
condos and stores in the high Sierra resort as a test case to
apply the law to privately built projects. In the suit, attorney

John C. McCarthy represented Friends of Mammoth, led by former Olympic skier Andrea Mead-Lawrence. The group contended that even though a private developer was planning to build the condo complex, the development was not exempt from the environmental law. The case went all the way to the state supreme court, which ruled in favor of the Friends of Mammoth.[49] Panic gripped the state's business community and building ground to a halt. The Irvine Company alone froze twenty-one projects. The giant landholder scrambled to get environmental impact studies of its plans to bulldoze orange groves and erect houses along Interstate 5 and the new San Diego Freeway in south Orange County.[50]

For Ed Koupal, it must have been a moment of vindication. His ballot initiatives and the environmental lawsuits signaled that support for nonstop economic growth and progress—a long-held bipartisan doctrine in California, and in America— was crumbling around Reagan. The governor watched in bafflement as wealthy Republicans in his own Pacific Palisades neighborhood elected Tom Bradley, who had run on a slow-growth platform, as L.A. mayor. The former police officer was a prominent Democrat and became the first black mayor of the city. "As the city land is zoned today," he said, "you could move the whole population of New York City in our boundaries. That is a nightmare. There is no way our air, our streets, our soil, our energy could support so many people. We must set reasonable limits or we face environmental disaster."[51] Soon Bradley would challenge Reagan on land-use and auto-use control issues. In a letter to the governor, the new mayor proclaimed: "I endorse . . . the state's responsibility to create adequate authorities and mechanisms to interrelate air pollution control and land use and transportation planning." He called such an approach "long overdue."[52]

Through more court battles and through campaigns for local and state offices, the antigrowth and environmental movements also shut down freeway construction in Los Angeles by the early 1970s. Freeways meant to interconnect different areas of town were left partially constructed. Activists upended the California Transportation Department's efforts to create a "gray carpet" throughout Southern California.[53] There were some negative side effects, though: more than thirty-five years later, some California freeways still come to an abrupt end, creating traffic gridlock in residential areas on narrow streets never intended to carry such high volumes of cars.

But Koupal's victories were limited. In 1972, his grand plan to clean up the air—the Clean Environment Initiative—suffered a bitter defeat at the polls after Reagan weighed in. Until two months before Election Day—which included elections for the presidency, as well as several state initiatives and offices, though not the governorship—Reagan had managed to stay largely above the fray. He maintained his popularity and credibility with his charming, telegenic manner. Then, in April, he took off the gloves and delivered a resounding blow to Koupal, calling the People's Lobby initiative little more than "political pollution, born of hysterical pollution." In its place, the ex-GE pitchman called for a "balanced common sense approach" that was "compatible with the goals and philosophy of a free society."[54] Reagan was joined by a big-money industry campaign lead by Standard Oil and a San Francisco political campaign firm that quickly outflanked Koupal and his band of everyday citizens in their bid to end conflict of interest, better monitor emissions, and enforce clean air rules on polluting industries.[55] In the face of the well-financed publicity blitz, voters turned down Koupal's initiative at the polls. However, the ragtag activist achieved some satisfaction when

California voters passed the political reform measure of the People's Lobby in 1974, which limited the power of big corporations like Standard Oil in state politics. By requiring public disclosure of political contributions of fifty dollars or more, it shined a new light on the links between money and politics in California.[56]

In 1976, Koupal—who was remembered for his line "Don't let your meat loaf. We gotta get boogien'"—died of colon cancer at age forty-seven with wife Joyce and friends at his side sharing the wine that the hellraiser had always loved. Joyce soon resigned as head of SOS and left L.A. for the bluer skies of Marin County, north of San Francisco.[57] Though Koupal suffered much defeat in his life, everything in his Clean Environment Initiative actually became a reality. In California, what begins as blasphemy often ends as orthodoxy.

BROWN VS. BROWN

AS RONALD REAGAN PACKED HIS BAGS TO LEAVE THE GOVERNOR'S mansion, his replacement slept contentedly on a mattress on the floor of a $250-a-month rental apartment in Sacramento. Jerry Brown, a thirty-seven-year-old Yale-educated attorney, former divinity student, iconoclast, and big thinker, was the son of former governor Pat Brown.[1]

The elder Brown had led a public infrastructure-building boom that delivered more water to Southern California, paved new freeways, and dramatically increased the size and number of campuses of the University of California and California State University systems. He had begun his career during the Great Depression and was a strong advocate for working-class people. With the memory of lean times always on his mind, as governor he set the stage for an era of unprecedented economic growth and prosperity in California throughout the 1960s. A self-made man who put himself through law school, Pat Brown presided over California as it surpassed New York to become the most populous state in the nation.[2] He championed a ten-billion-dollar, ten-year-long state freeway-building program in 1959 and within five years California built 1,500 miles of new freeways.[3]

But in the eight years after Brown left office early in 1967, the world changed radically. America was wracked by an unwinnable Vietnam War, shaken up by the Arab oil embargo of 1973, and in the grips of "stagflation"—a description cooked up by politicians and economists for an economy in which about the only things growing were the prices of goods and services. It was a new time that called for new leadership, so Californians turned to Pat Brown's young son. He brought an outlook on the nature of society and governance that was dramatically different than his father's.

While Pat had championed growth, Jerry ushered in an era of limits, which was supposed to mean more to Californians. Where the father was ready to spend, the son preached the virtues of frugality. State spending under Jerry Brown decreased an average of 5.2 percent a year, compared to an average growth of 5.7 percent a year under his father and even 3.1 percent a year under Reagan.[4] Jerry even denied a pay raise to the unionized state workers who backed him in his election run. And he admonished environmentalists that they too were subject to limits in their ambitions. "We are in an era of limits," Brown told the Sierra Club not long after taking office. "To clean up the air and clean up the water is going to be expensive, and I think the price is worth paying. But we have to recognize there are costs and jobs are displaced."[5] In many respects, Brown lead California by example. He eschewed tradition—serving yogurt and fruit at official state breakfasts instead of the standard bacon and eggs. He preferred a powder-blue Plymouth Satellite to the governor's official limousine, which sat idle in a state garage throughout most of his eight-year tenure as the state's chief executive. He flew coach class, ending the state lease on the private jet that his predecessor had favored.[6] Unlike Reagan, who was said to run staff meetings much like a corporate CEO, allotting a fixed time to discuss a policy item before making his executive decision, Brown burned the midnight oil in the governor's office.[7] He would hold his staff there to engage in wide-ranging discussions that examined policy issues from every conceivable angle before taking a position. After these sessions, he would frequent a local political dive in Sacramento known as Frank Fat's, where he sat and joked with anybody who happened to still be there.[8]

When in Los Angeles, the tall and handsome Brown was known for carrying on political discussions late into the night at Lucy's Cafe el Adobe on Melrose, a family-run Mexican restaurant where he met his girlfriend, folk-rock singer Linda Ronstadt. Their meeting made the restaurant famous.[9] At the annual Governor's Prayer Breakfast in 1976, Brown brought a Sufi choir, male dancers, and an anthropologist to deliver the keynote address. In his own benediction, Brown would say: "I think we have to realize that our technology can take us only so far, that our government can only give us so much, and that all of us are connected and dependent on one another."[10] He later quipped, "There is a limit to the good things we have in this country. We're coming up against those limits. It's really a very salutary exercise to learn to live with them. Everybody looks for politicians to come up with the solutions to the society's problems. It really is a rather totalitarian urge if you analyze it. Maybe the answer is the Ten Commandments."[11]

Brown fashioned this new idea—that human expectations must be limited rather than endless and that to solve problems people must sacrifice and change their ways—out of a mixture of his learning at a Jesuit seminary, his meanderings through Zen theology, and the new economics of the day as outlined by economist E.F. Schumacher in the book *Small is Beautiful*. He summarized the work of Schumacher by saying that "it is not that bigness is necessarily bad, but that the small has a role, too, particularly where bigness has overreached itself."[12] It was a fitting description of the problems facing Los Angeles at the time, particularly the roots of the air pollution crisis.

The youthful governor represented a complete departure from Reagan's style, even as both responded to an economy under stress and a people in turmoil. While Reagan had been the ultimate corporate-establishment governor, convinced that the free market and time-tested traditions would carry the day in the face of crisis, Brown soon came to be dubbed America's first "counterculture governor." Comedian Bob Hope joked, "Jerry Brown's getting a big following among rock fans. He'll get a lot of votes if he can keep 'em from smoking the ballots."

But Brown had developed personal discipline during his years at the Sacred Heart Novitiate, from 1956 to 1960,[13] and he had a commanding presence. Indeed, the young Brown had the same drive as his self-made father, and one of his first orders of business in office was to make good on his campaign promise of "blue skies over California."[14]

*   *   *

When Brown took office, the air in the Los Angeles region remained so foul that some high school and college students passed out after vigorous games of basketball and awoke with pounding headaches that would last for the rest of the day. After a hard day of breathing polluted air, asthmatics would wheeze at night and patients with emphysema and other lung diseases would gasp for breath, desperately reaching for their oxygen tanks. Industrial and automotive fumes blanketed the region by day and morphed into other noxious chemicals— like acid fogs—at night. Ronald Reagan's policies hadn't made much of a dent in the smog problem.

Near the end of his term in office, Reagan was preoccupied with how to bring *more* oil into California despite a warning from Air Resources Board chairman Haagen-Smit that the region simply could not tolerate any more polluting energy facilities. When Haagen-Smit concluded his impassioned briefing to the governor, Reagan replied with a non sequitur: "I raise horses for a living."[15] Reagan's mind, it seemed, had wandered from the subject of his constituents' lungs. He became preoccupied with the televised images of a panicked public stuck in gas lines throughout the state. The lines were the result of the Arab oil embargo, which was threatening to disrupt the never-ending progress he had promoted for so long. So Reagan ignored the great scientist's advice and went on to pressure state bureaucrats to make way for a "super-port" so petroleum companies could land Alaskan North Slope crude in Los Angeles.

And when the Air Resources Board was finally—to the delight of Gladys Meade—ready to require retrofit pollution-control devices on old cars, Reagan fired the whole board.[16] Retrofit devices represented a very costly affront to Reagan's sense of personal liberty. After dismissing the board one weekend, he replaced it on Monday with new members who would vote against the retrofit rule.

*   *   *

When Jerry Brown appointed his campaign manager Tom Quinn to chair the Air Resources Board at age thirty, automakers who had grown accustomed to Reagan's style were in for a shock. "Quinn," remembers his spokesperson Bill Sessa, "started making pronouncements left and right." His priority, Sessa elaborated, was to change the image of the state air agency, which was widely perceived at the time "as a passive board that took more counsel from the car industry than it gave."

Quinn was a former journalist and political operative, and he had little patience for long hearings on regulations and the drone of auto industry lobbyists seeking delays. "Quinn would gavel the meeting and he'd disappear," said Sessa. "It used to infuriate the car industry." Yet Quinn was not bothered: "Tom had a style. Tom would look you straight in the eye and tell you to go to hell with a smile and without animosity." This style, Sessa recalled, allowed him to dismiss a lot of the auto industry's arguments about why they couldn't build cleaner cars.[17]

Sessa recalled a particular meeting of the state air agency on tighter auto standards in Los Angeles, one which threatened to drag on late into the evening before the board got to the vote. Quinn spent most of the day working in a room adjoining the hall rather than listening to the testimony. As the day wore on, he directed Sessa to tell reporters that they would have a decision by 5 p.m. In the late afternoon, the TV crews gathered and set up the cameras in the hall as the testimony continued. At 5 o'clock sharp, Quinn walked in and took his chairman's seat in front of the rolling cameras. He cut off the speaker, who was still testifying to the board, and called for a vote then and there. The board approved the tougher auto standards without further discussion and Quinn got up and left.[18] It was vintage Quinn—and such tactics earned him a reputation for being heavy-handed.[19] He was "a ruthless Democratic politician from the word go," according to Gladys Meade, who had served on the Air Resources Board with Haagen-Smit under Reagan.[20] Yet, where some saw abuse under Brown and Quinn, others saw leadership. Sessa, who served at the air board for thirty years under numerous governors, credited Brown and Quinn with being "the political face who gave [the state air] board the power" it needed to clean up autos. "Quinn really understood the connection between public policy and how to make it popular with the public."[21]

"I grew up in L.A.," Quinn remembers. "I guess I remember the 1950s when most days of the summer your eyes would sting and hurt. Smog had been a part of my life from my earliest memories, an unpleasant part of my life." During Brown's campaign for governor in 1974, Quinn remembered walking one day with his son, who asked: "Dad, when Jerry wins can you do something to get rid of smog?" Quinn said it was at that moment that he decided to seek a post at the Air Resources Board if Brown won the election. "It got me to thinking how rewarding it would be to do something that's lasting," he said. "We believed we could remake the world. We were idealistic."[22]

A cornerstone of the new administration's idealism was the increasingly popular concept of "technology forcing" regulations. Rather than wait for the automakers to develop emissions controls before requiring them, under Quinn the Air Resources Board set reasonable standards and insisted that the automakers meet them. It was a huge shift from the Reagan days, when the companies stonewalled regulators at the board with excuses. Quinn wouldn't stand for it. "The auto companies just fabricated statements." The carmakers had also whipped up opposition to clean air standards among their dealers, who would come to Sacramento to lobby and testify against clean air standards.[23]

Soon after taking the helm at the Air Resources Board, the young chair ordered Chrysler Motors, which was near bankruptcy, to recall 21,000 model 1975 cars because they did not meet his new emissions standards. Quinn said the pollution from the tottering company's cars constituted "massive and unprecedented violations of our anti-smog laws."[24] Fed up with auto company tactics and attitudes, he said, he flew with Mary Nichols, whom Brown had also appointed to the air board, to Detroit to meet with Henry Ford II. They both asked him to change the tone of his representatives before the air board. Ford

Motor Company changed after that, said Quinn. "They stopped being obstructionist." Then Quinn won support for auto cleanup measures from the United Auto Workers. "That meant we had the political room to move," he said.[25] With that room, the air board accelerated the pace of cleanup. They required automakers to install catalytic converters by 1975 and to redesign car engines so that they put out less pollution in the first place. This led to innovations like "clean burn carburetors" to cut the release of hydrocarbons when gasoline was mixed with air under the hood.[26]

Brown and Quinn also pushed for new energy technology to address the oil crisis of the 1970s, which had drivers waiting in gas lines. While Reagan was still in office, Standard Oil of Ohio had proposed building a new import terminal in the port of Long Beach. The oil giant wanted to bring tankers full of Alaskan crude to the port and pump the oil into a pipeline that would take it to Texas for refining. Brown and Quinn were worried that the fumes resulting from pumping huge volumes of oil would worsen pollution across the L.A. Basin, just as they were on a roll to clean it up.[27]

Brown and Quinn brokered a deal under which the company agreed to offset the pollution it would emit by cleaning up even more pollution at a Southern California Edison power-generating plant in the L.A. area. In the end, the complications drove the company to drop its whole plan, even in the face of the Iranian oil cutoff of 1979.[28]

Instead of bringing in more oil and building nuclear power plants, Brown envisioned a future of decentralized solar energy, which would, he felt, be more consistent with America's "Jeffersonian ideals."[29] To that end, Brown pushed and won passage of legislation in California to create a $3,000 income tax credit for solar energy systems on homes. He imagined cities that stayed within their existing borders,[30] an urban strategy that would cut the need to drive everywhere, also reducing air pollution. It was the very opposite of his father's vision: Brown Senior might have just sought to build more freeways. "He was of a generation where the environment was just not part of his consciousness," said Quinn. "It was build, build, build and think about the consequences later."[31]

Jerry Brown also encouraged energy conservation by major industries and regular citizens alike. His administration required power companies to cut the voltage of their electric lines by five percent, which cut fuel burning at power plants by three million barrels of oil in 1977. Brown appointees also set energy-efficiency standards for refrigerators. People at the time considered it a goofy idea, but in the long run standards for appliances kept the cost of energy lower for consumers and minimized the need to build new polluting power plants.[32]

*   *   *

When Quinn took office, he was surprised to find that the facility that APCD inspectors gave the most tickets was not a smoking power plant or oil refinery, but a takeout restaurant next door to the agency's office in downtown Los Angeles known as "The Kosher Burrito." Inspectors would ticket the place when they walked out of the building for the smoke coming out of its grill at lunch, but would call ahead to schedule an appointment to inspect major polluters, like oil refineries and factories. "It was preposterous," he said.[33]

Brown saw dirty air as a "crime" and he expected agencies such as the APCD to act aggressively to control industries that spewed pollution. But first he had to instill vigor into the local agencies that were responsible for regulating stationary sources of pollution in greater Los Angeles: the refineries, power plants, factories, and other facilities that still spewed out a witch's brew of sulfur, nitrogen oxides, hydrocarbons, soot, and toxic chemicals into the air. "The APCD in Los Angeles was not in very good shape," said Quinn. "It was under weak leadership and there was no enforcement on stationary sources. It had lost a sense of mission."[34]

That was putting it mildly. Ed Camarena, a long-time smog-warrior, who at that time served on the Orange County Air Pollution Control District, started hearing rumors about the Los Angeles inspectors. When the county Air Pollution Control districts eventually were merged, he found the rumors to be true: a few of the inspectors were involved in graft and impropriety. A private detective photographed one inspector tending bar during work hours, another peddling jewelry out of the trunk of his government car, and another, who disguised his official vehicle with a panel over its door insignia, was caught apparently picking up a prostitute. "When we were done with the investigation, about fifteen people were fired or quit," Camarena recalled. "Afterwards, I had people tell me it was about time." To professionalize his roughly 170-person department, Camarena had inspectors undergo additional training in enforcement, technology, and ethics. Boosting morale was easier: he had air conditioning installed in their cars.[35] The investigation came after lawmakers began to widely view smog as a health menace that had to be ended. Conservative Republicans from the inland counties, where residents suffered from L.A.'s upwind emissions, teamed up with Democrats to pass a bill forming a regional, multi-county agency.[36] About the only people opposed to this were the powerful industries in Los Angeles and those organizations more or less controlled by them. The Los Angeles area Chamber of Commerce was against the bill, saying it would "give free reign" to the social philosophy of one small group "under the pretext of controlling air pollution."[37] The California Manufacturers Association called the idea "premature and unnecessary" and said that the move would provide "questionable benefits at higher costs, where the basic problem is automotive emissions."[38] Los Angeles County officials claimed that the formation of a new agency would violate "the concept of home rule," strip power from its board of supervisors, and stifle economic growth.[39] L.A. County officials denied that pollution even drifted downwind into neighboring counties. In one case, according to Camarena, an otherwise ethical technician fudged data to show that a sample L.A. air parcel did not travel to the Inland Empire.[40]

However, with the support of mayors from the inland counties, and even Los Angeles mayor Tom Bradley, these objections amounted to little.[41] The bill eventually passed and, with the stroke of a pen, Brown signed it into law, giving birth to a new regional agency. Abner Haldeman, of the city of Upland in San Bernardino County, spoke for many of his colleagues when he said that the new agency would give his wheezing and bleary-eyed constituents "some fighting chance of representation."[42] The bill, AB 250, which merged the APCDs of Los Angeles, Orange, Riverside, and San Bernardino counties, created what became known as the South Coast Air Quality Management District. The new regional agency instituted emissions fees that industries had to pay on each ton of pollution. The fees, while low, constituted the nation's first tax on pollution. The district also went about establishing a regional road map for clean air, which included an inventory of emissions and the use of computers to model how much raw pollution from cars and industries the air could tolerate under stagnant weather conditions and still not rise above the health limits established by the EPA in 1971. The young Southern California agency quickly adopted a landmark rule to require gas stations to put so-called "vapor recovery systems" on gas-pump nozzles to capture fumes that would otherwise leak into the air.[43] All the while, though, Quinn derided the agency for not doing more, claiming that Los Angeles had become the cancer capital of the nation due to air pollution, and that its rules were still too weak and influenced by corporations.

Camarena claimed that these attacks and the California Air Resources Board audits tattered the Los Angeles County Air Pollution Control District's enforcement program with misrepresentations, which undermined public confidence. He admitted, however, that the harsh critique did galvanize a new regulatory zeal. Camarena found that some refiners were deliberately ignoring equipment maintenance and regulations in order to save money. The new regional district fought back by targeting the worst offenders. Inspectors zeroed in on gas stations, dry cleaners, auto-body shops, chemical plants, foundries, refiners, you name it. They launched raids on the weekends and in the evenings, when company supervisors were gone and the temptation to circumvent controls was stronger.[44]

With both bureaucracies and major industries falling into line, Brown turned his attention to private citizens. He needed to get Californians to change their ways: they needed to use their cars less by carpooling or taking buses to work. So on March 15, 1976, the Brown Administration opened L.A.'s first "diamond lanes" on the jam-packed Santa Monica Freeway, which ran between downtown Los Angeles and the Pacific Ocean. The freeway carried 240,000 motorists a day and was the third busiest in the nation. The diamond lanes would allow carpoolers and transit buses to speed ahead of solo drivers, and they were the first of their kind in America.[45]

The diamond lanes were only operational during the morning and evening rush hours, when 120,000 commuters drove to work, usually at about twelve miles an hour. The new lanes, indicated by white diamonds, were expected to more than triple the speed with which buses could ferry commuters home. There were no stoplights on the freeway on-ramps leading to the diamond lanes, so the carpoolers and buses could whiz past cars waiting to get onto the regular lanes—one at a time as the light on their separate on-ramp changed. The strategy, of course, was to reward carpoolers and deter others from driving alone.[46] It backfired.

Perhaps it was because the operation began on the Ides of March, but the diamond lanes set off a wave of public rebellion that was noticed across the nation. The very next day, the freeway was snarled by unusually huge traffic jams, a rash of accidents, and seething motorists. Solo drivers found their commute had doubled in time, with waits as long as fifteen or twenty minutes just to get on the freeway. Some dared to jump into the diamond lanes to get around the traffic, until they were headed off by frantic California Highway Patrol officers, who would ticket the offenders. Others tried to cover up the white diamonds on the carpool lanes by splashing bags of paint over them, and the truly crafty discussed evading law enforcement officers by purchasing mannequins to double as passengers in their cars. Transportation officials, despite all this, hailed the opening as a success and bus riders raved about their shorter commutes.[47]

Almost immediately after the lanes opened, the conservative Pacific Legal Foundation—an organization dedicated to protecting personal property rights—asked a federal court to close them down. The foundation based its suit on the California Environmental Quality Act, the same law that environmentalists had used to mitigate the impacts of land developments and new industrial projects. The foundation claimed that the Brown administration had failed to analyze the social and environmental impacts of the diamond lanes.[48] There was a

16.9 percent increase in traffic on streets parallel to the free-way, which city engineers said was responsible for a thirty-percent increase in traffic accidents. The lanes had engendered what is now called "road rage," as solo drivers acted like rats in an overcrowded cage scrambling over one another to get to work or dinner.[49] By fall, a judge had ordered the lanes shut down and restored for use by solo motorists until proper studies were completed.[50] Brown's transportation secretary Adriana Gianturco, who for five months was steadfast in the face of the public outcry and stream of bad publicity, appealed the decision. She won federal support for the appeal from the Urban Mass Transportation Administration for a while, but eventually the Brown administration found itself alone in its drive to change the behavior of motorists in the name of energy conservation and reduced air pollution. The young governor's team ultimately ceased its appeal, but the stigma of the episode would remain.

Later, when Brown's presidential ambitions became known, conservatives resurrected the "diamond lane debacle" as proof that the governor was out of step with the majority of Americans. A stinging editorial in William F. Buckley's *National Review* summed up the criticism: "In a state whose economy is built around its marvelous mobility of people and goods, Brown proposed at the beginning to take the people out of their cars and put them on foot and/or public transportation and to reorganize the society of 21 million people into a system of collective communes. His blueprint for this pastoral community was his Orwellian State Transportation Plan. To ride shotgun on this project he brought in as Transportation Director an aging hippie carpetbagger from Massachusetts, Adriana Gianturco, who, in blue jeans and bare feet, assembled a huge task force and threw 3,413 pages and $60 million at the plan."[51]

But metered freeway on-ramps and carpool lanes did not fade away. Today, they are standard on almost all Los Angeles freeways and are credited for moving more people with less energy use and pollution than could be done by adding additional lanes for solo motorists. Brown and his young team may have made mistakes in how they put the concept into practice, but with time his idea—like his initiative for energy efficiency standards for refrigerators—was proven sound. Perhaps, Californians later thought, there was some kernel of truth in the governor's slogan that "less is more." So, in 1978, they returned Brown to his pad in Sacramento for another term as governor.

*   *   *

"There is an old adage," remembers Bill Sessa: "In the West you don't mess with a man's gun or car."[52] But in 1977, Congress amended the federal Clean Air Act to require that in smoggy areas like Los Angeles, motorists have their cars repaired if they fail a regular emissions test. At the time, California had an inspection program known as "smog check," but it only required cars to be checked when they were sold. Congress wanted it done at least every two years, preferably every year. Federal and state regulators knew that a more regular smog check could cut hydrocarbon emissions to the air by ten percent, eliminating a lot of the raw stuff that formed ozone in one fell regulatory swoop.[53] "It was designed to capture gross polluters," said Sessa. "The people who drove those cars were the ones least able to afford to get them fixed."[54] This made the strategy socially and economically contentious. However, pollution was so serious that Brown pursued all options, despite the fact that some required individual sacrifice.

Ultimately, it took a career cop to get L.A. motorists to submit to regular smog checks. State senator Robert Presley, formerly a sheriff, now represented downwinders in Riverside, east of L.A. He had pressed smog check legislation for years, but other lawmakers always either watered it down or refused to pass it in a form that the federal EPA would approve. Ultimately, though, he prevailed, with the help of the federal government and Jerry Brown. Impatient with Sacramento lawmakers and eager to help Presley in his unpopular stance, in 1979 the federal EPA invoked "sanctions" against the state, banning new industrial construction. The move put on hold forty-five projects in greater L.A. alone—petroleum refinery expansions, cleaning compound making facilities, and others. The EPA also threatened to cut off federal funding for highways. "It's ironic that California is having this problem," said Doug Costle at the time, who headed the federal EPA under President Carter. "They've usually been the leaders on a tough political issue."[55] Brown responded by saying "I am way out front on this war against smog and pollution. It just so happens we have a lot further to go."[56] The next year, Brown pulled his support for a smog check bill after lawmakers watered it down again by allowing cars made after 1982 to get tested every other year instead of annually. But lawmakers, reluctant to require their constituents to submit to the annual tests, persevered, and in 1982 Brown capitulated, signing a bill requiring checks for cars only every two years.[57] The requirement remains in place today.

*   *   *

In 1980, Jerry Brown threw his hat into the ring for the Democratic nomination for president. He lost the nomination to the incumbent Jimmy Carter, who was promptly turned out of office to make way for President Ronald Reagan. In his campaign, Reagan said that air pollution was a problem that "has been substantially controlled" and that trees and other vegetation were responsible for more emissions than cars.[58] Meanwhile, that year smog in Los Angeles reached four times the level considered healthful.

As Reagan took the reigns in Washington, Brown released them in Sacramento and entered a period of study, reflection, and service. He spent time working with Mother Teresa in India, tending to the sick and hungry. He opened a cultural center in Oakland and hosted the "We the People" talk show on Pacifica Radio for years. California elected a Republican governor to replace him. Los Angeles became a boomtown again under Reagan's Strategic Defense Initiative, a military buildup that brought billions in federal contracts to L.A. aerospace companies. While Brown contemplated, Angelenos again became preoccupied with bigger houses, bigger cars, and bigger steaks on the grill.

To many, Brown would be remembered as Governor Moonbeam, the nickname given him by columnist Mike Royko because he wanted California to launch a communications satellite to serve the state government's telecommunications needs. "People made fun of Jerry ultimately," said Quinn. "Maybe Jerry was too frank."[59]

Even so, the ideas that Brown advocated—energy efficiency, forcing technology through regulations, and the need for personal responsibility in the face of environmental crisis— became firmly implanted in the public mind. And Brown himself only laid low for a little while—in 1998 he become mayor of Oakland, and eight years later won election to a post his father once held: Attorney General of California. As the state's top cop, Brown would pick up where he left off by pressing counties and cities again to limit growth, become more energy efficient, and get people out of cars, this time to reduce greenhouse gas emissions. History would soon repeat itself.

THE WIZARD
OF OZONE

By 1986, Ronald Reagan had all but declared "mission accomplished" on the smog wars. The beast still blighted the skies of the Los Angeles area more days than not, but like their president, the region's leaders seemed to have all but forgotten the noxious cloud that hovered above. After the doldrums of 1970s stagflation and the strictures placed by Brown on business and state spending, L.A. was booming again. The freeways were full of out-of-state license plates. Defense companies the likes of Lockheed Martin Corp., Northrop, and Hughes Aircraft were attracting young engineers to help outflank the Soviet Union in weaponry and defeat the bastion of communism once and for all. Steven Spielberg and Disney's new CEO Michael Eisner were bringing in newly minted "imagineers" from the nation's art schools to work in Hollywood film studios. Business was booming for the renowned chef Wolfgang Puck at Spago's, as well as for other restaurateurs. Despite all this, the air remained a brownish-orange. It burned eyes and lungs alike, but most Angelenos looked at smog as the price they paid for the good life of cars, patios, hot tubs, and barbecues.

Reagan's EPA administrator Lee Thomas was working for a boss who had little interest in air pollution, but tremendous gusto for unleashing private enterprise from the restraints of government regulation and taxes—and Thomas was not about to spoil the show that L.A. had become under the Hollywood star. When Los Angeles had lagged in the past in cleaning up its air, previous presidents had slammed the region with cut-offs of federal funding and construction bans. Now it was just a year before Los Angeles faced the federal Clean Air Act's 1987 deadline for meeting health standards, and clearly the region had no chance of doing so. But neither Reagan nor Thomas seemed very bothered.

In fact, a full decade after it was formed, the South Coast Air Quality Management District still had not developed a plan to fully achieve healthful air. The AQMD had by then for-gotten all about Jerry Brown's technology-forcing approach and his call for personal restraint. Like Lee Thomas himself, the district was reluctant to disturb the self-satisfied residents of Reagan's West Coast hometown, who had found new wealth in federal defense contracts and making movies for the "Me" generation. California had turned from the social concerns of an earlier era to a passion for personal diversion and acquisi-tion—particularly of real estate. In offices, at pool parties, and at chic restaurants all over L.A., hardly a conversation went by without mention of real estate.

In this atmosphere of self-contentment, the district pre-sented a deficient clean air plan that fell far short of showing how or when the air could be made healthful again. Rather than pressing for costly clean air measures that might upset the applecart, Reagan's man sought to approve the half-baked plan under a new regulatory category known as the "reasonable extra efforts program." The EPA, Thomas announced, could approve the plan on the grounds that it would at least make *progress* toward reducing pollution if followed.[1]

By the mid-1980s, Brown's notion of "living within limits" was long gone. Small was no longer beautiful, particularly in a city where most people were in hot pursuit of bigger salaries, bigger cars, bigger homes, and bigger televisions. Predictably, those representing these people on the AQMD's board had likewise become disinterested in adopting new smog-fighting rules, or even in attending board meetings regularly. The city council members and county supervisors who sat on the board simply sent staff members in their place. They had more important issues to attend to, like approving new housing developments, shopping malls, and office parks in their respective cities and counties. Their dutiful staffers would sit through regulatory hearings, but when it came time to vote they either supported their bosses' growth initiatives or abstained—to do otherwise was to risk unemployment. As a result, new regulations to deal with the growth effectively were put on hold. With more cars, booming factories, and more homes and buildings puffing out fumes from paints and cleaning fluids and exhaust from lawn mowers, furnaces, and fireplaces, progress on air pollution had stalled, even as tighter motor vehicle standards had taken effect. After Brown left office, there had been no clear pattern of improvement in the air. Ozone drifted down a bit one year and up a bit the next. In 1986, for instance, ozone reached dangerous levels on 164 days, and there were other days when particulate, carbon monoxide and nitrogen dioxide reached unhealthful levels even while ozone remained in the healthful range.

Only hardcore environmentalists seemed to care anymore about pollution: people like Harvey Eder, a long-haired Vietnam veteran who would ride L.A.'s almost non-existent public transit system thirty-five miles from Santa Monica to El Monte to attend the monthly AQMD board meetings. After hours on the bus, Eder would wait hours more until the public comment sessions came

at the very end of the meetings. Then he would get his three minutes to address the board and the assembled industry lobbyists.
In his wrinkled corduroy pants and plaid shirt, Eder would walk
to the podium, with a limp from a war injury, to lambaste the
board for not embracing solar energy, his pet cause. While he
spoke, board members would pack their briefcases and chat as
they prepared to file out of the hall. Other environmentalists,
however, demanded more attention than Eder.

One was Mark Abramowitz, who was then executive director of the Hollywood-backed Coalition for Clean Air. Unlike the
disheveled Eder, he favored the buttoned-down look, wearing
dark conservative suits and ties. But he understood air pollution law and policy and knew how to talk about them, and he
was frustrated by a lack of action in El Monte. So when Thomas
approved the air district's clean air plan, Abramowitz filed a
lawsuit against the federal agency. He argued that the federal
Clean Air Act did not allow the EPA to approve any plan that
failed to show how cities and states would meet health standards for ozone, carbon monoxide, particulate, and other pollutants. Moreover, the district had failed to meet a 1987 federal
deadline for achieving health standards. Abramowitz had
shown that the EPA's acceptance of L.A.'s air plan clearly was
illegal, so Thomas had no choice but to backtrack. The law
required the EPA to develop a federal strategy for cleaning up
the air of any region that could not develop its own, so Thomas'
EPA reluctantly began to prepare one. Because the EPA was
remote and had limited power, local leaders and state lawmakers knew that any federal plan would include blunt, draconian
measures that would threaten growth.

Feeling the pressure of savvy environmentalists, the federal vice grip, and worried legislators in Sacramento, the AQMD
board knew it would need somebody with a strong hand and

good ideas to successfully fend off the federal government and maintain local autonomy. So at the end of 1986 they turned to a six-and-a-half-foot Tennessean, James Lents. A physicist and aerospace engineer by training, he had cleaned up smoke in Knoxville early in his career and gone on to shrink the brown cloud in Denver before landing in the "Super Bowl of Smog" in Los Angeles. He was brought in as the number two executive at the AQMD with the promise he would be promoted when that agency's long-time chief Jeb Stuart retired. Lents worked with lawmakers in Sacramento to reorganize the AQMD board and expand its powers despite its initial opposition. The scientist would guide L.A. toward cleaner air for ten years, scoring many successes and eventually accumulating a long list of enemies that would succeed in his ouster.

Like Jerry Brown before him, Lents was motivated by an unwavering belief that nobody had a right to impose poisonous air on others. He was fond of sharing the story of how he got involved in air pollution when he was a young scientist in Knoxville. There, he said, soot from coal power plants would cover windows, furniture, and laundry hung out to dry, not to mention the lungs of the people living there. Outraged by the health threat this posed to residents, including his young wife and child, he was drawn out of the world of aerospace engineering to apply for a job with the local air district, where he eventually won a requirement for coal plants to install pollution controls that would cut their soot emissions.

Looking for new challenges, Lents went to Colorado to head the state's air pollution control office. In Denver, he dealt with tougher and more complicated problems. To reduce the "brown cloud" of pollution that enveloped the city in the winter, when the air was stagnant, he promoted a volunteer carpool program to cut auto emissions. "It just became the thing in Denver," said Lents, recalling how the media jumped on the bandwagon to promote carpooling. The idea was to get people to commit to carpooling one day a week to cut emissions. The first year, the state found the program cut pollution by five percent, but the second year there was no reduction. "The lesson I drew from that is that voluntary campaigns don't work," Lents admitted.[2] So when he arrived in Los Angeles, he had his mind set on binding rules that would reduce the pollution emitted to the atmosphere each day by some seventy to eighty percent to meet health standards.[3] Every citizen had a moral duty to contribute to the cleanup effort.

The California bureaucracy saw things differently. "The South Coast Air District Board was pretty weak," remembered state Senator Robert Presley, an ex-cop who represented the smoggy inland area of Riverside. "They weren't very effective and the members weren't taking it very seriously," he said.[4] To help people in his area, he authored legislation to expand the agency's powers. The AQMD board immediately opposed the bill because it would give the governor the power to appoint more members, and thereby dilute the power of the local county supervisors and city council members, who had long been dominant. "I can't imagine what their thinking is, why they think it is so urgent to jump in there and oppose it at this early stage," said Presley at the time. "I really think the legislature is going to feel we have to improve that board. It needs restructuring and redoing. We can't sit around here and fiddle while Rome burns."[5] Presley's 1987 bill passed despite opposition, and it reorganized the AQMD board and banned members from sending their staff assistants to the monthly meetings. It also expanded the agency's powers to require the operators of fleets of trucks, taxi cabs, rental cars, and other vehicles to burn only clean fuels. It gave the board the power to ban trucks on freeways and busy boulevards during rush hour. Soon, the board had the power to require employers and businesses to pay cash to workers and patrons who rode the bus and carpooled to their offices, factories, stores, theaters, schools, and stadiums. Building complex owners were required to operate transit shuttle services to and from train lines and bus depots to facilitate use of public transportation by employees and shoppers. (All of these initiatives stemmed from measures Los Angeles mayor Tom Bradley and the air district took during the 1984 Olympics to keep the air tolerable for athletes engaged in world-class competition.)[6]

Once he was in charge of the agency, Lents wasted little time deciding how to use his new powers. His first mission was to write a comprehensive plan outlining the rules, technologies, and lifestyle changes Angelenos would need to face up to if they really wanted to breathe healthful air. But he immediately ran into a roadblock—in his own office. "The first fight I had was with the staff," recalled Lents. "Our job is to tell people how to clean up the air," he remembered telling them. They argued that it would be impossibly expensive. Somebody on the staff sent anonymous letters to the media and to new staff members that threatened to reveal dirt on Lents. But he was determined, so he labored over the weekend with the few staff members willing to work with him on a complete plan to clean up the environment. Together, they developed a brochure called "The Path to Clean Air." After it was published, his planning director resigned.[7] The brief, glossy document outlined a full frontal assault on smog. It called for rules to regulate small businesses. It envisioned pollution-free paints, cleaning fluids, printing press inks, and other materials used in households and manufacturing. It promised a crackdown on big industries and a shift to cleaner fuels for trucks, cars, and other equipment. It contemplated a sweeping car-pooling mandate, a ban on drive-through restaurants, the requirement of clean air barbecue lighter fluid, and even an end to the charbroiled hamburger due to the smoke that the grills produced. The plan foresaw a day when the transportation system would rely on electric vehicles powered by windmills and solar energy. Many of the measures called for technological breakthroughs and behavioral changes that had never been tried. Suddenly, forcing technology and the notion of personal sacrifice were back in the battle against smog.[8]

Despite resistance, Lents recalled, "I was able to put my stamp on the staff." He advanced the plan, which the federal EPA eventually approved. In short order, he succeeded in getting the agency's board to raise fees on regulated businesses. He hired more engineers, rule writers, planners, inspectors, and prosecutors to fully carry out the plan. Along the way, he fired Jim Birakos—long known as "Mr. Smog"—from his post as chief public spokesperson and deputy executive officer for the agency, and hired a new executive and public relations team to trumpet his revolutionary blueprint to the world. The outgoing Birakos blasted Lents in the press, claiming that the new man in town lacked "emotion" for fighting smog and that, under the new top smog cop, the agency had taken on a "corporate personality."[9]

Yet Birakos' judgment rang hollow. A new building was planned to house the smog cops and regulators who filled the agency's increasingly cramped headquarters in El Monte. The new $78 million facility was built in Diamond Bar, a suburb thirty miles east of downtown Los Angeles, closer to the geographic center of the four-county area the agency oversaw. A six-story building with an elaborate laboratory, an auditorium, and an atrium lobby, it featured walls painted with low-polluting paints, motion detectors that turned out the lights in unoccupied rooms, a solar carport to charge electric vehicles, and a hydrogen-powered fuel cell to provide electricity and hot water. The building sent a message that the public sector was serious about breaking the back of smog, once and for all. Lents' opponents quickly called the edifice the "Taj Mahal," alluding to the cost of building the facility. "The building is going to make them the aristocracy of the bureaucracy and they are going to live like kings," complained William Huston, chair of the Watson Land Co., who feared the costs of Lents' aggressive stance on his land development business.[10]

Lents had anticipated opposition to his ambitious new clean air plan from businesses, elected officials, and labor. So he had his board commission a study to put a price tag on the health effects of smog. The results of the study called to mind Oscar Wilde's observation about cynics, who "know the price of everything and the value of nothing." They showed that eliminating pollution would create $9.5 billion a year in health benefits, or $711 per year, per resident. Reducing smog, the study said, would put far more money in the pockets of residents, businesses, and schools than it would take out; it would limit employee and pupil absences, cut down on medical and prescription bills, and minimize expensive treatments of serious respiratory and heart disease. At the same time, the study said that Lents' blueprint would accommodate a fifty-five-percent growth in the number of jobs in the region by 2007 as regulators gradually put the plan in place. Most important, the plan would save an estimated 10,000 lives a year in the smoggy basin.[11] Opponents of the tough plan were caught off guard.

With a new pro-environment board, a bigger staff, positive public relations, a strong regional economy, and greater authority under state law, Lents had effectively consolidated his power. He had created what some saw as a stream roller that could crush the sources of smog. Within a few years, he scored numerous successes with new rules on big industry: power plants, oil refineries, glassmakers, aerospace companies, steelmakers. The AQMD board adopted clean air standards for barbeque lighter fluid, prompting one dissenting member to say: "Use a barbecue, go to jail." Meanwhile, Lents and his agency pushed the state to set tighter standards for cars, and to develop new standards that would require oil refiners to produce cleaner fuels. His team worked to reduce smog-forming fumes from aerosol spray cans and other common household products. Even nail polish came under clean air standards. Borrowing a page from the old Los Angeles County APCD, the AQMD launched a "smoke patrol" to ticket smoking vehicles and a toll-free number—1-800-CUT-SMOG, promoted on billboards and radio commercials—to which motorists could report the license plate numbers of smoking trucks and buses. The AQMD would then send letters requesting the owners to fix their cars, although repair was voluntary.

Lents and his encyclopedic strategy for cleaning up the air produced dramatic results. By the time he left office in 1997, the number of days that L.A. surpassed the federal ozone standard had declined from 164 a year to 68. The peak level of the pollutant had been cut by forty percent. The new rules continued to reduce pollution through the remainder of the decade, eventually cutting the number of days above the ozone standard to forty in 2000, and the peak level in half. In effect, his clean air plan brought the biggest and fastest improvement in air quality in the history of the region, making smog almost a nonissue in Los Angeles by the start of the new millennium. However, it did not come without a cost to residents, businesses, and to Lents himself.

The Tennessean's moral conviction was perhaps based in his religiosity and humble background. He grew up fairly poor in

Knoxville, the son of parents who had eighth-grade educations.[12] His tastes reflected his background: he was fond of eating popcorn at meetings with his executive staff and he preferred the quiet, orderly suburbs to the bustling urban core. He carpooled regularly or road his bike to work to minimize pollution. He used low-polluting products in his home and mowed his own grass with an electric lawn mower. It wasn't long before Lents' earnest, unpretentious style began to irritate his colleagues in the cutthroat world of California politics and business.

Among the many regulations he pushed was one requiring makers of wood furniture and other products to use lacquers, varnishes, and paints with minimal amounts of petroleum solvents—a key ingredient of smog. The rule was one of the first to target small and medium-sized businesses, many of them owned by families and ethnic minorities. It was an industry that provided opportunities for high school-educated workers at a time when the foreign-import, big-box economy was taking root, and any new regulations were seen as a threat. Furniture makers argued that the new water-based coatings would not provide the sheen their customers wanted. Moreover, furniture would take longer to dry, so bigger floor spaces or expensive, energy-intensive dryers would be needed. The rule, they said, ultimately would make it impossible for small business owners to compete against big companies outside California who did not face the same requirements.

Lents was undaunted. To counter the industry's arguments, he and his rulemaking team planned a press conference to show the media that the new water-based coatings would have the same aesthetic characteristics as the traditional petroleum-based finishes. They commissioned a midwestern company that made water-based products to coat some children's furniture and ship it to the AQMD. As the day for the press conference approached, the furniture still had not arrived. Finally, the day of the press conference, the furniture made it to the UPS depot, but too late for it to be brought to the conference. So the agency sent a staff member to the UPS depot in the wee hours of the morning to retrieve it. Upon opening the boxes just hours before the press was expected, Lents and his team found that the children's furniture had a dull, pitted coat of varnish, unsuitable for prime time. Improvising, his team substituted a number of flat pieces of wood they already had on hand that had been carefully coated with the water-based products in place of the furniture and the press conference went forward. Within days, the board adopted the rule. However, the adoption of the rule would come back to haunt Lents.

The AQMD also adopted rules requiring all employers of one hundred or more people to pay incentives for carpooling or riding public transit. Companies were to submit annual rideshare plans and reports to the AQMD outlining their incentives and the level of ridesharing among their employees. They were to work up to an average of 1.5 people per vehicle in their parking lots. At first the program was popular, said John Dunlap, who was in charge of administering it for the AQMD.[13] "It was a time when not much [transportation] infrastructure was being built," he said, so people saw it as a way to stretch highway capacity during rush hour as well as cut air pollution. Traffic had become so thick and slow on freeways that motorists burned three million gallons of gasoline each day while idling at a standstill.[14]

At first the rule applied only to large companies, but as it was phased in to cover smaller companies and small cities, resistance grew, admitted Dunlap.[15] Businesses and cities objected when the AQMD pressed employers to provide their employees with more "incentives" to encourage higher levels of carpooling to meet the rule's goals.

The backlash against carpooling became part of a larger resistance to Lents and his air pollution program. Opposition from businesses, labor, and politicians grew after a recession gripped the nation following the first Gulf War under President George H. W. Bush. Unemployment began to climb amid a downturn in defense spending after the war and a seeming onslaught of foreign imports and outsourcing by U.S. companies. Amid the weakening economy and a growing divide between the haves and have-nots, in 1992, an all-white suburban jury acquitted four white police officers in the case of the Rodney King beating. In an eruption of rage, thousands of L.A.'s poorest residents participated in what was variously called a riot, a rebellion, or a civil disturbance. Merchants trying to protect their stores shot from their rooftops at rioters below, who returned fire. Families crouched inside their homes and apartments just hoping not to get hit. There were no police to be seen. Smoke blanketed the region, carried by the wind more than thirty miles to the east. As it cleared, it became clear that rioters had burned down 5,000 buildings, leaving areas from South Central Los Angeles to Koreatown gutted. With neighborhood stores lying in rubble, people suddenly had to drive or take the bus for miles just to buy groceries.

As political leaders tried to understand what was happening to the economy and what was fueling the racial tensions revealed by the Rodney King incident, many pointed their finger at the AQMD's tough rules on business. They claimed that companies had been leaving the area to escape the cost of complying with the smog rules, stranding workers in the process and creating animosities along class and racial lines. "There was a widespread perception that South Coast [AQMD] was too tough on stationary sources," recalled Dunlap. In response, AQMD's board formed a commission to examine the impacts of the agency's smog cleanup program on the local economy. Dunlap headed it. "I was assigned to do [it]. Nobody wanted it," he recalled, adding that Lents resisted the commission. Dunlap ran seven public hearings anyway to collect testimony about the economic effects of the agency's program. Yet he received little support and remembered that when he came back to make recommendations for changes, "I had a problem getting heard."[16]

Small businesses had to pay heavy penalties for minor violations of air quality rules after already having shelled out substantial amounts of money to buy new, low-polluting equipment. One of many stories that came out as the hearings progressed was of a small company that was fined $5,000 because one of its employees had dripped paint.[17]

The backlash stemmed not only from the tougher, costlier rules, but also from actions Lents took to toughen the AQMD's enforcement program after being criticized by the Air Resources Board for laxity. In the past, the district had handed out mild penalties for pollution infractions, and businesses even were known to intimidate air quality inspectors. In one such incident, remembered Ed Camarena, a newly hired inspector called on a medical waste incineration company in Orange County, only to have an executive there throw a bag of waste at her feet. In another instance, a carwash owner, subject to inspections of his gas pumps for leaks, opened a drawer and laid a gun on his desk when an AQMD inspector called on him.[18]

To address such intimidation and get the upper hand in enforcing smog standards, Lents hired a chief prosecutor and a team of deputy prosecutors and investigators to rout out wrongdoing. Soon, the district racked up major penalties—a $1 million settlement with Lockheed Martin for 6,500 violations; a $550,000 settlement with ARCO for misreporting emissions to the agency; a $30,000 settlement for Humana Hospital after it failed to follow AQMD's carpooling rule.[19] The penalties kept rolling in, month after month. Big business didn't like it, though they found little sympathy with the public. But when AQMD's prosecutors took a similar tough approach with small business, it backfired in the court of public opinion.

Even Lents admitted that his team often was too zealous in enforcing rules. He recalled one day finding "an older black gentleman who was standing in the hallway crying" at the agency's new headquarters. The man was Woody Phillips, founder of family-run Woody's Barbecue in South Central Los Angeles. The AQMD hearing board had denied him a variance from a rule requiring restaurants to eliminate smoke from their operations.[20] Phillips faced having to possibly close his restaurant and lay off employees, some of whom had worked with him since he'd opened his beloved BBQ joint some twenty years before.[21] After some time, the AQMD was able to help him comply with the rules and Phillips remains in business today. His experience with the AQMD was not unique and was seized upon as a cause célèbre by Lents' growing number of opponents. In 1993, unemployed workers held a twilight candlelight vigil outside the front door of the agency's big headquarters in Diamond Bar to protest clean air rules. The event was orchestrated by the construction industry, timed for local evening news broadcasts and a good photo opportunity for the morning papers. As the sun set, AQMD executives nervously eyed the demonstration outside their office windows. In Sacramento, city officials and business owners and managers alike sought relief from the legislature and the governor.

Even before the riots, Lents tried to respond to growing criticism of his clean air program on the economy by ordering a kinder and gentler approach to regulating small businesses, one of which focused on technical assistance and flexibility instead of harsh enforcement.[22] In 1995, he and his board rolled back the controversial carpooling rule, letting employers buy their way out of it for $110 per employee per year.[23] He conceded to Los Angeles mayor Richard Riordan and deferred the timetable for rules to cut emissions from diesel equipment—such as trains and trucks—at the ports of Los Angeles and Long Beach, just as they were poised for major expansion under liberalized trade agreements put in place under President Clinton:[24] Lents laid off 204 staff members as revenues dipped during the recession. He also embarked on a controversial new emissions trading program, known as the Regional Clean Air Incentives Market, or RECLAIM, to ease the cost of pollution controls for the major industries that supplied the sprawling region with power, gasoline, chemicals, and other basic materials and products.

The RECLAIM program had been lobbied for by a sophisticated lawyer named Robert Wyman, who put together his own environmental affairs group and called it The Regulatory Flexibility Group. Wyman's coterie represented most of the major industries in the region, including the influential *Los Angeles Times*, with its huge printing presses and truck delivery fleet, both of which poured toxins into the air each day. The handsome, bright, young attorney, often quoted in the paper's stories about air pollution, argued that using market forces instead of "command-and-control" regulations would spur needed innovation and reduce the cost of pollution control. He won the ear of Lents and the AQMD board. Soon the agency formed a large task force to devise an emissions trading program that would supplant pollution control rules already on the books for the biggest industries in Los Angeles.

The board approved the program late in 1993, over the vehement objection of environmentalists. It was aimed at cutting both sulfur oxides, which form acidic particles in the air, and nitrogen dioxide, which forms both ozone and particle pollution. Under this program, each of 390 facilities was assigned an annual cap on emissions of each pollutant through 2010. Those caps declined each year. For each pound of pollution included in the caps, the AQMD granted the companies emissions credits that could be traded: operators that could reduce pollution below their annual caps could sell their resulting excess emissions credits to those who chose not to meet their caps. As long as every operator had enough credits to cover their emissions, air regulators could be assured that RECLAIM would reduce emissions each year until the air was clean. However, should a business exceed its cap and not be able to purchase credits to cover those excess emissions, it would be in violation of RECLAIM.[25] Environmentalists warned that the program would open the region's air pollution program to fraud by unscrupulous businesses and traders and that it would be difficult for regulators to police. They turned out to be right, but that would only become evident later.

The immediate effect of RECLAIM was to make irrelevant some of the cleanup rules that the AQMD had on its books, particularly for power plants that would have been required to install state-of-the-art pollution controls by the mid-1990s. Those rules would have required plant operators (specifically Southern California Edison and the Los Angeles Department of Water and Power) to completely modernize their plants, not only reducing pollution but also making them more energy efficient and lengthening their useful lives.

However, when the AQMD adopted the RECLAIM program, it caved to pressure from business and handed out grossly inflated quantities of credits to power plant operators and other industries. With electricity deregulation on the horizon, Edison could foresee that it might eventually unload its plants, so it had no motive to spend millions of dollars to clean them as long as it had enough credits to wait a few years. No surprise, then, that Edison was a major supporter of RECLAIM. When the state legislature deregulated utilities in 1996, it required Edison, the major utility for the area, to sell its power plants to out-of-state merchant generators. In doing so, the company unloaded a major pollution control liability. As the new companies took the reins, air pollution credits were the last thing on their minds, particularly by the time the energy crisis hit California in 2000.

Deregulation opened the door to manipulation of energy markets, allowing energy trading companies and generators to bilk Californians out of billions of dollars, drive Pacific Gas and Electric into bankruptcy, and drive Southern California Edison to the brink of insolvency. It was also bad for air quality. With money to be made as the price of electricity shot up, generating companies worked their aging plants overtime to provide power and make a handy profit. However, their emissions caps finally declined to the point where their surplus credits had evaporated. So power plant operators bought all available credits on the open market, causing their price to soar. Meanwhile, other businesses also had waited to clean up their plants. Suddenly it seemed just about everybody was emitting more than allowed under the RECLAIM program. Lents was gone by then, but with its back to the wall, the AQMD had no choice but to let the power plants continue to exceed their emissions. The agency fined a couple companies, but let the others off as long as they agreed to install controls on negotiated schedules that the old command-and-control rules would have required in the mid-1990s. To make those extensions legal, the agency amended its rules to temporarily remove power plants from the RECLAIM program. Eventually, the AQMD was able to bring RECLAIM back on track and document that it had achieved the promised emissions reductions, but only after years of delay and latitude for businesses.

There was another fly in the ointment as well. A Wall Street-style pollution market without intensive oversight exposed RECLAIM to outright fraud, as the saga of one of its infamous brokers illustrates. In the early 1990s, Anne Sholtz had been a go-getting Caltech economist and entrepreneur helping the district to structure its revolutionary air pollution bazaar. As a member of AQMD's industry task force, the ambitious young woman suggested, among other ideas, ways to sequence the trades to stem confusion and paperwork headaches.[26] Sholtz, in many respects, was just what early L.A. smog generals envisioned: a fresh thinker who could motivate companies to make deep emission-cuts by dangling flexibility and profit incentive before their eyes.

Known for her slick presentations and revealing dresses in an otherwise staid tableau, the thirty-something businesswoman from the Midwest seemed to be queen of her very own technical kingdom. She claimed to hold a Ph.D. from Washington University in St. Louis, and heralded her brokerage for its employment of cutting-edge software—originally developed for deep-space exploration—to analyze and optimize clients' trades. As competition grew, she affiliated her companies, EonXchange and Automated Credit Exchange, with big-name financial institutions. Internet-driven pollution trading was the buzz and she had a talent for it. Major manufacturers—defense companies, power-generators, energy interests—signed up with her. By the late 1990s, flattering media attention showered her as a "New Economy" success. From her spoils, she built a lavish, 8,000-square-foot estate along the San Gabriel Mountains.[27]

It wasn't until after Lents departed AQMD, though, that evidence seeped out that Sholtz was not the dynamo she appeared. Soon came the revelation that she had no Ph.D., as was cited in her involvement with Belgium and the Netherlands in a 2001 simulated pollution-trading exercise.[28] Then the entire RECLAIM system shook when in 2002, the district logged complaints from nine companies that she'd defrauded them out of millions of dollars. EPA criminal investigators were notified, and they zeroed in on her dealings with a New York-based energy investment firm called AG Clean Air and what is now ExxonMobil Corp.

Sholtz had convinced AG executives they could sell Mobil roughly $17.5 million in credits the oil giant needed for a handsome windfall. When in December 2000 AG queried Sholtz why it had only received $9 million in proceeds, she began manufacturing excuses and covering her tracks. As the Feds later concluded in their probe, she'd organized a magnificent sham. She, and possibly a mysterious, smooth-talking cohort named Jimmy Keller, had impersonated Mobil executives and even forged documents to trick AG into believing the Mobil deal was legitimate.[29] Was this the tip of the iceberg? As the EPA traced Sholtz's moves, they turned up evidence of eighty potential counts of wire, mail, and false-statement fraud. AQMD and other environmental officials who'd rubbed elbows with her felt embarrassed and betrayed. The collapse of her companies triggered a monster bankruptcy, where firms and investors registered as much as $80 million in claims. In one shady transaction involving powermaker Intergen North America, she'd blamed the 9-11 terrorist attacks for destroying important paperwork inside the obliterated World Trade Towers.[30]

Even with all that, the U.S. Justice Department charged her with only a single felony count involving the phony AG deal. She pled guilty and in April 2008 received what some observers considered a surprisingly lenient punishment: one year of home detention and five years of probation.[31] Today, her descent from eco-business phenomenon to convicted criminal makes her a cautionary tale about the perils of boutique environmental exchanges as the nation clamors for similar markets to curb greenhouse gases.

Even as Lents eased up on business to the extent that somebody like Sholtz eventually could take advantage of smog rules for profit, he still had accumulated a long and unforgiving list of enemies and had stepped on so many toes in his drive to clean up the air that he had a diminished circle of friends. Conservative Republicans were concerned about the impact of his anti-smog program on the economy. Some Democrats were worried, too, particularly about the impact on furniture makers and other small manufacturing operations that employed the area's growing population of upwardly mobile Latinos and new immigrants, who were eager to improve their economic standing.[32] To rein in the AQMD, Governor Pete Wilson named a series of members to the board who were hostile to Lents. Dunlap—who by then chaired the Air Resources Board in Sacramento—helped Wilson choose whom to appoint.[33] Legislators sponsored a series of bills aimed at clipping the agency's wings. Republican lawmaker Curt Pringle, who sponsored some of the legislation, saw it as a matter of protecting the rights of the individual against "the tyranny of the majority." Small businesses, the former lawmaker recalled, had "a diminished ability to respond to the strength of the district."[34] In a desperate attempt to protect the AQMD's power against an onslaught of bills, Lents took the suggestion of one of his new board members, William Burke. Burke, who had been appointed by legendary Democratic Speaker of the Assembly Willie Brown advised Lents to hire a woman named Layne Bordenave to lobby for the district in Sacramento in order to "garner support for district policy, agenda, and mission." The board approved a $53,000 contract.[35] After several months, it became clear that Bordenave was doing very little—and then it became clear why. "I found out we had hired one of Willie Brown's mistresses," said Lents. "I felt manipulated." Lents said he met with Burke to talk about it, but Burke was unconcerned because Brown had promised to "bottle up" anti-AQMD bills. Lents told Burke, "It just doesn't feel right to me."[36] Indeed, records filed by Bordenave with the California Secretary of State in 1995 show that she lobbied on no particular bills and had no clients other than the AQMD. In fact, she filed reports only after that office repeatedly threatened to fine her for failing to disclose her lobbying activities. In her first report, which she wrote in July 1995, she said "I am a new lobbyist. This was my first client. I did not know that if you did not have anything to report, that you have to file. I did not have any activity."[37] Despite her lack of lobbying activity for the AQMD, however, Brown kept his word and prevented passage that year of any bills to trim the AQMD's power. Soon after the incident, Lents said Burke tried to "get rid of me."[38]

Burke said, "It had nothing to do with Layne Bordenave and everything to do with Jim Lents." Burke acknowledged recommending Bordenave after Lents asked him for suggestions about how to fend off bills in Sacramento. He said she had extensive experience working for legislators at both the state and federal level and that he did not pressure Lents to contract with her. Burke said the real reason he sought to remove Lents was because he had failed to clean up the air in low income communities. Moreover, others had criticized him for being insensitive to local governments and small businesses.[39] However, the Bordenave incident marked the ascension of corruption at AQMD.

"It really didn't amount to anything," said Bordenave of the contract, awarded while she acknowledged she was in a "relationship" with Willie Brown.[40] Soon, Burke, who is black, teamed up with other minority Democrats and conservative Republicans, including Governor Wilson's appointee Cody Cluff, to terminate Lents' career.[41]

Cluff, who sported a shaved head and wore black turtlenecks and sunglasses to meetings, would later plead no contest to embezzlement that took place while he was head of the Los Angeles County's Entertainment Development Corporation, a public office aimed at promoting the film industry. He narrowly avoided prison time by striking a plea deal with prosecutors, though the county probation department recommended he go to prison because of his "corruption and greed."[42]

By 1997, Lents knew he had reached the end of the road. With his clean air strategy yet to be fully achieved, he could not muster the seven votes he needed from the twelve-member board to renew his contract. While the air was cleaner, many issues still were left unaddressed by Lents, including toxic pollution and a growing cloud of cancer-causing diesel pollution over Los Angeles as the area became a new gateway for cheap international imports. Many of his technology-forcing rules worked in the end, including his concept of emissions-free or low-polluting paints, inks, varnishes, and cleaning fluids. He also had finally laid the groundwork, although imperfectly, for cleaning up major industries. However, his call for lifestyle changes and personal sacrifice was largely rejected, even by his own staff. Today, the parking lot at AQMD headquarters in Diamond Bar is full of large sport utility vehicles that guzzle gas, emit pollution, and contribute to global warming. Where the AQMD stood in El Monte when Lents arrived there is now a fast food court full of the drive-through restaurants he once envisioned banning. Both are a rebuke to his unfinished agenda. They demonstrate that as much as Angelenos profess environmentalism, their commitment stops just short of personal sacrifice.

11
SEARCHING FOR PERPETUAL MOTION

ONE EVENING IN 1996, LOS ANGELES TELEVISION VIEWERS WERE taken by surprise by a new kind of commercial, one with no narrator and no dialogue. It opened with a dramatic crack of lightning that knocked out the power in a typical suburban house. As eerie *Star Wars*-like music played, appliances in the darkened home suddenly came to life—fans, toasters, lamps, and vacuum cleaners. They marched to the curb where they gathered with other automated housewares under the dark sky. Up the street, headlights appeared and a sleek car drove up and parked before the admiring crowd of appliances. As the commercial ended, the screen simply filled with these words: "The electric car is here."

With that commercial, General Motors introduced Californians to its EV-1, a production model electric car designed from the ground up that could go from zero to sixty miles an hour in 8.5 seconds. It was completely unlike other electric cars at the time, which took thirty seconds to reach freeway speed and basically consisted of conventional cars retrofitted with batteries and electric motors. The sleek and aerodynamic EV-1 had a driving range of seventy to ninety miles, depending on driving conditions, long enough to get most Los Angeles residents to work and back on a single charge. Unlike many other electric vehicles, it had air conditioning, dual air bags, and modern conveniences like power locks and windows. It could go up to 110 miles per hour, but the automaker had artificially limited its speed to 80 miles per hour. GM had designed and produced the car in response to the California Air Resources Board's "zero emissions vehicle" rule adopted in 1990.[1] Under the new rule, which made headlines around the world, major automakers were to make sure that, beginning in 1998, two percent of the cars they sold were "zero emissions vehicles." Each year after that they were to increase sales by an additional two percent until zero emissions vehicles comprised ten percent a year of their total auto sales in California by 2003.

There was some irony in trying to enforce such a rule in a city that had effectively crafted and sold the auto's image for the car industry. From the dazzling shots of cars spinning through the empty streets of downtown L.A. to the aerial views of beefy pickup trucks triumphantly climbing the red buttes of the stark and isolated landscape of the American West, it was Hollywood that produced most of the nation's car commercials. Automotive technology had seen plenty of glamour on the silver screen too, from the daring street races depicted in James Dean movies to the sophisticated beauty and gadgetry of James Bond's 007 sports car. Now it was all about to change.

Because of its severe smog problem, the state air board envisioned that most of the zero emissions vehicles would be sold in the Los Angeles area. In effect, the board's mandate meant that automakers had to start making battery-powered electric cars, since no other technology to date had been developed to make cars emissions free.

The electric car was hardly new. A Scotsman named Robert Anderson had invented an electric carriage in 1832. By the turn of the century, the electric vehicle out-numbered its more recent cousin, the gasoline car. France and Great Britain were the first nations to see electric vehicles commonly used in the late 1800s, but by 1897 they had become the car of choice for taxi drivers in New York City. Cabbies and other drivers preferred electric vehicles over gasoline- and steam-powered ones for a number of reasons.[2] First, electric vehicles started right up. Drivers had to hand crank gasoline-powered vehicles to start them and it could take up to forty-five minutes to get water boiling on a cold morning before taking off in a steam-powered car. It was difficult to shift gears, too. Electric vehicle drivers, on the other hand, did not even have gears; they were clean and quiet, with none of the smoke, noise, and vibration common to gasoline- and steam-powered vehicles. Driving range was not as much of an issue since most vehicle use was for local trips.[3] In fact, at the turn of the century, city dwellers usually could walk to small corner markets to buy much of what they needed. People from the small towns that surrounded Los Angeles would ride the Red Car and make a day out of visiting downtown. As for visiting neighboring towns or far-away friends, there was simply no easy way to make the trip in a car, as connecting freeways did not exist.

Los Angeles in those days was more like New York, which began building its comprehensive subway system in 1900 by piggybacking it onto a rail system already in place. Throughout America, businesses still commonly delivered groceries and ice to people's homes, and even in smaller towns, people still could walk downtown. There were milkmen, vegetable and fruit sellers, ice cream vendors, bakery deliverymen, and door-to-door Fuller Brush men, peddling a wide array of domestic products. These homespun marketing networks persisted into the 1960s, but eventually gave way to the regional shopping malls made possible after construction of a massive freeway network. Local downtowns became engulfed by suburban housing tracts with the coming of a new freewheeling lifestyle born in Los Angeles.

From the beginning, it was the development of new highways and the opening of new vistas that propelled the popularity of the car. Early in the 1900s the nation began to develop its network of roads to connect cities. This change suddenly made a car's driving range more important. A refillable gasoline car could take people hundreds of miles away from home, and an electric car could not. Meanwhile, the auto industry made improvements in gasoline-powered vehicles. In 1912, the industry developed electric starters, eliminating the need for the hand crank to fire up gasoline vehicles. Henry Ford then figured out how to mass-produce gasoline-powered cars for between $500 and $1,000 with a continuously moving assembly line. While still a lot of money, the price of Ford's Model T substantially undercut the price of an electric roadster, which sold for $1,750 at the time. Throw in falling gasoline prices with the discovery of gushing crude oil in Texas and gasoline easily won out against electric-vehicle technology. But the electric car never really went away; it just went underground.[4]

*   *   *

The reappearance of the electric car was actually engineered in 1987, nearly a decade before GM debuted its futuristic machine. By then, pollution had made breathing a chore in Los Angeles. On virtually any sunny day the air was chock full of particles, ozone, acidic gases, and hydrocarbon fumes.

The AQMD's brochure, "The Path to Clean Air," had just been released and the call for zero-emissions technology was among its most controversial demands. But under James Lents, the board envisioned a binding plan that would call for automakers to make and sell pollution-free devices and products by a certain future date, thereby giving companies a strong incentive to invest in such innovations. Lents and his team fleshed out the brief brochure into a full-fledged legally binding clean air blueprint in 1989 under the federal Clean Air Act. The California Air Resources Board approved it and sent it on to the federal government. There the EPA gave the document and its myriad clean air measures the force and weight of federal law.

The blueprint promised that if Los Angeles motorists went electric, they could breathe fresh air within a generation. The prospect captured the world's imagination at a time when free markets were spreading like wildfire. Communism had fallen and the glimmer of the American lifestyle had begun taking root in places like China, India, and Indonesia. Workers dreamed of cars, freeways, and roomier homes full of appliances and gadgets in these nations, where rapid industrialization was bringing terrible air pollution, just as it had in Los Angeles a generation before. Media, academics, environmentalists, and government agencies were attracted to "The Path to Clean Air" because it raised the prospect that these developing countries could technologically leapfrog right past the fume-belching gasoline-powered car. Locally, entrepreneurs, engineers, and designers began to "think green"—both in environmental and cash terms. A cottage industry of electric vehicle technologists grew in Los Angeles, as inventors hoped that they and Los Angeles could become to the twenty-first century what Henry Ford and

Detroit were to the twentieth century. All they had to do was bring back the electric car. With a regulatory mandate behind them, sales would be all but guaranteed in Southern California, the biggest auto market and trendsetter in America. Soon the nation and world would follow.

The AQMD itself could not require electric vehicles—only the state Air Resources Board had the power to regulate autos in California. And with the bang of a gavel in Sacramento in 1990 the board adopted the state's zero emissions vehicle mandate. They had put Detroit on notice: eliminate pollution once and for all or take a hike when it comes to selling cars in California. If Detroit didn't comply, officials felt confident that California could make its own cars. After all, the state had the technical know-how and manufacturing capacity to produce the *Star Wars* weapons. How hard could it be to make electric cars, particularly when the basic technology had been known and used, at least in a limited way, for a hundred years?

*   *   *

Regulators understood that it would take time to make a transition from gasoline to electric cars. They required automakers only to gradually phase in the new vehicles, beginning with some test cars, before actually meeting the two percent sales target in 1998. And the automakers responded, at least with research and development vehicles. Environmentalists were feeling vindicated and optimistic when an unlikely harbinger of doom arrived in Los Angeles. Suddenly, more than clean air seemed to hinge on the development of an electric vehicle.

It was an early spring day in 1992 when General Colin L. Powell swung through town. He had come to deliver a blunt warning: "Everyone needs to wake up and smell the coffee.

Anyone who thinks this is cynical, I think is mistaken. It is not cynical. It is a fundamental restructuring. It is going to affect many regions throughout the county, but especially here, in Southern California." He was referring to the coming disintegration of L.A.'s defense industry establishment, which had long been one of the major pillars of the region's economy. Powell announced that the U.S. government would shrink its defense budget after the fall of the Soviet Union. "For forty years we have chased Soviet technology and have felt the hot breath of Soviet technology on our back. We were always trying to stay ahead of it, because we were a smaller force and quality was our difference. . . . Our whole industrial base, and their whole industrial base, kept churning out. That is gone."[5]

Ronald Reagan had presided over the largest military buildup in the nation's history in a final showdown with the Soviets during the 1980s. Its economy fatally weakened by pouring so many of its resources into weapons, the Soviet Union effectively surrendered in the Cold War. The Berlin Wall came down and the world celebrated. But the wall's collapse signaled the collapse of an entire industry, as well.

Smogtown was about to suffer economically. A report released just a few days before Powell came to town predicted that the region would see the demise of a web of companies— including household names like McDonnell Douglas, Lockheed Martin, and Northrop, as well as small job shops—that made everything from screws to sophisticated satellite surveillance systems and stealthy composite materials for B-2 bombers. The report, which came from the Los Angeles County aerospace task force, warned that Los Angeles County alone could lose 420,000 jobs by 1995 and lose $84.6 billion in personal income as a result of the end of the Cold War. "Los Angeles County is facing a severe decline of a key industry," said the report. "The effects will be long-lasting. County communities will be affected by relocation, tax revenue loss and economic ripple effects. More tragically, the lives of hundreds of thousands of persons within Los Angeles County will be painfully disrupted. Employment opportunities for tens of thousands of workers will be severely limited." In desperation, the county sought federal assistance for retraining the displaced workers, but for what?[6] Enter Lon Bell, a man with a plan.

Bell, a lifetime engineer who had earned a B.S., an M.S., and a Ph.D., all from the Caltech, had spent much of his life as president of an automotive components manufacturing concern that he started in 1967 and sold to TRW in 1986. The company produced crash sensors used to deploy air bags in cars, as well as other types of electronic controllers that incorporated computer technology into vehicles. After the state adopted its zero emissions vehicle mandate, the energetic Bell formed a new company called Amerigon, which worked out of rented quarters in the heart of the smoggy San Gabriel Valley, directly east of Los Angeles. On the strength of Bell's engineering and automotive background, the startup won a $375,000 grant from the AQMD to build a prototype electric vehicle.[7] But Bell realized that simply building a prototype would not be enough to create the excitement he would need to create a viable electric vehicle industry in the L.A. area. Bell thought bigger. He knew he needed to win the hearts and minds of politicians from Washington to Sacramento, so he produced a report entitled "Advanced Electric Transportation Technology Commercialization: A California Plan." He released it with great fanfare the day after Colin Powell delivered his "wake up and smell the coffee" speech.

Bell's timely report heralded the state's zero emissions vehicle mandate as the cornerstone for a new economy in

Southern California that could create 20,000 electric car jobs in 1995, and 65,000 by 1998, the first year the standard was to be enforced. After that the burgeoning industry would see annual job growth at a fifty percent compound rate. Bell believed that California's aerospace talent and plants were well positioned to provide many of the components that automakers at home and abroad would need to assemble electric cars—everything from heaters to instruments.[8] In a move that caught media attention, Bell joined with labor unions and politicians to propose that a closed-down Lockheed Martin plant in Burbank be transformed into a manufacturing center for electric vehicle components. Eventually, it would house a consortium of companies known as CalStart, which was to become the nexus of a new clean transportation industry that could fill the new and frightening void in the region's economy.[9] By the time CalStart moved into the facility, with much fanfare, unemployment in L.A. was pushing eleven percent and housing values were in free-fall.

In another effort to replace disappearing defense work, Northrop Corp. hatched a plan to begin making buses and train cars for use in mass transit. After all, the fuselages of aircraft are very similar to those of transit vehicles. Other companies began to move in a similar direction.[10] When GM rolled out its EV1, it was based on a prototype designed largely by Hughes Aircraft and Aerovironment, both Los Angeles area companies. Environmental leaders were elated, the car's $35,000 price tag notwithstanding. GM justified the high price by noting that it had spent $350 million to develop the car.[11] The company targeted the vehicle largely to well-educated, affluent residents with household incomes of more than $125,000 and a garage in which they could have a specially-built battery charger installed.[12]

Enamored with the promise of the new technology, politicians and environmental regulators rushed in with untold millions in subsidies to help early adapters buy their new electric cars. Soon there were tax write-offs, rebates, and a subsidized network of battery chargers installed at public expense in the basement parking garages of law firms and corporations throughout Los Angeles. State and local air pollution agencies supported automakers with generous research and development grants to advance electric vehicle technology. Indeed, there were so many subsidy programs that the Air Resources Board could not tally how much public money went to support the electric vehicle.[13] Despite these hefty incentives, California motorists showed little interest in driving electric vehicles, turning instead to the large sport utility vehicles and pickup trucks that clog state highways today. The range of the electric car was just not long enough to meet all the needs of motorists—such as taking long weekend trips or vacations—and few could afford to own an electric vehicle just for commuting. By 2003, there were just 3,000 freeway-capable electric vehicles on the state's highways and 9,000 glorified golf carts, marketed as neighborhood electric vehicles, to meet the state requirement. That same year there were 23 million cars in the state.[14]

As a result, the jobs promised by Lon Bell failed to materialize. A study done in 2000 by CalStart found that only 767 new jobs in California could be directly attributed to the development of the electric car and that the 134 companies that had some role in the electric vehicle industry employed just 3,500 workers. Total sales at those companies were estimated at a relatively meager $400 million a year.[15] But all this didn't matter much to economists. By then, another industry was well on its way to filling the gap left by the departure of defense and aerospace manufacturing. California had become the import capi-tal of the United States, the port of choice for the arrival of electronics, food, and other consumer wares from overseas to stock the shelves of Wal-Mart and Target stores throughout the nation. The unemployed aerospace workers had found new jobs, many in the booming shipping industry, working in ware-houses that were now gobbling up the region's remaining farm-land. Housing values were on the rise, credit was easy, and gas was cheap. The growth of imports buoyed an economy that had been submerged, seemingly ready to drown, at the begin-ning of the 1990s. Chevrolet Suburbans and Ford Explorers with unlimited driving ranges were easy to buy, and for those who owned big houses in inland areas far from where they worked, that was preferable to paying just as much to live in cramped apartments in the urban core, where an electric vehi-cle might have met most of their automotive needs.

Unwilling to accept this reality, electric vehicle aficiona-dos—in their genuine concern for the planet—complained that GM had conspired to hold back new batteries that would have made the electric car practical for more people, and even that the company had withheld vehicles from anxious buyers. In fact this was true, but only because the initial cars had sold so poorly. It was a product that had little future in the land of long commutes. The lack of demand for the EV1 had become a drag on GM's bottom line.

But the company could not easily step away from the EV1, because with their zero emissions vehicle mandate, California's air quality regulators had in fact created a sacred cow. The mandate, hollow as it was, remained on the books, even though the state had repeatedly backed off from enforc-ing it. What GM needed was a strategy to rid itself and other automakers of the money-losing mandate. So the carmaker set out to do just that, with a little inside help from an old friend, William Burke.

Burke by then was not only chair of the AQMD in Los Angeles, but had also been appointed to the Air Resources Board by Governor Gray Davis. He came to the state board as it was making midcourse corrections in the zero emissions rules, and he made the most of the opportunities that timing presented. GM was already in his good graces because the company had agreed to sponsor the L.A. Marathon, an annual for-profit extravaganza that Burke had won the bid to operate. (None of the other bidders had lined up major corporate sponsors.) GM later backed out of the deal, but without the company's initial commitment it was unlikely that Burke would have been able to close the deal with the city.[16] The company exploited its relationship with him again in 2000, when it asked Burke for help in gutting the board's electric vehicle rules in an attempt to free automakers from the world's toughest clean air standard.

The effort came in the context of one of the state board's periodic reviews of how the technology was developing before it enforced a requirement for larger numbers of electric vehicles. As the 2000 review approached, the majority of board members assumed they would give automakers more time to develop the clean air vehicles, but still pressure them to keep working for that zero emissions technology.[17] "It's the vision thing," explained Catherine Witherspoon, a key staff member of the Air Resources Board at that time who would later come to lead the agency. "It's what we're aiming for." Indeed, the state's insistent vision of a day when most Californians would drive pollution-free cars had been an inspiration for people across the nation and around the world. "It has been monumental," said Bill

Moore, editor of *EV World*, who began following the development of electric vehicles in 1998. "Without it, nothing would happen.[18]

Burke saw things differently—especially after a private meeting with General Motors "vice president of environment and energy," Dennis Minano. Minano recalled that Burke "was willing to look at new approaches to getting air-quality benefits." From his perch on the Air Resources Board, Burke pushed a proposal to allow the company to buy its way out of the standard with millions of dollars.[19] After their private meeting—just five months before the air board would vote on the future of the state's zero emissions vehicle standard—Burke joined Minano in announcing the AQMD-GM "Community Clean Air Partnership." Under that partnership, GM was to settle a contract dispute with the AQMD involving a project to clean up diesel locomotives: GM, one of two major locomotive builders in North America, had failed to deliver a test model of a clean-burning, natural-gas locomotive for the Los Angeles area. As Burke publicized the partnership with GM, however, it became evident that it was little more than a divide-and-conquer strategy aimed at pitting environmental justice advocates against the zero emissions auto buffs and even the state mandate itself.[20]

Burke also met with Tom Soto, of P.S. Enterprises. "I was a consultant to GM," Soto recounted. "I helped design a plan that would work as an alternative to the zero emissions vehicle mandate." Under that plan, Soto explained, GM and other automakers would make a cash payment to the state to buy their way out of the zero emissions vehicle requirement. The money would be used to clean up diesel vehicles, including school buses, a chief concern of environmental justice advocates. Burke, Soto said, supported the plan, believing it would enable the state to continue its diesel cleanup program, which was beginning to run out of money at the time. "It was very bold of him to take that position," said Soto.

In January of 2001, the Air Resources Board met to consider an extended timetable for meeting the zero emissions vehicle standard. As the daylong hearing progressed, Burke told his fellow board members, "Now you know, I make deals for a living. I'm going to vote for this thing now, so I'm not trying to make a deal here and change anything on here. I'm a zero emissions vehicle advocate, but I'm also a realist." He continued, "I'm the only one on this board with only one lung. I'm the only one on this board with a diminishing capacity in the other lung. Two years ago when I really got sick, going to the bathroom from my bed was a two-stop trip." The implication, of course, was that he had a deeply personal stake in improving California's air quality, but in fact Burke had developed trouble breathing due to a spinal injury that was compressing a nerve that controlled one of his lungs. He underwent spinal surgery, which largely corrected the problem.[21] What Burke did not reveal to the public that day, however, is that he had sent letters to his fellow board members asking them to *delay* acting on the amendments to the zero emissions vehicle mandate and to consider further softening the standards. On January 9, Burke wrote to the board's executive officer Michael P. Kenny urging "the board to fully consider the industry's alternative"—namely the plan devised by GM to let automakers buy their way out of the standard by paying to clean up diesel vehicles instead. He also urged Kenny and other fellow board members to delay acting on the amendments until the state could conduct "an extensive energy audit of the impact that the zero emissions vehicle mandate might have on California's energy situation."[22] The concerns Burke expressed in those letters were the concerns GM had voiced, about how charging electric vehicles would affect the electricity grid in the midst of the state's energy crisis of 2000 and 2001. The letter struck a nerve with many because the state had been suffering from rolling blackouts due to an ostensible power shortage. (It soon became evident, however, that companies like Enron had caused the shortages to jack up electricity prices.) Reflecting on Burke's letter a few years later, David Freeman, who Davis had appointed as the state's energy czar at the time and had spent a career managing electric utilities, called it an "outrageous" tactic. The grid, he said, could have easily supplied enough power to charge up the number of electric vehicles required under the zero emissions vehicle mandate.[23] Burke did his best to conceal his involvement with GM until the last possible minute. Just before the board voted, Burke said, "I instructed my staff assistant I didn't want to talk to anybody on this. . . . She did an excellent job and she let only two slip through." They were, he said, Minano of GM and Tom Soto of P.S. Enterprises.[24]

AQMD's chief executive Barry Wallerstein, who replaced James Lents, said that the Los Angeles area agency supported GM's proposal to buy the company's way out of the mandate, since it would provide $400 million a year to the state and the AQMD to clean up diesel vehicles. As a member of the California Air Resources Board and chair of the AQMD, Burke would have substantial control over that money. "Once I have control of the money," Burke told *LA Weekly*, "you can't pull the wool over my eyes. End of story." He called backing the GM plan "the best move I ever made in my life."[25]

However, as he continued in that interview, "We couldn't do that without CARB's permission. So I called up Alan Lloyd [chair of the CARB] and said, 'Look, here's the deal: They're willing to do this. Can we do it as a pilot project?' And he said, 'No,' so I said, 'Okay,' but told him that battery electric vehicles were going nowhere. Alan Lloyd says, 'I have orders from the [Gov. Gray Davis] administration to continue to pursue battery technology.'"[26] This appears to be untrue. Asked about whether he had orders from the administration or governor, Lloyd simply replied: "Not correct. I never got a call from the governor. In all my time I got one call from the governor, and that was not to tell me what to do. I didn't see any merit in having a company buy its way out of the standard." He went on to say it was "the start of a slippery slope" to allow a company to buy its way out of a regulation.[27] In the state legislature, the GM lobbying campaign led by Tom Soto inspired key members of the state assembly to send letters to the board questioning the zero emissions vehicle program. They also urged the state air board to give automakers greater flexibility in meeting the emissions standards.[28] Typical of the letters was one sent by lawmaker Herb Wesson—who would soon become speaker for the assembly—who wrote on January 12, 2001, "California's communities need a regulation that will further the objectives of the zero emissions vehicle mandate, namely cleaner air and healthier citizens, while giving regulators and businesses a flexible framework that can consider new ideas."

Lloyd said he welcomed the voicing of the legislators' concerns. "What I was surprised about," he said, "was the explicit reference at the hearing that some of the legislators were sitting on our budget." Legislators had made veiled threats that unless the board conceded to GM they would cut the agency's funding.[29] Addressing the concerns of legislators and automakers, the air board gave automakers credit toward meeting the zero emissions standard by improving energy efficiency in their gasoline-powered cars. "It was an attempt to extend flexibility," recalled the Air Resources Board's Witherspoon. "The surprising part was when they filed the lawsuit."[30] It should not have come as a shock. In a three-volume submission to the air board just days before the 2001 vote, GM warned that it would sue the state if the board adopted the revisions to the standard that were before it. But nobody discussed the warning at the hearing, and air-board staff members did not recall reading the document. The board approved the revisions, including the last-minute energy-efficiency language its staff had devised in part to allay the concerns of state legislators. This gave GM just what it needed to finish off the mandate once and for all. The Detroit giant quickly joined DaimlerChrysler and a group of Central Valley auto dealers to challenge the revised regulations with an argument that stood the notion of states' rights on its head: they claimed that the federal Energy Policy and Conservation Act pre-empted states from setting fuel-efficiency standards for autos. A federal district court agreed, and issued an injunction preventing the board from enforcing the 2001 standards. Ultimately, the air board settled out of court and, early in 2003, effectively removed the zero emissions vehicle requirement from the state regulations, except to require the automakers to produce a handful of hydrogen-powered, fuel-cell vehicles.[31]

Electric car diehards were convinced that the standard was overturned just as the electric vehicle was poised to gain commercial success thanks to a breakthrough that had occurred in battery technology. "It was like telling people to scale Mount Everest and, when they were a foot from the top, telling them, 'No, we didn't mean it,'" said Steve Kirsch, the

founder of Infoseek, whose foundation pushes development
of electric vehicles. "Everyone supporting the climbers just
packed and left."[32] In the end, the state air board "got nothing," said Wallerstein. After beating back the standards,
Dennis Minano retired from GM, and the company never
delivered any money to the state or the AQMD to clean up
diesel trucks, buses, or trains. In a defensive comment, Burke
said, "They made a bad decision in Sacramento, but I guess
the governor paid for that because he got recalled." Burke
would have preferred to see the buyout go forward because
he said it would have provided cash to clean up diesel vehicles. Later, however, he would admit that tighter controls on
auto emissions are needed. "If you don't control the mobile
emissions, we're fighting a standoff and will be overcome,"
he said.[33] Burke missed the point, though. The larger lesson
behind how the auto industry ridded itself of an unwanted
and unprofitable regulation revolves around the limits of
technology itself in achieving environmental goals. The truth
was that the EV1 performed as warranted and GM made a
substantial commitment to developing the car and marketing
it. But the vast majority of Southern Californians were willing to breathe petroleum fumes if it meant they could live in
the suburbs and drive in big, comfortable cars powered by
cheap gasoline. It wasn't that the EV1 was unaffordable to
motorists, who gladly shelled out as much on their Chevy
Suburbans. It was that they didn't seem to care. Instead of
thinking about the self-inflicted damage to their health,
Californians seemed to be dreaming about cooking dinner at
home on barbecues stoked up with toxic lighter fluid that
spread the reek of kerosene through their neighborhoods. No,
technology was not the problem, but neither was it the ultimate answer. Deep down, smog remained a problem of the

culture itself, a product of human values that were mis-placed, and an economy that was spinning out of control, threatening to burn up the planet under a cloud of gases. Rather than change its values and way of life, the state soon would pin its hopes on a new technological grail: Governor Arnold Schwarzenegger's "hydrogen highway."

HE GOT THE GOLD MINE, THEY GOT THE SHAFT

HUDSON ELEMENTARY SCHOOL IN LONG BEACH, CALIFORNIA, LIES along the busy Terminal Island Freeway, which carries trucks from the ports of Los Angeles and Long Beach. Across the highway there's a rail yard where diesel locomotives, like the trucks barreling past, carry cargo containers from the twin-port complex. Emissions from the trucks and trains, not to mention from nearby ships, oil refineries, and other industrial facilities clustered around the port, have made the location of the elementary school one of the most polluted points in sprawling Los Angeles.[1] On a daily basis, diesel soot creeps into the lungs of young students, increasing their rate of asthma and respiratory infections and laying the groundwork for long-term health risks like cancer and heart disease before they get even to high school.

The twin ports of Long Beach and Los Angeles are the largest and busiest in the nation, spanning more than sixteen square miles. In 2004, almost 6,000 ships visited the complex, transporting 13.2 million twenty-foot-long containers. Each day it takes scores of cranes, thousands of pieces of yard equipment, 30,000 trucks, and hundreds of locomotives to keep the goods moving. Giant ships arrive from Asia stacked with as many as 8,000 metal containers crammed full of imported goods. Workers lift the containers off the freighters with huge cranes and use off-road trucks and other equipment to jockey them around in terminal yards.

About half the goods arriving here are shipped east in containers—including some then transferred onto ships bound for Europe. The other containers go to warehouses, where crews break them down and repack the goods in trucks destined for stores throughout California and the rest of the West. Diesel emissions occur all the way down the line, from the incoming ships to the outbound trucks and trains on the east end of the metropolitan area.

A little farther along the Terminal Island Freeway and closer to the gigantic port complex stand a growing number of empty steel shipping containers stacked six high. Their paint fades and peels. Many have small engines that were once used to power refrigerators keeping the fish and other food from Asia frozen on its journey across the Pacific to the freezer cases of U.S. supermarkets like Safeway, Ralph's, and Trader Joe's. The refrigerator units on the containers show signs of rust and may well be leaking refrigerant compound, a powerful global warming gas—all this at a time when California Governor Arnold Schwarzenegger beams from the cover of national news magazines heralding his state's new climate protection law.

The air pollution from the port operation doesn't stop at the waterfront or nearby communities. It stretches far into the inland areas of Southern California, blanketing communities like Mira Loma in Riverside County with soot and other pollutants. There, trucks inch along Etiwanda Boulevard, puffing diesel smoke as they jerk forward in heavy traffic. Low-slung warehouses bearing the Wal-Mart, Black & Decker, Costco, and

Honda brand names now cover the farms and dairies that once thrived along the banks of the Santa Ana River. Above Etiwanda, trains rumble across a bridge to a Union Pacific rail yard, delivering shiny new cars that will be transferred to trucks and whisked away to auto dealerships. Idling locomotives permeate the adjacent Field of Dreams youth sports complex with cancer-causing exhaust as students walk home from nearby Jurupa Valley High School.

Mira Loma is but one small pocket of Southern California's so-called logistics industry, which exploded in the wake of international trade agreements like GATT and NAFTA in the 1990s. Those agreements have triggered a rising tide of cheap imports and a cloud of toxic diesel exhaust from the armada of ships, trucks, and trains that move goods through the ports to inland warehousing centers and on to big-box retailers. The Los Angeles area has effectively become what environmental activists call "the driveway to the nation."

*   *   *

Responsibility for the cloud of cancer-causing diesel pollution that has sullied communities around the port and warehouse centers—as well as along the roadways and rail lines between them—can be laid at the doorstep of the AQMD. In the midst of the deep economic recession that gripped the nation during the 1990s, L.A. mayor Richard Riordan pressed the AQMD to delay tough measures to cut pollution from trucks, trains, and other equipment involved in shipping goods. Riordan knew that forestalling the cost of cleanup would make it easier for the region to capitalize on its strategic position as a port of entry on the Pacific Rim. In effect, America's growing trade deficit became an economic opportunity for Southern California that could replace the aerospace industry bust. With this in mind, the AQMD delayed the measures in 1994. However, the measures still hung like the guillotine over the head of the new import-driven regional economic development strategy.

So in 1997, while James Lents was preoccupied with saving his job, the city of L.A. struck again at the port measures, seeking to have them excised from the official clean air plan. Doing so would allow unbridled expansion of the ports of Los Angeles and Long Beach. Sympathizers with this plan at the AQMD found a willing ally in Barry Wallerstein, the agency's director of planning at the time. It was his job to update the 1997 clean air plan and to decide which measures were necessary and which were not. The first step in that process was to determine how much pollution the air could tolerate and still meet federal health standards, which is called the "carrying capacity" of the air. Wallerstein's staff ran a computer model that simulated the basin's environment, taking into account emissions of pollution in time and space, the region's geography, and the weather.

But Wallerstein's air modelers threw out the worst case-scenario weather that had historically been incorporated into these computer models to predict how much smog would form as emissions changed. The planning department basically assumed that the weather in the future would not be as stagnant as it had been in the past, and therefore would not promote the buildup of pollution as readily. Presto: they had dramatically increased the carrying capacity of the air basin. By eliminating the "worst case weather day" from their assumptions, they were able to create a model that showed the air could tolerate almost twice as much nitrogen oxide pollution—the key compound emitted by heavy duty diesel equipment—than what was shown by the modeling for the 1994 clean air plan. With the new modeling results in hand, the AQMD was able to eliminate calls for electrifying trains at the port, and a number of other tough and expensive steps for the international shipping industry.

In an unprecedented response, nine of the eleven members of the AQMD's outside scientific advisory panel resigned en masse, charging that the plan devised under the new model would not clean the air. They called the predictions underlying the plan unreliable.[2] The AQMD's board was unruffled. It largely ignored the independent scientists, and adopted the plan. Wallerstein defended it, saying it was based on "state-of-the-science analysis." For his efforts, when the AQMD board finally fired Lents that same year, they chose Wallerstein to replace him.[3]

Environmental groups soon sued to strengthen the plan and the groups reached a settlement in 1999, but by then the weak strategy had already done its damage to the cleanup effort. Progress in fighting smog had stagnated by 2000 and diesel pollution, by all measures, was growing worse.

The 1997 plan effectively set the stage for a huge expansion of international trade throughout the region. Immediately, port activity surged. Records show that since 1998, shipments through the twin ports of Los Angeles and Long Beach—the biggest in the nation—have doubled and are projected to quadruple in the next twenty years. Diesel emissions will increase dramatically unless major steps are taken to control them. Yet nobody has figured out how to reduce this health menace—only to keep it from growing any worse. And even that comes at a cost of billions of dollars, much of which California officials are planning to stick to the taxpayers. Long Beach mayor Bob Foster estimates it will cost $10 billion to bring to heel the air pollution mess at the ports.

*   *   *

The diesel cloud in port communities like Wilmington, California, represents a double pollution burden. Not only does the area suffer from the soot emitted by all of the trucks, trains, and equipment used in the surrounding port, but it also bears the burden of emissions from oil refineries. At night, the huge industrial complexes cast a strange flickering illumination in the sky with their glowing flares. Their rotten egg odor of hydrogen sulfide and heavy hydrocarbon fumes frequently hang in the air over this largely residential community, which is increasingly populated by low income Latino workers and their families.

In fact, the birth of environmental justice in Los Angeles might be traced to a gray Saturday in Wilmington in the early 1990s. That morning, people arrived in the parking lot of the Wilmington Elementary School for a meeting about pollution in their community. Down the quiet residential street on which the school stood, the Texaco refinery loomed in the background. Teachers, students, and parents all believed the giant industrial complex—with its pipes, tanks, boilers, and smokestacks that hissed and roared—was the source of the toxic fumes that had overwhelmed them. They came to the meeting for a chance to tell air pollution regulators face-to-face about the frequent odors that hung in the air on the campus. They came to tell about their illnesses, which they feared had been caused by air pollution from the refinery.

As people milled about the parking lot and auditorium waiting for the meeting to begin, two cars eventually pulled up to the school. Both were uncharacteristic in this dense working-class neighborhood lined with old cars and small houses. One was a shiny Mercedes Benz. The driver, Pat Nemeth, was a red-haired ex-nun in charge of industrial regulation and enforcement as an executive for the AQMD. Conservatively, yet sharply, dressed in a style native to the well-to-do Laguna Beach area where she lived, Nemeth came that day to defend her agency.

Next, gray-haired Eric Mann pulled up in his Lexus. Mann, tall and fond of wrinkled sport jackets and baggy pants, had been organizing the neighborhood along with a small band of activists to mount pressure on Nemeth and other air pollution regulators to clean up industrial pollution in places like Wilmington.

They entered the auditorium like opposing prize fighters. Nemeth—an architect known as the "dragon lady" by her staff because of her exacting expectations and controlling manner—led off with a presentation outlining the agency's regulatory plan and "process" for cleaning up pollution. Mann—a Cornell-educated figure whom industry lobbyists had dubbed a "Lexus liberal"—waited for his chance to attack. In a strong and insistent voice, he charged that while regulators were making progress on smog to help middle-class suburban folks in the San Fernando and San Gabriel valleys, they had neglected the toxic pollution that was causing cancer in poor and working-class neighborhoods in central Los Angeles County. Like Wilmington, these towns were mostly populated by racial minorities and surrounded by refineries, factories, power plants, and other industries. Not only were these neighborhoods subject to frequent puffs of hydrogen sulfide, which can quickly cause people to vomit and gasp for breath, but also to benzene and other cancer-causing chemicals emitted all day, every day, 365 days a year. Mann had studied the problem and published a book, *L.A.'s Lethal Air,* about it. He had assiduously organized the Wilmington neighborhood around toxic air pollution. That day, he caught Nemeth off guard. After that meeting, the air pollution regulators knew they had to address the issue Mann had raised and soon began working on studies of the toxic air pollution problem. Ultimately, though, the solutions would have to be approved by the political appointees on the agency's board.

*   *   *

Mann and his Labor Community Strategies Center, along with another grassroots California environmental organization known as Communities for a Better Environment, were creating a sea change in Los Angeles. They re-energized the environmental movement, which had grown stodgy and technocratic like the regulatory agencies charged with controlling pollution—fond of wool suits and overhead slide presentations. Together, the two small organizations walked neighborhoods and talked directly with residents to enlist new participants in the debate about air pollution.

They came from the gritty industrial hulk of Los Angeles, where Latinos and African Americans lived next to heavy industrial complexes and increasingly busy rail yards, freeways, and ports. Residents who became engaged wanted the AQMD to put an end to the soot and pollution that were causing an epidemic of disease in their communities, from cancer to asthma, and creating the injustice of unequal protection under clean air laws. The organizations and their members stood outside the mainstream of the environmental movement, lacking the expertise of the large environmental groups and the snappy ties of the corporate lobbyists who freely roamed the halls of the AQMD each day. But what they lacked in sophistication, they made up for in tenacity and boisterous enthusiasm. By late 1993, under the banner of "Environmental

Justice," this new movement had become a power that had begun to rival mainstream environmental groups.

This movement in Los Angeles arose against the backdrop of a hollowed-out industrial core, where residents received second-rate public services and education. There was little economic opportunity after President Reagan had broken the union movement in 1981. Economic internationalization and free-floating monetary exchange rates had begun to undermine the economies of old U.S. manufacturing areas like South Central Los Angeles. Large industrial plants that made tires, cars, steel, and other products closed down, unable to compete with the new imports arriving from Asia and Latin America. 75,000 jobs were lost in the area, most of them high-paying unionized positions. The community suffered as a result, seeing the rise of gangs, drug trafficking, and crime. Later in the 1980s a flood of immigrants from Central America came, seeking to escape the wars Reagan had supported in Nicaragua, Guatemala, and El Salvador. Desperate to support themselves, the new immigrants were easily exploited by businesses in the garment industry, one of the few remaining bastions of manufacturing in Los Angeles, and the growing service industry of hotels and restaurants catering to the wealthy. Meanwhile, the aerospace and defense industries boomed under Reagan's Strategic Defense Initiative buildup in the final push to win the Cold War with Russia. This created prosperity for much of Los Angeles, but also an increasing divide among the haves and have-nots. The result was an increasing frustration and social breakdown in the central core of Los Angeles, as the list of grievances grew longer and longer to include everything from a lack of health care, jobs, and parks, to crime and urban blight, not to mention pollution. Then, in 1992, an all-white jury acquitted Los Angeles police officers in the case of Rodney King. Los Angeles exploded into a rage that went on for days.

*   *   *

When the devastation resulting from those riots became clear, a major shift began in Los Angeles as minorities rose to power in the state legislature and on boards like the AQMD. The all-white agency began to change as new African-American, Asian, and Latino members, who were sympathetic to the environmental justice movement's push for more say over air quality policy, were appointed to the board. Key among them was an African-American man who had begun his long political career in the mail room at City Hall, a man on whom many activists and minority residents pinned their hopes: William Burke.

The issue came to a head one day in 1994, when the environmental justice activists organized by Mann and Communities for a Better Environment arrived at a hearing in the AQMD auditorium ready to fight—ready to charge the dais—in the name of cleaning up toxic pollution from factories around the Los Angeles area that the air district itself said would cause cancer in 10,000 people.

Unlike the neighborhood activists who had formed the environmental justice movement, William Burke had been able to successfully parlay his political connections into profit: he bought a silver Mercedes and a large yacht with proceeds from the Los Angeles Marathon, which he heads to this day. He used his access to corporate cash to wield political influence behind the scenes in the legislature and Los Angeles City Hall. However, on that day in 1994, Burke faced his first major decision on the AQMD board: whether or not to adopt a strict rule to cut toxic pollution. Would he be a man of the people, or a servant of the corporate barons who ruled the region's economy?

Clad in blue jeans and T-shirts, the boisterous crowd of workers, parents, and students waved signs and marched outside. They sensed that victory was within their reach.

But Burke surprised them. He cited the cost of the new rules to businesses and sided with the free-market capitalists. He backed a hollow alternative that required little, if any, action, by most factories for years to come. As Burke made his position clear, Labor Community Strategies Center organizer Chris Mathis, an African American who had brought scores of people to the hearing, marched to the front of the room and yelled, "You're no brother!" Burke lurched over the dais at him, shouting back, "Fuck you!" The hearing erupted into a near-riot until Los Angeles County sheriff's deputies rushed in and cleared the hall, bringing the meeting to a sudden close. Within months, the agency's board adopted rules prohibiting people from bringing signs into their meeting room, where they kept sheriffs stationed to quell any outbursts of emotion.[4] But they were not as quick to take any action at all against the cancer-causing pollutants in L.A.'s poorest neighborhoods.

*   *   *

Nearly ten years after that event, the toxic emissions causing ill health in urban communities and working-class suburbs remained largely unaddressed. Deep disparity in health protection under Los Angeles' clean air program continues to abound. Take the Maris Street neighborhood in the quiet city of Pico Rivera, east of downtown Los Angeles. Exhaust stacks of a large auto body repair and paint shop cast a shadow over the backyards of residents in this mostly Latino suburb. Residents complain of odors of paints and toxic solvents wafting into their yards, and they have organized a group known as "Residents of Pico Rivera for Environmental Justice."[5]

"The city planners do what they want, figuring people up here won't do very much," said Joe Caballero, a retired man who serves as vice president of the group. He became concerned about the facility when his two granddaughters, who lived in his home for many years, developed respiratory problems and eventually were diagnosed with asthma. For five years, the residents have been fighting to clean up the facility, which is only one of five auto body shops in a square-mile area full of homes and schools. They finally persuaded the AQMD to form a task force to address their concerns, but the facilities still operate amid their homes.[6]

Further east, in the heart of Los Angeles County's sprawling San Gabriel Valley—home to some two million people—lies the Torch Middle School in La Puente. The school is part of the Basset Unified School District, where officials have been worried for years about odors and emissions from a facility known as Light Metals, immediately adjacent to the south end of the campus. "I was concerned about the odor at the plant and I contacted AQMD and they have been monitoring the company since that time," said the school principal, Robert Nero.[7] However, AQMD officials never mentioned the cancer-causing hexavalent chromium emissions emanating from the metal plating facility just south of Light Metals. Nor did the company bother to inform the school district of its toxic emissions. The firm in question, Size Control Plating Co., Inc., which had imposed on its neighbors a cancer rate higher than 100 in a million, lies not only next to the Torch Magnet School, but just a couple doors west—upwind, that is—of a residential neighborhood.[8] Under air district rules, the plant was perfectly legal. That's because the district decided to exempt chromium plating plants from regulations requiring firms posing a cancer risk of greater than 10 in a million to notify their neighbors.[9] Under severe pressure by environmental justice groups, the air district finally ended the exemption for the company and other metal plating firms and forced them to take steps to reduce the cancer risk they imposed on their unknowing neighbors. But it took fifteen years of organizing by people like Cabellero, Nero, and countless others to bring about this change.

*   *   *

Years after his first betrayal of anti-smog activists, Burke still dominated the AQMD board, and environmental justice advocates still voiced many of the same complaints about the unbearable air pollution and odors in their neighborhoods. The record is mixed at best. To his credit, Burke worked hard to clean up diesel vehicles—from buses to trucks—a major cause of lung cancer and a prime concern for environmental justice advocates. However, the rules passed by the AQMD affected only a small fraction of these vehicles, leaving the vast majority untouched and failing to address the growth in their numbers. That growth quickly overwhelmed the benefits of the AQMD cleanup rules, which covered only government vehicles.

Mostly, Burke has remained a friend to business throughout his tenure on the AQMD board. Most telling, perhaps, was the day in 1999 when Burke intervened with the staff of the AQMD to support a bid by the televangelist Pat Robertson to reopen the closed-down Powerine oil refinery in the mostly Latino suburb of Santa Fe Springs. Environmental justice groups bitterly opposed this, but Burke called on the AQMD staff to move forward, which it did. It was only President Clinton's federal EPA that eventually squelched the project after finding that the AQMD under Burke had skirted the laws in reactivating permits for the closed-down facility, rather than making Robertson apply for fresh permits that would have required new pollution controls. It didn't matter much to Burke. For his trouble, the reverend already had given Burke a cut of a gold mine he owned in Liberia. To paraphrase that country western classic: Burke got the gold mine; the community got the shaft.[10]

That's why Angelo Logan, a young Latino man with a neatly trimmed beard, still complains about the pollution in the Bandini neighborhood where he grew up just off Washington Boulevard in the City of Commerce. The area lies just south of downtown Los Angeles, and at 8:30 a.m. on a weekday it looks like many other residential areas in Southern California. Rows of houses with well-trimmed lawns line the streets. People drive their cars to work. Things are quiet at the local elementary school, the children settling down for the morning lesson.

However, residing in Bandini is far different from living in most other places in California. Pollution is actually increasing in this city. Just beyond the neighborhood's residential streets lie two of the busiest intermodal shipping facilities in the nation—one operated by the Burlington Northern Santa Fe Railroad and the other by the Union Pacific Railroad. More than 30,000 trucks rumble through this neighborhood to its rail yards each day, spewing diesel soot all the way. From the ports of Los Angeles and Long Beach, they carry shipping containers full of goods once made in Los Angeles, now made in China. The neighborhood also lies along Interstate 710, a freeway that the California Department of Transportation has proposed double-decking with special lanes to accommodate a projected doubling of freight trucks serving the port complex over the next decade.

The environmental assault is palpable in Logan's home neighborhood. The freeway roars, trucks rumble along Washington Boulevard, diesel train engines hum, bright lights in the train yards illuminate the area like a football stadium at night, and, even on a blustery day, the acrid odor of diesel exhaust pervades the air. Just west, on Washington Boulevard, stands a row of factories, including a chemical plant, a chrome-plating shop, and two lead-smelting companies. To the east, a refuse-to-energy facility burns garbage across the street from apartments. Chemical drum recycling shops, with barrels stacked two stories high, are tucked between the factories. Across from the Burlington Northern Santa Fe yard is a large animal-rendering plant. Drivers on the congested boulevard can smell whiffs of odors from the plants, as well an indescribable stench that covers a wide area—perhaps from the rendering plant, which processes the carcasses of dead cows into meal for pet food and tallow for candles.

In the Bandini neighborhood, the 2000 census showed that residents are ninety-five percent Latino, predominantly speak Spanish, have a median annual household income of $33,065, and have a one-in-five chance of living below the poverty line. Despite Burke's promises to help such folks, Bandini remains a forgotten pocket under a heavy bombardment of toxic air pollutants. "Health should be a priority and commerce should be secondary," says Logan, who has organized Bandini residents into a group known as the East Yard Communities for Environmental Justice. "I grew up in the neighborhood. A lot of my family and friends were sick. Even as a young child I noticed that this is not a normal environment. The pollution in this area was disproportionate to other neighborhoods."[11]

Unfortunately, even after fifteen years of "environmental justice," Bandini is hardly the only such neighborhood in the

Los Angeles area. It is only one of countless communities in which one of every 250 people will get cancer due to the heavy assault of diesel soot and other toxic compounds from traffic, factories, and shipping yards. Industries and government agencies have found it easier to locate polluting facilities in poor communities because their residents lack the political clout of upscale communities. "Political power matters," says Manuel Pastor, an economist at the University of California at Santa Cruz who directs the Center for Justice, Tolerance, and Community. He has studied the pattern of the location of hazardous waste facility sites and factories that emit toxic pollution in California, and as he puts it: "No matter how you slice or dice it, there's a racial disparity."[12]

To achieve equality, the environmental justice groups have long argued for a more holistic approach to environmental protection, one which goes beyond setting limits for individual pollutants and facilities in isolation. Standards, they argue, must take into account the cumulative effect of all pollutants in the environment. An AQMD study published in 2000 showed wide disparities in the risk of cancer from outdoor air pollution in the sprawling region of fourteen million people. The lifetime cancer risk ranged from as high as 1,700 cases per million residents in highly toxic neighborhoods to as low as about 300 per million in affluent Malibu Beach. The finding, later revised upward for areas around the region's ports, has led the AQMD to discuss how to set an acceptable level of cumulative health risk from toxic air pollution like diesel soot, and a series of new requirements to be imposed on sources of air pollution when that level is exceeded in individual neighborhoods. One option for reducing excessive cumulative risk would be tighter restrictions placed on businesses in polluted areas than those applied to the same types of businesses operating in cleaner areas. Businesses seeking to locate in areas with high cumulative risk could be rejected, or they might face extra requirements, which in some cases may make it more economical to locate in a cleaner location.

However, the discussions have been under way since 2002. Nothing substantive has happened yet because environmental justice advocates face a powerful array of vested interests. California businesses claim they are not convinced that the assessments will show any disproportionate pollution exposure among low income, minority neighborhoods, now commonly known in air pollution discussions as "environmental justice communities."

"It is important to determine if there are communities being exposed to a much higher level of pollution," acknowledges Cindy Tuck, former general counsel for the California Council for Environmental and Economic Balance, and now a high-level official with the California Environmental Protection Agency. The council, which former California governor Edmund Brown, Sr., helped form, is a consortium of big industries and labor unions that maintains that the movement for clean air must be tempered by economic considerations. Business representatives like Tuck believe that environmental agencies should carefully identify which communities actually bear disproportionate exposures to toxic pollutants before rushing to regulate them. She warns that unless good data on cumulative exposure is developed, any new rule could have "a very serious impact on jobs and new businesses."[13]

Environmental justice advocates have had some successes, though. In 1999, the state enacted a law requiring "fair treatment of people of all races, cultures, and income levels, including minority populations and low-income populations." In 2000, the legislature required the California EPA to identify

and address environmental justice "gaps" in existing programs. This has resulted in an effort to determine the cumulative exposure to toxic pollutants that Californians receive in
the food, water, and air.

In response to the new legislation, state environmental regulators pledged to do a better job of integrating environmental
impacts with land-use decision making in the years ahead.
"Almost all of the decisions that are most damaging are made
at the local level by city councils and county boards of supervisors," notes attorney Luke Cole, an environmental justice
advocate. Likewise, the AQMD has promised to badger local
land-use decision makers to avoid locating toxic facilities next
to residences, schools, and hospitals.

Still, despite the state laws and pledges by agencies, not
much has changed. Drive around Los Angeles and you'll see
plenty of housing tracts right next to freeways, and it is not
unusual to find day-care centers next to gas stations and
"risky" businesses.[14]

In the final analysis, state and regional environmental
agencies have only an advisory role in land-use decision
making. That's why so many environmental injustices
abound today. Unless the legislature changes the law, and
nobody is standing up to do so, local city councils and county boards of supervisors will continue to have the final say on
projects, and developers will continue to wield what many
see as undue influence at city and county hall. The forces of
economic growth will always have the upper hand, particularly when people like William Burke are regulating L.A.'s air
pollution.

So as time marches on, Pico Rivera's Joe Caballero,
Bandini's Angelo Logan, Torch Magnet School's Robert Nero,
and hundreds of other neighborhood activists continue to toil

in the shaft of highly polluted working-class and poor neighborhoods in Los Angeles, hoping to turn them into gardens of environmental justice that will bring a sweet harvest of improved health, at least for their children. Meanwhile, Burke and other politicians pay lip service to their cause, but then get back to tending their gold mines, both literal and figurative.

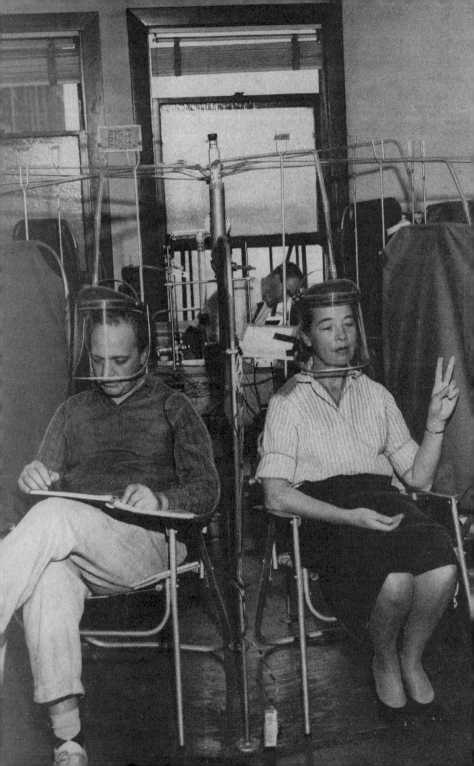

13
ACTION HEROES?

IN 2003, A NEW FIGURE BURST ONTO THE SCENE IN CALIFORNIA. He was an unlikely leader for the environmental movement, known more for his muscles and equally oversized cars than for his green thumb. It was none other than Arnold Schwarzenegger, the Hollywood action hero who ran and won on the Republican ticket against Governor Gray Davis in the 2003 recall election. Environmentalists decried the recall of Davis and announced themselves as sworn opponents of Schwarzenegger. Soon, though, he'd make them change their tune. That's because the Terminator had a surprise up his sleeve. At a press conference near Santa Barbara, in the heat of the election campaign, Schwarzenegger unveiled a hydrogen-fueled Hummer, declaring himself a converted environmentalist. The actor-turned-activist outlined an ambitious plan to move away from petroleum. His vision, heavily influenced by his wife Maria Shriver, would accomplish two major goals. It would seek to end the scourge of air pollution once and for all and to attack the phenomenon of global warming head-on.

Schwarzenegger announced himself as an environmentalist sixty years after smog first seized Los Angeles. By many accounts, the region had made remarkable progress cleaning

up the air, even though much work remained. Days exceeding
the old one-hour federal ozone standard had fallen to 68 a year,
compared to 124 in 1993 and 152 in 1983. Key to the progress
were not only controls on so-called "stationary sources of air
pollution and consumer products," but also standards that the
California Air Resources Board set during the 1990s for motor
vehicle emissions and cleaner gasoline. The electric vehicle
never materialized, but the low emissions vehicle standards
set by the state board, coupled with a standard requiring refiners to produce cleaner-burning gasoline in the mid-1990s, have
cut the amount of pollution the average new car emits today by
ninety percent from the level in 1990. Overall, the cumulative
effect of California motor vehicle standards since the state air
board was formed is that cars today emit ninety-nine percent
less measured pollution when they roll off the assembly line
than cars made before that time. Of course, the vehicle emissions controls degrade over time. The progress has also been
tempered by growth. The population of people owning cars
has increased some five-fold and the number of miles driven
has exploded due to suburbanization and long distance commutes in the L.A. region. Also, there are more trucks, aircraft,
trains, ships, and construction equipment in the area, all of
which still have relatively dirty engines and have been subject
to less regulation than passenger cars.

And science shows that air pollution is worse than previously believed. Scientists have delved further into the
chemistry of airborne pollutants and how they act in the
body to reveal dark realities. In the seventh decade of L.A.'s
struggle with air pollution, doctors have learned that smog is
responsible for a growing list of health ills: stunting children's lungs, contributing to asthma and heart attacks, and
weakening the immune system. Studies show that pollution

still kills 9,600 people a year statewide, the vast majority of them in greater Los Angeles. The chief culprit in the deaths is not ozone, the target of so many of the region's pollution control efforts for decades, but ultra-fine particles that carry molecules of toxic, cancer-causing chemicals, like benzene, right through the tissue of the lung into the body. Once in, they create a wide variety of biochemical reactions that can lead to heart attacks, strokes, respiratory diseases, and cancer. They are even suspected of contributing to Alzheimer's disease. In areas around the busy ports, like Long Beach, scientists expect that one in every two hundred residents will ultimately succumb to cancer just from the involuntary act of breathing the air in their home. The particles—invisible to the eye, part liquid and part solid—are blown out of tailpipes and smokestacks, forming an aerosol, much like that from a spray can. They are so small that as many as a million can be contained in the amount of air that could fit inside a marble. Moreover, their level in the air has been increasing in many areas since 1997, due largely to increasing traffic volume. Automotive pollution control equipment appears to be ineffective at controlling these tiny particles, for which there are no vehicle emissions standards or applicable measurements. Some suspect this equipment might even increase their production in exhaust from internal combustion engines. Ozone may be down, but ultra-fine particles represent possibly the worst element of pollution.[1]

Los Angeles is hardly alone: the ultra-fine particles are a national problem, particularly in urban areas with heavy traffic. Scientists are just beginning to understand these tiny culprits and search for ways to control them.[2] Meanwhile, ozone is a worse respiratory irritant than initially thought. Ongoing studies of the pungent gas led the EPA to tighten the ozone health standard in 1997. The studies showed that that the federal agency's one-hour standard was not protective enough of human health. Eleven years later, the agency further lowered that standard based on more recent medical evidence showing that ozone much above background levels in the atmosphere harms human health.

Even though the problem of smog remains only partially solved, Californians—even the environmentalists among them—seem to have largely forgotten about air pollution as they take up a new cause: global warming.

After winning the election against Davis, Schwarzenegger took the national environmental movement by storm, championing renewable energy, alternative fuels, and the nation's first legislation to fight climate change. However, as his environmental agencies began to struggle with how to reduce greenhouse gas emissions, it became increasingly evident that previous decisions in the war against smog have hemmed these efforts in at the start of a new century. Just as Los Angeles had been the template for creating smog, it now represents "the perfect storm" in a warming world.

It could have been different. Los Angeles could have turned toward a different lifestyle and become like a Mediterranean city after the first smog siege, with rich urban neighborhoods where people walk on the promenade at night. Instead, Angelenos bought into the idea that suburban living—with two cars in every garage—marked progress, as General Electric and Ronald Reagan insisted. More gadgets marked the advancement of civilization. The monumental and seemingly immovable edifice of this corporate-driven culture again and again forced Los Angeles smog warriors to rely largely on technological weapons against air pollution. This way they could let Angelenos persist in their dreamlike state, pursuing a subur-

ban Eden, predicated on the notion of an everlasting entitle-
ment to cheap resources and a conviction that bigger lifestyles
and more consumption are the mark of both individual and
cultural superiority.

Today, we have almost completely tapped the last vein of
technology to reduce smog-forming pollution in an economy
that remains almost totally dependent upon fossil fuels. So
with the ensuing growth, not only does the air pollution
remain, but so do huge volumes of greenhouse gas emissions,
which are wreaking havoc on Earth's climate. Global warming, like much of the remaining smog in Los Angeles, stems
from suburban land-use patterns: lifestyles organized around
freeways and cars and a preoccupation with shopping at malls
for cheap goods, produced in factories powered by coal and
shipped across the ocean, burning fossil fuel all the way. The
sixty-year pattern of suburban development that is synonymous with Los Angeles is creeping farther and farther inland
into hot desert areas, where land is cheap. In these communities, Angelenos can afford to buy large tract homes at affordable prices. As long as they can own a single-family home
with a backyard, they put up with traffic that is jammed from
the moment they get onto the freeway until they get all the
way to their distant jobs. It is not unusual for people to commute 40, 50, even 80 miles one-way to work. Understandably,
these commuters have developed a taste for big, comfortable
vehicles, even though they get terrible mileage and emit huge
quantities of greenhouse gases, as well as more smog-forming
air pollutants. Altogether, their big air-conditioned homes,
large cars, and long commutes have exploded energy use, off-
setting in part not only the benefits of cleaner cars and power
plants under air pollution rules, but also causing emissions of
carbon dioxide to grow. Throw in the penchant for buying

goods shipped from halfway around the world, and it's easy to see why people in poor nations tell places like Los Angeles to get their own house in order before talking to them about the need to cut greenhouse gas emissions. It all adds up to make the average Angeleno responsible for ten times more greenhouse gas emissions per capita than the average person in the world.[3] Like smog, greenhouse gases are one of the major by-products of the deeply entrenched culture and economy of Los Angeles—the continuation of which is heavily aided and abetted by carmakers, oil companies, home builders, banks, and major retail chains. State politicians and regulators still claim that global warming can be easily solved at little or no expense, just as they claimed smog could be quickly eliminated three generations ago. The technology is at hand, they promise. Little will be required of individuals to meet the state law's dramatic goals of cutting greenhouse gases by thirty percent by 2020 and eighty percent by 2050. All people will have to do is use all the available technology. As they do, the economy will grow, as will lifestyles. Nobody will have to sacrifice.

Yet the road may not be so easy. Researchers at Princeton have outlined how to reduce emissions enough to keep the Earth's average temperature from rising by more than 3.6 degrees over the next fifty years. Cars will have to get the equivalent of sixty miles per gallon. Average auto usage will have to decline to 5,000 miles a year. Reliance on wind and solar energy will have to be increased by 2,500 and 70,000 percent, respectively. Coal power plants, including those in the deserts of Utah, New Mexico, and Arizona that serve Los Angeles, will have to be closed down. Massive amounts of cropland will have to be converted to growing plants from which ethanol and other biofuels can be made. Additional wind-power farms will have to be erected to make hydrogen out of water to power many vehicles. A conversion to organic farming will be necessary. Beyond fifty years, new technologies will be needed to stabilize the world's climate.[4] In response to climate change, California's leaders again beat the drum for more fuel-efficient vehicles, energy-efficient appliances, solar energy, and "smart growth" favoring density and public transit over sprawl. Yet in their fight to control global warming, everything old is new again. They find themselves revisiting many of the same roads they walked in the war against smog, seizing upon ideas expressed twenty years ago in James Lents' "The Path to Clean Air." They return even to the environmental ideas championed during the energy and environmental crisis of the 1970s, when motorists lined up for gas and the air hung heavy with a hydrocarbon haze.

Even some of the same characters are involved. In Washington, Representative John Dingell (D-Michigan) is again reticent to let California enforce its own emissions standards on autos, this time resisting the state's plan to limit greenhouse gas emissions from tailpipes. Jerry Brown is back, too, now as California Attorney General. He has filed a series of lawsuits against cities to force them to reduce auto use and suburban sprawl. Early on in the office, he scored a small success in settling a case with San Bernardino County, one of the fastest-growing areas in California, where suburbanization is spreading between Los Angeles and Las Vegas. The county has agreed to pursue higher-density development, fees on developers to help fund public transit, better energy efficiency in buildings, and solar rooftops on new homes.[5] It will be helpful, but in a county where people frequently must drive five miles to get a loaf of bread and commute over a mountain range to make a living, that help will be limited. Few seem likely to ride public transit. Moreover, no matter how energy efficient, each new home represents an increase in greenhouse gas emissions.

The reality is that just as in the war against smog, growth remains the double-edged sword of global warming. Without it, it is difficult for environmentalists to make progress because businesses faced with the cost of cleanup complain to politicians, who put the kibosh on regulators. With growth, for every two steps forward, the environment takes at least one step back.

That doesn't stop politicians from striking the confident pose for the camera, though. California's photogenic governor plans to harness the power of the market to provide incentives for reducing greenhouse gases. Regulators are busy developing the ground rules for an emissions trading program, not unlike the one put in place in the hopes of controlling smog in Los Angeles fifteen years earlier. The concept at that time was sound in principle, perhaps, but its administration had problems because of politics. Under pressure from business in the midst of a recession, the AQMD handed out grossly inflated quantities of credits to power plant operators and other industries. With more than enough credits in hand when the program began, companies simply used credits to cover their emissions instead of cleaning up. Soon companies exceeded emissions standards under the trading scheme, which also was dogged by fraud. It left many companies asking where their clean-air money went.

In the worst case, Anne Sholtz, the once-hard-charging credit broker convicted of wire fraud, was interested in a lot more than RECLAIM trades, documents indicate. EPA investigators and other officials, in fact, contend she was involved with big-money international financial schemes using federal-reserve notes, currency, gold, and high-yield investment programs, among others.[6]

Sholtz in 1998 even tried to ferry "gold and currency" into the United States under cover of a diplomatic flight from the Philippines, according to records pieced together by the lawyer for the court-appointed bankruptcy trustee in her case. To finance this venture, Sholtz sold RECLAIM credits belonging to Chevron, Mobil, and Aera Energy to Southern California Edison. (Chevron and Mobil were unaware of the missing credits until later.) With the nearly $2 million from Edison, Sholtz then paid three outfits—including a Philippine holding company and charter airline, "Air America Holdings, Inc."—to execute the operation.[7] "Operation Bald Headed Eagle" was its name.

For the trip to bring $20 million into the U.S., Air America Holdings wanted $500,000.[8] The records don't address whether the outfit was connected with Air America, the charter airline that the CIA secretly owned and operated to supplement military operations during the Cold War. The airline was especially active—and controversial—in Laos during the Vietnam War. Similarly, the records don't specify whether it was cash or gold she was attempting to snatch.

Either way, Sholtz tried orchestrating the flight—or a series of them—through "Gold Ray Group Limited," which she described as "an international charitable organization" registered with the United Nations out of the Caribbean island of Nevis.[9] She expected the plane would receive special handling in the Philippines. In her instructions to the holding company about the Manila-Las Vegas trip, Sholtz stressed the goods-carrying plane should not be subject to inspection by customs or immigration officials because it was a "diplomatic flight."[10] Everything was ready in Nevada. "The items and personnel flying to Las Vegas will do so under a specially arranged entrance/exit system," she wrote, referencing an earlier Air America memo that she said a "special person" signed. "You can rest assured that all precautions have been taken to assure not only your safe passage but also your security while in our country."[11]

Evidently, Operation Bald Headed Eagle never panned out, and it's not apparent if Sholtz herself was conned. The Justice Department never charged her for her role in it, meaning local air regulators probably didn't know about the clandestine scheme. Besides, by Fall 1999 Sholtz had a different destination in mind. Organizers of a United Nations conference on climate change in Bonn, Germany listed her as a participant under the auspices of an emissions-marketing organization.[12]

As her actions telegraph, there can't be a respected pollution market for greenhouse gases or smog-constituents without foolproof policing to keep criminal activity from ruining its legitimacy. Carbon markets may hinge on it.

Today, the emissions trading program being developed by California regulators to control greenhouse gas emissions will be even more complicated than the one developed by the AQMD. Not only must it control emissions within California, but also at power plants outside the state that feed Los Angeles and other major California cities. Moreover, the trading program is likely to allow for so-called "emissions offset projects" carried out, perhaps, anywhere in the world. Some envision, for instance, that to offset its emissions, a company in California could plant trees in the jungle of Central America or seed the middle of the Pacific Ocean with plankton to absorb the same amount of carbon dioxide from the atmosphere that it emits. But California officials would have to police these distant projects to make sure that the trees and plankton were actually planted and remained living for generations to come.

In a proposal equally reminiscent of some of the early grandiose schemes to rid Los Angeles of smog, the Palo Alto Research Center (owned by Xerox) has suggested that California environmental officials help fund development of a machine that could extract carbon dioxide from the atmosphere. The carbon dioxide then would be permanently stored underground or converted into methanol to be used as a transportation fuel. The project would cost about $1 billion, and would involve using 19.3 square miles of membrane packed into cylinders that would effectively filter the carbon dioxide out of the air. It would be designed to capture as much carbon dioxide as is produced by burning the greenhouse gases from the gasoline made at an average-sized oil refinery each day. But it is dubious whether the plant actually would be able to reduce carbon dioxide levels in the atmosphere unless it was run with nuclear power or renewable energy. Otherwise, the laws of thermodynamics show it to be a net energy user and a net carbon dioxide emitter.

In addition, the trading program Schwarzenegger favors must control so-called "leakage," meaning the shift of production of power, cement, and myriad goods and crops out of state to evade the law's emissions limits. Leakage could result not only in increased greenhouse gas emissions, but also higher levels of ozone and other pollutants in the ocean breeze. Already, that breeze at times contains ozone equivalent to almost half the level allowed under the federal health standard. And finally, in the face of industries able to move willy-nilly to other states or nations, in the next

economic downturn it seems doubtful regulators and politicians will be able to stand up to businesses when they claim
they cannot afford to reduce emissions. Instead, history is
likely to repeat itself. Just as regulators and politicians
backed off on smog, they are likely to back off on greenhouse gas emissions.

Schwarzenegger also has called for a low carbon fuel standard as a way to reduce greenhouse gas emissions from cars.
The standard might be a boon to plug-in hybrid vehicles,
which can run on batteries charged up off the grid for the average daily commute in Los Angeles and draw on auxiliary gasoline-powered engines for longer trips. Plug-in electric vehicles,
which now are custom-made, use technology developed during the state's press to commercialize battery electric vehicles,
like the GM EV1. But it appears that the low carbon fuel standard will be heavily weighted toward ethanol, most of it made
from corn at first.

In favoring ethanol, California is not alone. In the face of
rising gas prices and limited supplies of oil, like the rest of
the nation, the Golden State is making a major turn toward
ethanol without fully examining the health and economic
consequences. Ethanol proponents are creating the mistaken
perception that biofuels can lead the way toward energy
independence and that they emit less of the carbon dioxide
that causes global warming. Yet rapid growth of the heavily
subsidized ethanol industry will lead to higher food prices,
overuse of water, water pollution, and soil erosion. And it
will not help clean the air. It could even increase air pollution, particularly in smog-clouded Los Angeles. A Stanford
University study found that ethanol poses the same health
risks—or ones that are even worse—as gasoline.[13] Ethanol-
fueled cars also get poorer mileage than gas-powered cars—

up to twenty-five percent worse—and a gallon of ethanol costs roughly the same as a gallon of gasoline. Summing up the case against ethanol, Earth Policy Institute president Lester Brown says, "Ethanol euphoria is not an acceptable substitute for a carefully-thought-through policy. Do we really want to subsidize a rise in food prices?" With increased demand for ethanol, corn prices doubled from 2006 to 2007 on the world market, triggering tortilla riots in Mexico.[14] Undaunted, state politicians remain convinced that ethanol will bring quick cuts in greenhouse gases. Recent legislative handouts include the approval of millions of dollars in direct subsidies to the ethanol industry under jacked-up fees on state motorists for smog checks and car registrations, and an easing of clean air standards, not to mention the "Governator's" order that the California Air Resources Board adopt preferences for low carbon fuels. These favors for ethanol come even after studies by the state air board showed that boosting the amount of ethanol in gasoline to ten percent will increase hydrocarbon emissions by 118 tons a day during the summer. In the smoggy Los Angeles area, the increase could be as great as forty-two tons a day, more than four percent. The studies also found that emissions of toxic pollutants, including cancer-causing benzene, would increase under some weather conditions. Finally, more ethanol in gasoline is expected to increase nitrogen oxide emissions, which form not only ozone but also dangerous fine-particle pollution in the air. Statewide emissions are expected to grow by twenty-one tons a day and by eight tons a day in Los Angeles, a boost of almost one percent. Aside from making the air over Los Angeles more dangerous, the increase of ethanol content in gasoline also will cost motorists an extra $600 million a year, about $36 per driver, because it will cut mileage by 1.3 percent, according to the air board. Convinced that more ethanol will cut greenhouse gas emissions, though, the board changed its fuel regulations to lift the cap on the amount of ethanol allowed in gasoline from six percent to ten percent. The change will allow sales of ethanol to go from 900 million to 1.5 billion gallons a year, enough to support as many as twelve new ethanol plants in California, which typically produce fifty million gallons a year. One farmer has proposed plants that would convert one-third of the farmland in the Imperial Valley near Los Angeles to grow sugar cane for ethanol. The vegetables now grown there during the winter— lettuce, asparagus, broccoli, and many others—would instead be grown abroad and shipped to Los Angeles and other markets on ships, blowing out greenhouse gases all the way across the ocean. They may well be grown on land cleared of forests for that purpose, thereby releasing a torrent of carbon dioxide to the atmosphere. Once the low carbon fuel standard is written and put in place, regulators are likely to further raise the limit on the blend of ethanol in gasoline to fifteen percent or more, requiring even more farmland to grow crops to make the biofuel and emitting even more smog-forming pollutants, if not even more greenhouse gases.[15] The addition of ethanol, however, is unlikely to reduce the amount of gasoline state motorists actually burn, only prevent it from growing, as auto use is projected to increase and, likewise, demand for motor fuel. Ethanol is little more than a scheme to allow the continual spread of the suburban culture for which L.A. is both renowned and reviled.

In fact, demand for energy is growing so rapidly that state energy officials have voiced concerns about a new energy supply crisis in California. To clear the decks for new supplies of fossil fuels, AQMD officials are making air credits available to energy companies so they can build new power plants and new liquefied natural gas and oil import facilities at the region's ports. In 2007, Los Angeles area air quality regulators made the same pollution credits available to a number of gas-fired power plants. They plan to extend the credits to oil and natural gas import terminals soon. The companies need the credits under the federal Clean Air Act, which specifies that industrial projects only can be built or expanded in smoggy areas if they line up credits for smog-forming emissions. The companies can either purchase the credits on the open market from others who have over-controlled their emissions, or earn them by cutting their own emissions more than required at an existing plant. But now the AQMD has opened up a pool of credits for these highly profitable energy companies, a pool that is normally reserved for essential public services provided by the government. Reluctant to stand in the way of an adequate supply of fossil fuels for Angelenos, the smog fighters eased their rules for the energy industry, just when the credit shortage would have forced energy firms to make major investments in renewable power to meet new demand. If they had stood their ground, the price of gasoline might have gone up and begun to hem in the suburban sprawl that is the source of so much air pollution and greenhouse gas emissions.

At least a couple AQMD board members complained. One member, Jane Carney, voiced concern about making the credits available for fossil fuel plants when there are doubts about how much power the region will need. She cited competing proposals to develop renewable energy, build new transmission lines, and increase energy-efficiency programs. "I don't think it's right for these pollutants to be put into the basin absent the showing of an energy crisis," said Carney. Board member Joe Lyou—an environmental justice advocate whom

Schwarzenegger had just appointed to the board—denounced the plan as an unfair subsidy for fossil fuel plant builders. Just as prices for pollution credits were going up and tilting the power market in favor of renewable energy and energy efficiency, he observed, the air district was changing the rules to give fossil fuel plants a break. "I don't think it's fair to the alternative energy providers," said Lyou. "They don't get the certainty they need."[16] However, board chair William Burke brushed aside their complaints, saying they did not constitute any major concern because "the marketplace" will prevent projects from producing excess power and pollution. "As our region continues to grow, we will need more clean energy to prevent rolling blackouts," said Burke.[17] The amendments were approved by an eight-to-three vote.

Right now, panic is building about global warming after Hurricane Katrina, extreme summer heat in California, pictures of glaciers collapsing into the ocean, etc. The state has little choice in confronting the issue, just as it was forced to confront smog in the 1940s. Global warming is actually increasing smog in California in strange ways. Summer "heat storms" are increasing the demand for electricity to power air conditioners. It is a matter of life and death for some, as in each of the past two summers people living with no air conditioning died when temperatures soared as high as 116 degrees in coastal valleys. The increased use of power forces electricity makers to turn on fossil-fueled peaking power plants that increase emissions of smog-forming pollution and greenhouse gases. Hotter weather increases the need for water, too, which must be pumped out of wells or over mountains to keep lawns and crops growing. This requires burning more fossil fuel, sending more emissions into the air. Watersheds are threatened in California as less precipitation falls. Increasingly, there is rain in the winter instead of snow, and that rain must be released from dams to prevent flooding. While snow would normally have been stored in the mountains well into the summer, now the precipitation runs to the ocean, so California has less stored water. This requires more energy to pump water or to recycle it within cities. Likewise, rising sea levels threaten to make the Sacramento-San Joaquin River Delta—the source of much of the state's fresh water—salty. Solving this problem will require more energy to filter the water in a state that already uses more than twenty percent of its energy to supply and treat water.

So as California stands at the crossroads trying to solve its remaining air pollution problems and tackle global warming, it faces difficult choices, many of which it has faced before. The challenge of paring back auto use in the heart of the car culture cannot be underestimated. It spells the end of the cherished suburban lifestyle for large portions of the middle class. Will politicians be more successful in getting Angelenos and other residents to make personal changes than they have been in the war on smog? Only time will tell. Ultimately, though, it must be the people of Los Angeles who become action heroes and agents of change to bring about an end to air pollution and a solution to global warming. If, instead, the people act as they have in the past, Angelenos are likely to keep driving their cars to the detriment of their own health, the well being of people around the globe, and the long-term welfare of their own beloved children.

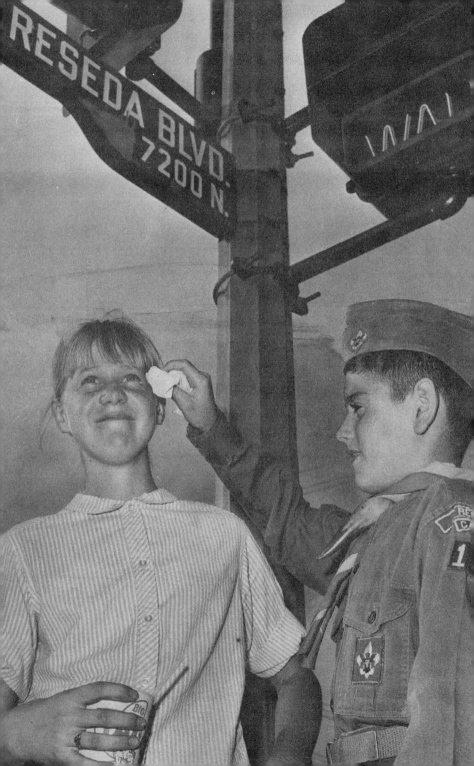

EPILOGUE:
CONJURING
HAAGY'S GHOST

As we draw the curtain on Smogtown, let us first pause for a moment of respiratory delirium. Southern Californians today can breathe easier than at any time since the beastly murk engulfed the West Coast's glamour city that fateful day in 1943. Ozone levels are one-third what they were in the chaotic 1950s. Where parts of the region once smashed federal health standards more than two-thirds of the year, the "bad" days now represent just about a quarter of the calendar. Where a low-lying ceiling of unburned exhaust regularly chafed the bodies and psyches of millions of suburbanites along the planet's first "smog belt," the gauzy blue sky there today is not a mirage.[1] Sure, Los Angeles remains stuck wearing the crown of America's metropolitan air-pollution capital. Just like yesteryear, the skyline and hills occasionally vanish behind that familiar russet patina. Yet, Smogtown's sixty-five years of revolutionary gadgetry, civic feistiness, hard-won regulation, and population survival constitute an enormous success, no matter its overshadowing by global warming and other scourges of modern civilization.

While inhaling is no longer the residential hazard that it once was, it doesn't mean the enemy has hit the bricks—not as long as our lifestyle remains auto-centric and technology-dependent. Rachel Carson's screed in *Silent Spring* over pesticide damage might've been written about the West Coast atmosphere. "As crude a weapon as the cave man's club, the chemical barrage has been hurled against the fabric of life—a fabric on one hand delicate and destructible, on the other miraculously tough and resilient, and capable of striking back in unexpected ways."[2] L.A.'s sixty years of pollution trauma bears witness to that: overload the ecosystem and hide for cover. Distressingly, even in the age of the Prius and the green factory, there's still no guarantee the L.A. area will fully meet state and federal clean air goals by 2023. There's no such doubt, conversely about air pollution's ongoing chockhold on health—or the public kitty. The airshed remains lethal. A power crisis here, a spurt of new autos there, and the beast has shown it will lunge again. In 2004 alone, treating air-pollution-inflamed heart disease, asthma, bronchitis, and the like cost Californians $22 billion. Just breathing fine particulates, even at levels below national standards, can strip two years off your life expectancy, a Harvard University study that followed people for sixteen years concluded. Those microscopic pebbles also can instigate strokes, aggravate diabetes, and who knows what else.

Essentially, what doctors have managed with some cancers and other awful diseases, we have managed to do with smog. Unable—or, more truthfully, unwilling—to vanquish it by shucking off our contaminating routines, we have learned to coexist with our filth. Look no further than the mega-sized ports of Los Angeles and Long Beach. They are way stations for the global goods-movement in a Wal-Mart world and the Southland's largest fixed source of pollution, including diesel particulates identified as cancer-causing years back. It is here history and karma meet. Partly because of stringent clean-air regulations, Southern California saw much of its manufacturing base head to the Far East. Yet now, we grapple with the emissions from cargo ships ferrying cheap exports *back* to the West Coast. We breathe carbon-soot over the Pacific from the industrializing Far East. Just as *made-in-L.A.* smog infected neighboring cities and states long ago, Angelenos are now getting what they gave, and just as a new population boom is underway.

The parallels with global warming are alarming. Both arise from mankind's dependence on emission-disgorging machines. Both threaten, albeit in different ways, how societies organize their cities, workforces, and economic production. Both offer us opportunities to re-imagine how we commute, electrify, manufacture, and achieve energy independence shorn of bloodshed and class strife. If the world misses the lessons from air pollution's beachhead as it races to slash greenhouse gases melting the Arctic and intensifying weather disasters, won't those chest-throbbing years in sun-shanghaied Los Angeles have been in vain?

The old ways don't cut it anymore. You can't maintain a healthful airshed in a horizontally configured juggernaut like L.A. if the fumes from its millions of cars don't billow away naturally. You can't hound manufacturers pushed to their technological cracking point without consistently requiring the citizenry to offer a proportional sacrifice. And you can't expect quantum gains without an engaged national government hellbent to put the people's health and welfare ahead of corporate agendas. Don't blame automakers, whose core mission is to profit from product sales, for resistance or attempts to influence science. Question what created the vacuum that allowed Detroit to manipulate and colonize the Los Angeles car market. West Coast scientists in the 1940s suspected the internal combustion engine was smog's parent, and with braver leadership, we could've been on our third or fourth generation of clean-running vehicles by now. It's always the people who pay one-way or another, anyhow. The twenty or so years of denial and delay in regulating automobile exhaust have trans-lated into omnipresent taxes on the average Southern Californian (at the gas pump, at the smog-check station), in consumer products yanked from stores (wood-burning fire-places, oil-based paints, old-style lighter fluid) and in their skyrocketing healthcare premiums. Call it the Smogtown law of trickle-down levies. Pinched as we are today, we at least should be grateful that by the late 1950s, the politicians got out of the way and let the science illuminate how we set the tropo-sphere against ourselves. From the old APCD came a smog chamber full of discoveries that rolled out faster than society's ability to accept them. But the turmoil was everlasting in the death of local agriculture, in the loss of good, blue collar jobs evident in the LA riots, in sowing mistrust between people and their government, in private miseries of folks dying in anony-mous hospital rooms of pollution-inflicted emphysema. The déjà vu is equally indisputable. Athletes gathering for the 2008 Summer Olympics in Beijing are jittery about their health and performance in the chunky, sooty air. They expressed the same reservations about the 1984 Summer games hosted in L.A.

It's all probably enough to make Arie Haagen-Smit, the indefatigable Dutch scientist who discovered the origins of photochemical air pollution, condemns us. A few years before he died of a lung ailment as "just an old soldier fading away,"[3] he spelled out in an article entitled "The Sins of Waste" why our contaminating ways mystify us. He was no tree-hugger or corporate apologist. His was a brilliance borne of noble intelli-gence and irrefutable common sense:

The venom sometimes directed at the internal combustion engine is actually rather silly. It is the use, not the instrument, that is the source of our troubles. . . . Who says that we must propel a 3,000- to 4,000-pound car to move a 160-pound person? Don't blame General Motors. We are the ones who make the decisions . . . Today when a baby is born, the good fairy endows him or her with two gallons of fuel oil and one gallon of gasoline per day for the rest of his life. Every time a baby comes off the assembly line, three cars do the same in Detroit . . . What Lewis Carroll's Alice foretold, when she said that she had to run twice as fast to stay where she was, is the effect of exponential growth . . . We need to educate, to inform people, to present them with alternatives . . . And I am not downhearted. A beginning has been made.[4]

We also reflect on one of California's favorite sons, Jerry Brown, who once suggested that people seek counsel in religious ethics rather than the halls of government to defeat self-inflicted air pollution. Just think what would have happened had leaders and the people found wisdom in the golden rule: "Do onto others as you would wish them do onto you." Imagine if we adapted to our ecosystem instead of gutting it and crying misfortune. As Brown learned when he tried reforming zoning and a creating a carpool lane on the Santa Monica Freeway, asking Americans to alter their entrenched, everyday behavior is almost begging for political suicide. Adding to the resistance that Brown and other crusaders met was establishment skepticism that ozone and its contaminant cousins actually prompted ill health, just like people resisted the notion that cigarettes caused disease until evidence became irrefutable. Perhaps it would have been different had a true smog emergency, like the ones in London or Donora, whacked Los Angeles in the 1950s, sickening thousands. A government reacting to a mass revolt after a mass sickness would've had the clout to force the automakers to diligently seek alternatives to the messy internal combustion engine.

Since cultural beliefs, the West Coast suburban idyll, and distaste for taxes hemmed in remedies, most of the politicians invested their faith in evolving technologies and the power of money to buy solutions to the environmental crisis as they genuflected at the altar of perpetual economic growth. At least inventors could make a buck off filtering-products. The citizenry had to face its own comeuppance. Like a middle-aged man stricken with hypertension and high cholesterol from a coach-potato lifestyle and affinity for junk food, Angelenos only took their medicine so they could forego changing diet and exercise patterns—choices that required self-restraint and self-discipline of the "no pain, no gain" philosophy. Smog, like high blood pressure and elevated cholesterol, was but a symptom of an untenable lifestyle and dysfunctional relationship with nature itself. As a result, the efforts to bolt better widgets onto smoke stacks and tailpipes, or develop less polluting hamburger grills, were nothing more than palliatives that masked a symptom of an underlying, self-induced disease.

Because Angelenos have continued hitching their environmental wagon to what the latest technology and engineering marvels can concoct, it's not just the beast lying in the background. On the horizon are converging storms threatening to blow into Los Angeles with the force of a category-five hurricane. Global warming is accelerating to the tipping-point, unleashing natural processes that likely will be far more devastating than humanity's own activity in propelling swift climate changes in the future. Methane, a powerful greenhouse gas long trapped in the permafrost of the Arctic region, is beginning to be released as the permafrost melts. Loss of ice cover is making the Earth darker, so that it absorbs more solar energy. Warming, like ozone, has now taken on a life of its own. On the resources front, oil production may have peaked and be on the precipice of a steady downward path. For the past three years world output has been relatively flat while consumption of motor fuel has expanded. The gap has been filled by converting corn and other food crops into fuel for the growing number of cars in the world. As a result, food prices have risen dramatically, triggering a series of food riots, first in Mexico, now around the world. More than a 100 million face starvation, and many have turned to eating mud cookies, a concoction made of vegetable oil and dirt, to fill their bellies. In L.A., we still drive, but even the conversion of massive amounts of crops to fuel has not stopped oil prices from reaching historic highs. The double whammy is undermining the economy.

In response, politicians in Washington and California attempt to soothe an increasingly anxious public with promises that a revolution in green technology will solve global warming and energy constraints and get the economy moving again. They call it "smart growth." Environmental groups sing in the chorus. Purveyors of systems to trap and pipe carbon dioxide from power plants into underground formations and to remove carbon dioxide from the air and make fuel for cars walk the halls of government looking for taxpayer money. Their promises are reminiscent of the smog sewer system proposed in L.A. in the 1950s to pipe the pollution from factories high into the mountains, where it would rise from smokestacks into the air well above the inversion layer. Scientists and inventors are still hoping they'll be able to manipulate the weather with artificial rainfall and such to offset some of man's devastation. A Dutch Nobel laureate scientist in 2006 evoked some of

Smogtown's wackier schemes, when he suggested firing smog-forming sulfates into the air—from balloons, of course—as a kind of shade to slow atmospheric heating.[5]

But as we gaze at the murky haze in *Smogtown*, something rings hollow in the promises of an imminent green and sustainable future. Whatever citizen revolt Californians mounted against the enemy of their own making, they continue driving as if the ozone is now cotton candy—a collective 825 million miles daily while burping out 5.4 *million* tons of pollutants and greenhouse gases. It's enough to fuel more than 1,600 round trips to the moon.[6] Thus, we find ourselves pondering an old lesson from Sunday school about not bowing down to false idols. As the Biblical commandment states, "For I the Lord your God am a jealous God, punishing children for the iniquity of parents, to the third and fourth generation of those who reject me, but showing steadfast love to the thousandth generation of those who love me and keep my commandments." Call it God or Mother Nature's thinning patience, but the planet can't afford to ignore the story of *Smogtown* as an admonition to live wisely.

NOTES

CHAPTER 1

1. "Grand Jury Checking Up On Fumes," *Los Angeles Times*, Oct. 7, 1943.
2. "Exhaust Fumes Hang Over City," *Los Angeles Times*, July 23, 1943.
3. "City Blamed For 'Gas Attacks,'" *Los Angeles Times*, July 28, 1943.
4. Betty Koster, *A History of Air Pollution Control Efforts In Los Angeles County* (Los Angeles County Air Pollution Control District, Aug. 31, 1956).
5. "Butadiene Smoke Again Blankets City In Haze," *Los Angeles Times*, Sept. 9, 1943.
6. "Grand Jury Checking Up On Fumes," *Los Angeles Times*, Oct. 7, 1943.
7. Marvin Brienes, "Smog Comes To Los Angeles," *Southern California Quarterly*, Winter 1976.
8. Brienes, *Southern California Quarterly*.
9. "Smog Closes Monrovia Lookout Tower," *Los Angeles Times*, Oct. 2, 1947.
10. "Smog Blanket Densest Here Since End Of War," *Los Angeles Times*, Sept. 14, 1946.
11. "Atmospheric Freak Holds Smog Over City," *Los Angeles Times*, Sept. 24, 1944.
12. Eugene Gacsaly, citizen correspondence to the City of Pasadena, Oct. 15, 1956.
13. "Smog Irritates Flyers On Nation-Wide Survey," *Los Angeles Times*, Dec. 5, 1946.
14. "Expert Says Smog Can Be Eliminated," *Los Angeles Times*, Nov. 28, 1944.
15. "Chlorine In Air Held Cause of Smog Tears," *Los Angeles Times*, April 18, 1946.
16. "Grand Jury Checking Up On Fumes," *Los Angeles Times*, Oct. 7, 1943.
17. "Children To Aid In Smog Drive," *Los Angeles Times*, Jan. 14, 1947.
18. "Howser To Sue Smog Creators," *Los Angeles Times*, Sept. 24, 1946.
19. "Directors Hope To Smoke Out Smog," *Pasadena Independent*, Sept. 21, 1945.
20. Koster, *A History of Air Pollution Control Efforts In Los Angeles County*.
21. Dr. Arnold O. Beckman, *Remarks At The John And Alice Tyler Ecology Awards Dinner For Arie Haagen-Smit* (Beverly Hills, May 3, 1979).
22. Kevin Starr, *California: A History* (Modern Library, 2005).
23. Starr, *California: A History*.
24. "The Pink Oasis," *Time*, July 4, 1949.
25. Kirse Granat May, *Golden State, Golden Youth: The California Image In Popular Culture, 1955-1966* (University of North Carolina Press, 2002).
26. "The Pink Oasis," *Time*, July 4, 1949.
27. "Hollywood-A Harvard Version," *Los Angeles Times* editorial, Dec. 19, 1946.
28. "Beautiful, Sunny California, Eh? Los Angeles Now No. 1 'Smog Town,'" *St. Louis Globe Democrat*, Oct. 9, 1946.
29. "Smog Drive Set To Get Under Way," *Los Angeles Times*, Sept. 28, 1947.
30. "The New World," *Time*, July 15, 1957.
31. "County Smog-Fighting Staff Traces Evil Fumes' Sources," *Los Angeles Times*, Oct. 18, 1946.
32. "Oil Refineries Found To Be Cause Of Much Smog In Los Angeles Area," *Los Angeles Times*, Dec. 5, 1946.
33. "Thirteen Civil Suits For Abatement Of Smog Filed By Dist. Atty. Howser," *Los Angeles Times*, Oct. 16, 1946.
34. "Move Chemical Plants To Nevada, Suggestion," *Pasadena Star-News*, Jan. 7, 1947.
35. "Times Expert Offers Smog Plan," *Los Angeles Times*, Jan. 19, 1947.
36. James E. Krier and Edmund Ursin, *Pollution & Policy: A Case Essay On California And Federal Experience With Motor Vehicle Air Pollution, 1940-1975* (University of California Press, 1977).

37. Krier and Ursin, *Pollution & Policy.*

38. "New Bill To Aid Officials In Battle On Smog Will Be Introduced Today," *Los Angeles Times,* Jan. 29, 1947.

39. Krier and Ursin, *Pollution & Policy.*
"Two Die As Fog And Smog Blanket Tangles up Traffic," *Los Angeles Times,* Jan. 25, 1947.

40. "Fumes From Dumps Endanger Health of 300,000, Mothers' Group Charges," *Los Angeles Times,* Feb. 13, 1947.

41. Koster, *A History of Air Pollution Control Efforts In Los Angeles County.*

42. "Smog Endangering Health, Physician Group Report," *Los Angeles Times,* Feb. 8, 1947.

43. "Fumes From Dumps Endanger Health of 300,000, Mothers' Group Charges," *Los Angeles Times,* Feb. 13, 1947.

44. "Smog Held Greatest Flight Hazard Here," *Los Angeles Times,* May 12, 1950.

45. "Student Flier Lands on Freeway Path," *Los Angeles Times,* Sept. 1, 1965.

46. "Smog Cuts Down Flying Time For Planes, Director Says," *Pasadena Star-News,* Feb. 25, 1948.

47. "Mayor Charges Smog Laxity; Supervisor Refutes Statement," *Los Angeles Times,* Sept. 9, 1949.

48. Edward Hummel, citizen correspondence to the city of Los Angeles, Nov. 10, 1958.

49. B.J. Lathshaw, citizen correspondence to the city of Pasadena, Aug. 20, 1947.

50. *Los Angeles Times,* Sept. 9, 1949.

51. "Oil Companies And Lumber Interests Reported Opposing Anti-Smog Bill," *Los Angeles Times,* May 17, 1947.

52. Harold W. Kennedy, *The History, Legal And Administrative Aspects Of Air Pollution Control In Los Angeles County* (Los Angeles County and Los Angeles County Air Pollution Control District, May 9, 1954).

53. "Governor Signs Anti-Smog Bill," *Los Angeles Times,* June 11, 1947.

54. "Smog Controller McCabe Arrives To Assume Duties," *Los Angeles Times,* Oct. 2, 1947.

55. "Anti-Smog Chief To Seek Industry Cooperation," *Pasadena Star News,* Oct. 2, 1947.

56. "Real Sunshine Greets Family Of 'Smog Man,'" *Los Angeles Times,* Nov. 12, 1947.

57. "$18,000 Smog Research By County Proposed," *Pasadena Star-News,* Nov. 11, 1947.

58. "How Goes The Smog Fight?" *Los Angeles Times* editorial, Nov. 22, 1947.

60. Koster, *A History of Air Pollution Control Efforts In Los Angeles County.*

61. Koster, *A History of Air Pollution Control Efforts In Los Angeles County.*

62. "Delay In Smog Program Asked By Industrialists," *Los Angeles Times,* Jan. 15, 1948.

63. Western Oil & Gas Association, memo to the Los Angeles County Air Pollution Control District, Feb. 9, 1948.

64. "Smog Relief Pads Offered," *Los Angeles Times,* March 23, 1947.

65. "How To Soothe Your Smog-Smitten Eyes," *Los Angeles Times,* Oct. 26, 1948.

CHAPTER 2

1. Betty Koster, *A History of Air Pollution Control Efforts In Los Angeles County* (Los Angeles County Air Pollution Control District, Aug. 31, 1956).

2. "Smog Blamed For Slump In Tourist Trade Here," *Los Angeles Times,* Jan. 20, 1950.

3. "Smog Blamed By Ex-Director For Heart Ills Death Rate," *Pasadena Star-News,* March 30, 1948.

4. George Schuler, citizen correspondence to Los Angeles County Board of Supervisors, Aug. 20, 1947.

5. Dr. Louis McCabe, official correspondence with City of Pasadena, July 16, 1948.

6. James E. Krier and Edmund Ursin, *Pollution & Policy: A Case Essay On California And Federal Experience With Motor Vehicle Air Pollution, 1940-1975* (University of California Press, 1977).

7. Harold W. Kennedy, *The History, Legal And Administrative Aspects Of Air Pollution Control In Los Angeles County* (Los Angeles County), May 9, 1954.

8. Los Angeles County Office of Air Pollution Control, *Annual Report Of the Office Of Air Pollution Control, 1946-1947.*

9. "Smog Thinning In 18 Months Predicted By Dr. McCabe," *Los Angeles Times,* June 1, 1949.

10. Dr. Arnold O. Beckman, *Remarks At The John And Alice Tyler Ecology Awards Dinner For Arie Haagen-Smit* (Beverly Hills, May 3, 1979).

11. "Lets Face Facts On Smog," *Los Angeles Times* editorial, Sept. 16, 1948.

12. "'Not So,' Oil Industry Replies To Smog Detectives' Finding" *Los Angeles Times*, Sept. 28, 1948.

13. "Smog Itself Exhibit A In Injunction Case," *Los Angeles Times*, Sept. 21, 1948.

14. Los Angeles County Air Pollution Control District, *Air Pollution Damage to Commercial Crops In Los Angeles County 1964*, Nov. 5, 1965.

15. "Trial Of Suits Charging Fumes Crop Loss Begins," *Los Angeles Times*, March 18, 1950.

16. "California Scientists Say Smog Kills Crops," *Argonaut* magazine, Sept. 24, 1954.

17. "Smog Rivals Frost In Damaging Crops," *Los Angeles Times*, April 5, 1953.

18. "Smog Damage In Southland Soars," *Los Angeles Times*, May 29, 1963.

19. APCD, *Air Pollution Damage to Commercial Crops In Los Angeles County 1964*

20. "No More Blue Skies: A Non-Progress Report On Air Pollution," *West magazine (Los Angeles Times)*, May 31, 1970.

21. "Thousands See Times Smog Film," *Los Angeles Times*, Dec. 12, 1948.

22. "Airborne Dump," *Time*, April 25, 1949.

23. "Threat of Disaster From Smog Hanging Over Los Angeles," *Los Angeles Times*, Oct. 16, 1948.

24. "Zanuck Purchases New College Life Novel," *Los Angeles Times*, Dec. 2, 1949.

25. "Hit Smog Two Ways," *Los Angeles Herald-Examiner*, Dec. 4, 1948.

26. "Smog Sleuth Finds A Friend—Leonardo," *Los Angeles Times*, July 1, 1949.

27. Krier and Ursin, *Pollution & Policy*.

28. "Death At Donora," *Time*, Nov. 8, 1948.

29. "No Sidetracking On Smog!" *Los Angeles Times* editorial, Nov. 23, 1948.

30. "Victory Over Smog To Take Time, McCabe Tells Council," *Los Angeles Times*, Nov. 27, 1948.

31. H.F. Johnstone, University of Illinois, *"Technical Aspects Of The Los Angeles Smog Problem. A Report Prepared For The Los Angeles County Air Pollution Control District,"* April 15, 1948.

32. Krier and Ursin, *Pollution & Policy*.

33. "Grand Jury Report Assails Supes' Smog Attitude," *Los Angeles Times*, Dec. 15, 1948.

34. "Officials Spend Five Years On Smog With No Result," *Los Angeles Herald-Examiner*, Dec. 5, 1948.

35. *Los Angeles County Air Pollution Control District Annual Report 1947-'48* (Los Angeles County Air Pollution Control District, Jan. 6, 1949).

36. "Smog Control Achieves High Scientific Plane," *Los Angeles Times*, March 10, 1949.

37. "Nationwide Fight On Smog Launched," *Los Angeles Times*, Oct. 8, 1949.

38. "Three Influences Can Wreck Smog Control, McCabe Says," *Los Angeles Times*, Nov. 11, 1949.

39. Koster, *A History of Air Pollution Control Efforts In Los Angeles County*.

40. "Smog Control Achieves High Scientific Plane," *Los Angeles Times*, March 10, 1949.

41. "McCabe Resigning County Smog Job For Federal Post," *Los Angeles Times*, May 11, 1949.

42. Koster, *A History of Air Pollution Control Efforts In Los Angeles County*.

43. "Aims Of New Smog Group Discussed," *Los Angeles Times*, Sept. 28, 1949.

44. "Aims Of New Smog Group Discussed," *Los Angeles Times*, Sept. 28, 1949.

45. "Mayor Charges Smog Laxity, Supervisor Refuses Statement," *Los Angeles Times*, Sept. 14, 1949.

46. "Mayor Charges Smog Laxity, Supervisor Refuses Statement," *Los Angeles Times*, Sept. 14, 1949.

47. "Mayor Charges Smog Laxity, Supervisor Refuses Statement," *Los Angeles Times*, Sept. 14,1949.

48. Advertisement, *Los Angeles Times*, Sept. 20, 1949.

49. "Smog Kills 104 Persons A Year In Los Angeles County, A Professor Of Medicine Testified Today," *United Press International*, Nov. 28, 1949.

50. Koster, *A History of Air Pollution Control Efforts In Los Angeles County*.

51. "Study Hints Smog Raise Respiratory Death Rate," *Los Angeles Times*, Nov. 27, 1950.

52. "Hospital Head Hits At Factory Fumes," *Los Angeles Times*, Dec. 6, 1950.

53. "Streetcar Crash In Smog Injures 22 Passengers," *Los Angeles Times*, Dec. 3, 1949.

54. "Night Romance Spells Doom For Late Mr. Riley," *Los Angeles Times*, Dec. 13, 1949.

55. "Supervisors Favor Curbs On Refineries," *Los Angeles Times*, Dec. 7, 1949.

56. Koster, *A History of Air Pollution Control Efforts In Los Angeles County.*
57. "Three Influences Can Wreck Smog Control, McCabe Says," *Los Angeles Times*, Nov. 11, 1949.
58. "Oil Industry Hits At Smog Charges," *Los Angeles Times*, Dec. 1, 1949.
59. Koster, *A History of Air Pollution Control Efforts In Los Angeles County.*
60. Koster, *A History of Air Pollution Control Efforts In Los Angeles County.*
61. "Grand Jury May Sidestep Gang Subject," *Los Angeles Times*, Dec. 9, 1949.

CHAPTER 3
1. Dr. Arnold O. Beckman, *Remarks At The John And Alice Tyler Ecology Awards Dinner For Arie Haagen-Smit* (Beverly Hills, May 3, 1979).
2. Beckman, *Remarks At The John And Alice Tyler Ecology Awards Dinner For Arie Haagen-Smit.*
3. Beckman, *Remarks At The John And Alice Tyler Ecology Awards Dinner For Arie Haagen-Smit.*
4. Beckman, *Remarks At The John And Alice Tyler Ecology Awards Dinner For Arie Haagen-Smit.*
5. "Think Of Him When The Sky Is Blue," *Los Angeles Times*, March 6, 1977.
6. "The Smog That Smothers Los Angeles," *Reader's Digest*, Jan. 1956.
7. "Think Of Him When The Sky Is Blue," *Los Angeles Times*, March 6, 1977.
8. Beckman, *Remarks At The John And Alice Tyler Ecology Awards Dinner For Arie Haagen-Smit.*
9. "A Bouquet To The Father Of Smog," *General Motors Quarterly*, Winter 1975.
10. "Haagen-Smit On Smog," *Westways*, Aug. 1972.
11. "A Bouquet To The Father Of Smog," *General Motors Quarterly*, Winter 1975.
12. "Puzzle Of Smog Production Solved By Caltech Scientist," *Los Angeles Times*, Nov. 20, 1950.
13. "The Air Pollution Problem In Los Angeles," *Engineering & Science*, Dec. 1950.
14. "The Air Pollution Problem In Los Angeles," *Engineering & Science*, Dec. 1950.
15. "The Smog That Smothers Los Angeles," *Reader's Digest*, Jan. 1956.
16. "Puzzle Of Smog Production Solved By Caltech Scientist," *Los Angeles Times* Nov. 20, 1950.
17. James E. Krier and Edmund Ursin, *Pollution & Policy: A Case Essay On California And Federal Experience With Motor Vehicle Air Pollution, 1940-1975* (University of California Press, 1977).
18. Betty Koster, *A History of Air Pollution Control Efforts In Los Angeles County* (Los Angeles County Air Pollution Control District, Aug. 31, 1956).
19. Ed Ainsworth, undated memo about May 1952 air pollution symposium, to his *Los Angeles Times'* editor. *Department of Special Collections, University of California Los Angeles.*
20. "Mystery Cloaking Smog 'Birth' Ends," *Los Angeles Times*, May 2, 1952.
21. "Bus Link To Smog Spread Analyzed, *Los Angeles Times*, Dec. 3, 1946.
22. Herman P. Roth and Engelbrekt A. Swanson, "Physiological Studies Of Irritant Aspects Of Atmospheric Pollution," School Of Medicine, University of Southern California, Oct. 15, 1947.
23. Herman P. Roth, correspondence with Ed Ainsworth, Department of Engineering, University of California Los Angeles, Jan. 19, 1951.
24. "Think Of Him When The Sky Is Blue," *Los Angeles Times*, March 6, 1977.
25. James Bonner, *Arie Haagen-Smit: Biographical Memoirs*, (National Academies Press, 1989).
26. Zus (Maria) Haagen-Smit, Oral History, Archives, *California Institute of Technology*, Interviewed by Shirley K. Cohen, March 16 & 20, 2000.
27. Beckman, *Remarks At The John And Alice Tyler Ecology Awards Dinner For Arie Haagen-Smit.*
28. Zus (Maria) Haagen-Smit, Oral History, Archives, *California Institute of Technology*
29. Krier and Ursin, *Pollution & Policy: A Case Essay On California And Federal Experience With Motor Vehicle Air Pollution.*
30. *Los Angeles County Air Pollution Control District Annual Report 1947-'48* (Los Angeles County Air Pollution Control District, Jan. 6, 1949).
31. "Think Of Him When The Sky Is Blue," *Los Angeles Times*, March 6, 1977.
32. "Auto Fumes Control Vital, Says Professor," *Pasadena Star-News*, Feb. 17, 1954.
33. "Smog Experts Attack Auto Exhaust Problem," *Los Angeles Times*, July 18, 1955.
34. Arie J. Haagen-Smit, "The Sins Of Waste," *Engineering & Science*, Feb. 1973.

35. Arie J. Haagen-Smit, "Smog Research Pays Off," *Engineering & Science,* May 1952.
36. "Four Fronts, Including You, Seen In Our Smog Problem," *Los Angeles Times,* Oct. 25, 1952.
37. "Smog To Stay Long Time," *Los Angeles Times,* May 6, 1952.
38. "Four Fronts, Including You, Seen In Our Smog Problem," *Los Angeles Times,* Oct. 25, 1952.
39. "No Matter What He Does, Smog Boss Isn't Popular," *Associated Press,* Dec. 21, 1952.
40. Koster, *A History of Air Pollution Control Efforts In Los Angeles County.*
41. "Ask Watchdog To Eye County Smog Inaction," *Pasadena Independent,* Oct. 29, 1952.
42. "Valley Cries For Smog Relief," *Los Angeles Times,* Nov. 16, 1952.
43. "Winds Dissipate Worst Smog In Recent History In Pasadena," *Pasadena Star-News,* Dec. 21, 1953.
44. "Supervisors Begin Search For New Smog War Chief," *Los Angeles Times,* Dec. 17, 1953.
45. "Smog Evacuation Threat Foreseen," *Los Angeles Times,* Nov. 25, 1953.
46. "Disaster Held Averted By Smog Law," *Los Angeles Times,* July 22, 1953.
47. "Supervisors Vote To Replace Larson As Smog Control Chief," *Los Angeles Times,* Oct. 16, 1953.
48. "Supervisors Vote To Replace Larson As Smog Control Chief," *Los Angeles Times,* Oct. 16, 1953.
49. Koster, *A History of Air Pollution Control Efforts In Los Angeles County.*
50. "Activities Of Smog Office Under Fire," *Los Angeles Times,* Feb. 2, 1954.
51. Arthur J. Will And Harold W. Kennedy, "Investigation Of The Los Angeles County Air Pollution Control District," *Los Angeles County,* March 15, 1954.
52. "Larson Fires Six Who Caused Investigation," *Los Angeles Times,* March 19, 1954.
53. "Dorn Smog Report Draws Fire," *Pasadena Star-News,* March 10, 1954.
54. "Our City," *Pasadena Independent,* March 17, 1954.
55. "4,500 Hear Demand For Smog Probe," *Los Angeles Times,* Oct. 21, 1954.
56. "Los Angeles' Legendary Smog Gives Citizens A Slow Burn," *Business Week,* Oct. 30, 1954.
57. Krier and Ursin, *Pollution & Policy: A Case Essay On California And Federal Experience With Motor Vehicle Air Pollution.*
58. "Poulson Urges Tax Aid In Smog War," *Los Angeles Times,* April 15, 1954.
59. "Politicians Using Smog For Smear," *Los Angeles Times* editorial, Oct. 23. 1954.
60. "Larson Tells Story To Grand Jurors," *Los Angeles Times,* Oct. 28, 1954.
61. "Larson Tells Story To Grand Jurors," *Los Angeles Times,* Oct. 28, 1954.
62. "Wife Sues Smog Chief Larson For Divorce," *Los Angeles Times,* Dec. 30, 1954.
63. "Air Pollution Foundation Reports On First Year," *Los Angeles Times,* May 20, 1955.
64. "Two Smog Groups Swap Charges Over Funds," *Los Angeles Times,* June 12, 1958.
65. "Research Group Will Begin Operations In Southland," *Los Angeles Times,* Aug. 10, 1948.
66. "Villainous California Sun," *Time,* Aug. 30, 1954.
67. Zus (Maria) Haagen-Smit, Oral History, Archives, *California Institute of Technology*
68. A.J. Haagen-Smit, memo to Evaluation And Planning Staff, Los Angeles County Air Pollution Control District, regarding "Evaluation of Stanford Research Institute Research Proposal No. PS 56-182," Nov. 1, 1956.
69. "Think Of Him When The Sky Is Blue," *Los Angeles Times,* March 6, 1977.
70. "A Bouquet To The Father Of Smog," *General Motors Quarterly,* Winter 1975.
71. Zus (Maria) Haagen-Smit, Oral History, Archives, *California Institute of Technology.*
72. "The Smog That Smothers Los Angeles," *Reader's Digest,* Jan. 1956.
73. "Freeway Fumes May Reduce Driver Ability," *Los Angeles Times,* Jan. 1, 1968.
74. "Freeway Users Told Of Poison Gas Dangers," *Los Angeles Times,* Jan. 1, 1965.

CHAPTER 4

1. "The Smog That Smothers Los Angeles," *Reader's Digest,* Jan. 1956.
2. "Smog Bothers One In Three Californians," *Associated Press,* Dec. 17, 1956.
3. "Bettors Get Hit By The Smog, Too," *Los Angeles Times,* Oct. 30, 1965.
4. "Smog Pushing Farther Into West Valley, Officials Said," *Los Angeles Times,* June 28, 1960.
5. "Student's Necktie Gets Gaudy New Hue In Smog," *Los Angeles Times,* Nov. 5, 1954.
6. "How Does Health Stand Up In Smog," *Associated Press,* Dec. 18, 1952.
7. "Smog Wanes As Illness Increase," *Los Angeles Times,* Nov. 4, 1953.
8. "The Smog That Smothers Los Angeles," *Reader's Digest,* Jan. 1956.
9. "Smog Seen As Favor In Mental Illnesses," *Associated Press,* Dec. 8, 1954.
10. "How Does Health Stand Up In Smog," *Associated Press.*

11. "Driver Daces Mental Tests In Auto Death," *Los Angeles Times*, Sept. 26, 1963.

12. Glendale Betterment Committee, Inc., letter to Los Angeles County, Nov. 7, 1958—check addressee

13. "Man Writes Note Assailing Smog, Then Ends His Life," *Los Angeles Times*, Sept. 20, 1956.

14. "Even Smog's Wonderful To Twice-Freed Convict," *Los Angeles Times*, March 7, 1954.

15. "Knight Won't Supersede Local Smog Agencies," *Los Angeles Times*, Oct. 17, 1953.

16. "Governor Won't Take Over Task," *Los Angeles Herald-Examiner*, Jan. 22, 1955.

17. "Federal And State Participation With The Air Pollution Control District In The Re-Evaluation Of Air Contaminants From Refineries And Power Plants And The Air Monitoring Program In The Los Angeles Basin" (Los Angeles Air Pollution Control District, Aug. 5, 1955).

18. Betty Koster, *A History of Air Pollution Control Efforts In Los Angeles County* (Los Angeles County Air Pollution Control District, Aug. 31, 1956).

19. "End Smog Quickly, Hinshaw Warns," *Los Angeles Times*, Sept. 29, 1954.

20. "Smog's Short-Change," *Los Angeles Herald-Examiner* editorial, April 3, 1957.

21. "Poulson Urges Federal Help To Combat Smog," *Pasadena Star-News*, April 15, 1954.

22. "Two Sent To Jail For Smog Violations," *Los Angeles Examiner*, April 18, 1957.

23. "Smog Sheriff Readies Tough New Crackdown" *Los Angeles Examiner*, Jan. 18, 1956.

24. "Long Fight Against Smog Seen By Control Director," *Los Angeles Times*, Dec. 28, 1955.

25. "New Smog Industries Ban Sought," *Los Angeles Examiner*, July 18, 1956.

26. "New Teeth Asked For Smog Control," *Los Angeles Times*, June 16, 1956.

27. "Secret Smog Papers Row," *Los Angeles Herald-Examiner*, June 29, 1955.

28. "Trains, Smog, Rockets Disrupt Indian Shooting," *Los Angeles Times*, Nov. 4, 1955.

29. "L.A. Will Have Special Smog Violations Court," *Los Angeles Times*, Feb. 3, 1955.

30. "Plan Outlined For Alerting Public On Dangerous Smog," *Los Angeles Times*, Dec. 2, 1954.

31. "The Polluted Air," *Time*, Jan. 27, 1967.

32. "Air Pollution Control Plan Hits Snag," *Los Angeles Times*, June 7, 1957.

33. "Knight Signs Air Pollution Emergency Bill," *Los Angeles Times*, June 3, 1955.

34. David E. Day, Richfield Oil Co., correspondence with Los Angeles County Air Pollution Control Board, Nov. 8, 1955.

35. M.A. Ennis, Liquefied Petroleum Gas Association, correspondence with Los Angeles County Board of Supervisors, June 17, 1956.

36. "Analysis of Shutdown Plans Submitted Under Regulation VII" (Los Angeles County Air Pollution Control District, July 25, 1956).

37. "Air Pollution Control Plan Hits Snag," *Los Angeles Times*, June 7, 1957.

38. "New Smog Industries Ban Sought," *Los Angeles Herald-Examiner*, July 18, 1956.

39. Koster, *A History of Air Pollution Control Efforts In Los Angeles County.*

40. "A New Report To You On Smog," *Los Angeles Herald-Examiner*, July 1, 1957.

41. "The Smog That Smothers Los Angeles," *Reader's Digest*, Jan. 1956.

42. Mr. And Mrs. F.G. Prater, letter to County Board of Supervisors About Incinerator Ban, June 6, 1955.

43. "The End Of Back-Yard Burning," *Los Angeles Times* editorial, Sept. 26, 1957.

44. Sheldon Davis, California Incinerator Association, correspondence with Los Angeles County Board of Supervisors Regarding Elimination of Single Chamber Back Yard Incinerators, June 9, 1955.

45. Walter Rosenbrock, Currier Enterprises, correspondence with California League Of Cities Regarding Elimination of Single Chamber Back Yard Incinerators, June 15, 1955.

46. "Smog Shakedown Charges Traced," *Los Angeles Times*, June 19, 1954.

47. "More Time Sought In Smog Inquiry," *Los Angeles Times*, June 22, 1954.

48. "Supervisors Call Mayor On Rubbish," *Los Angeles Times*, May 25, 1955.

49. "Racket Charged In Smog Trouble," *New York Times*, Oct. 2, 1955.

50. "Council Consider Defiance Of City Incinerator Use Ban," *Los Angeles Times*, Aug. 1, 1955.

51. "Long Fight Against Smog Seen By Control Director," *Los Angeles*, Dec. 28, 1955.

52. "Jessup Denise Secrecy Of Smog Health Report," *Los Angeles Times*, June 2, 1956.

53. "The Smog That Smothers Los Angeles," *Reader's Digest.*

54. Western Oil & Gas Association, "Economic Effects Of Banning The Use Of Fuel Oil On Supplies Of Energy Required In The Los Angeles Area" White Paper, Oct. 22, 1958.

55. Western Oil & Gas Association, Statement of R.L. Minkler to the Los Angeles County Board Of Supervisors, June 11, 1959.

56. "Long Fight Against Smog Seen By Control Director," *Los Angeles Times*, Dec. 28, 1955.

57. Silvia Talmadge, letter to Los Angeles County Board Of Supervisors Regarding Rule 62, Nov. 7, 1958.

58. C.H. And G. Rivers, letter to Los Angeles County Board Of Supervisors Regarding Rule 62, Nov. 11, 1958.

59. Vera Lehrer, letter to Los Angeles County Board Of Supervisors Regarding Rule 62, Nov. 12, 1958.

60. Frank Romano, letter to Los Angeles County Board Of Supervisors Regarding Rule 62, Nov. 12, 1958.

61. Citizens Anti-Smog Action Committee, letter to Los Angeles County Board Of Supervisors Regarding Rule 62, June 11, 1959.

62. S. Smith Griswold, correspondence with Los Angeles County Supervisor John Anson Ford regarding Southern California Edison, March 12, 1956.

63. "Industry Faces Fact: Spend to Cut Smog Or Relocate," *Los Angeles Herald-Examiner,* Oct. 17, 1959.

64. "New Smog Industries Ban Sought," *Los Angeles Examiner,* July 18, 1956.

65. "Stalingrad Praised In Smog Control Study," *Los Angeles Times,* June 27, 1959.

66. "New Smog Industries Ban Sought," *Los Angeles Examiner,* July 18, 1956.

67. "Industry Faces Fact: Spend To Cut Smog Or Relocate, *Los Angeles Herald-Examiner,* Oct. 17, 1959.

68. "Fontana Smog 'Coverup' Hit," *Los Angeles Examiner,* Jan. 15, 1959.

69. "Don't Relax In Battle On Smog, Dr. McCabe Warns," *Los Angeles Times,* June 29, 1959.

70. "Smog Partially Blamed For Spiritual Crisis," *Los Angeles Times,* June 26, 1959.

71. Koster, *A History of Air Pollution Control Efforts In Los Angeles County.*

72. "The Forecast—Clear," *Newsweek,* April 18, 1960.

CHAPTER 5

1. "Progress Report On Industrial Controls" (Los Angeles County Air Pollution Control District, Oct. 28, 1958).

2. "Cigarettes Found Contributing To Smog," *Los Angeles Times,* Oct. 3, 1956.

3. "Analysis of Progress By APCD In Fulfilling The Recommendations of the Governor's Report On Air Pollution Control (Beckman Report) of Dec. 5, 1958," (Los Angeles County, Aug. 18, 1958).

4. "L.A. Site Called 'Worst Possible' For Smog," *Los Angeles Times,* March 3, 1966.

5. "Gains In Smog Fight Offset By More Cars," *Los Angeles Times,* Dec. 5, 1965.

6. "Problems Associated With Forecasting Air Pollution Over An Urban Area," (Los Angeles County Air Pollution Control District, Nov. 6, 1961).

7. "Problems Associated With Forecasting Air Pollution Over An Urban Area" (Los Angeles County Air Pollution Control District, Nov. 6, 1961).

8. "The Southland's War On Smog: Fifty Years Of Progress Toward Clean Air," (South Coast Air Quality Management District, 1997).

9. Betty Koster, *A History of Air Pollution Control Efforts In Los Angeles County* (Los Angeles County Air Pollution Control District, Aug. 31, 1956).

10. "The Southland's War On Smog: Fifty Years Of Progress Toward Clean Air" (South Coast Air Quality Management District, 1997)

11. Interview with Edward Camarena, Feb. 26, 2007.

12. Interview with Jim Birakos, Feb. 1, 2007.

13. S. Smith Griswold, Testimony about Rule 64, June 25, 1959.

14. "Griswold Takes Two-Hour Test In Smog Chamber," *Los Angeles Times,* July 24, 1956.

15. "The Southland's War On Smog: Fifty Years Of Progress Toward Clean Air" (South Coast Air Quality Management District, 1997).

16. "Nobody Envies LA's Smoggy Griswold," *Sacramento Union,* Sept. 30, 1956.

17. "Big Turnover Of Smog Workers Blamed On High Pressure Of Job," *Los Angeles Times,* Dec. 4, 1959.

18. "Smog Detectives Sway On Scaffolds High In The Air," *Los Angeles Times,* June 20, 1955.

19. "The Southland's War On Smog: Fifty Years Of Progress Toward Clean Air" (South Coast Air Quality Management District, 1997).

20. "The Truth About Smog," *Los Angeles Times* editorial, Oct. 15, 1957

21. "Analysis of Progress By APCD In Fulfilling The Recommendations of the Governor's Report On Air Pollution Control (Beckman Report) of Dec. 5," and "Progress Report On Industrial Controls" (Los Angeles County Air Pollution Control District, Aug. 18, 1958).

22. "APCD Completes Job—All Except Auto Exhaust, *Montebello News*, Nov. 7, 1957

23. "Analysis of Progress By APCD In Fulfilling The Recommendations of the Governor's Report On Air Pollution Control (Beckman Report) of Dec. 5," and "Progress Report On Industrial Controls" (Los Angeles County Air Pollution Control District, Aug. 18, 1958).

24. "Smog News," Committee On Air Pollution Controls, *The American Society Of Mechanical Engineers*, Jan. 15, 1957.

25. "Airborne Radioactivity Monitoring Program," (Los Angeles County Air Pollution Control District, Oct. 1, 1958).

26. "Airborne Radioactivity Monitoring Program," (Los Angeles County Air Pollution Control District, Oct. 1, 1958).

27. John Mills, memo to Gordon Larson, Los Angeles County Air Pollution Control District, Relating to Radiological Training, Feb. 11, 1953.

28. "It Isn't Real Smog That Burns Eye, Group Hears," *Los Angeles Times*, Sept. 27, 1956.

29. "Navy Enlists Smog For A-Blast Defense," *Los Angeles Examiner*, March 19, 1961.

30. "Smog Filters Sun Photos," *Los Angeles Examiner*, Feb. 23, 1961.

31. "Evaluation Of Impact Of Proposed Nuclear Reactor Power Plant In Santa Clara River Valley Or Vicinity" (Los Angeles County Air Pollution Control District, Dec. 15, 1960).

32. "Toxics Law May Have Swayed Lockheed Case," *Daily News Of Los Angeles*, Aug. 26, 1996.

33. Interview with Jim Birakos, Feb. 1, 2007.

34. Interview with Jim Birakos, April 22, 2008.

35. "Smog Control Office Flooded With Imaginative Plans Of Inventors," *Los Angeles Times*, Sept. 5, 1950.

36. James E. Krier and Edmund Ursin, *Pollution & Policy: A Case Essay On California And Federal Experience With Motor Vehicle Air Pollution, 1940-1975* (University of California Press, 1977).

37. "Smog Control Office Flooded With Imaginative Plans Of Inventors," *Los Angeles Times*, Sept. 5, 1950.

38. Los Angeles County Air Pollution Control District, Anti-Smog Inventions' Files, Archived by South Coast Air Quality Management District.

39. "Firm Offers To End Smog In Three Years," *Los Angeles Times*, Nov. 25, 1954.

40. "Everybody Has A Smog Remedy," *Los Angeles Times*, Nov. 12, 1953.

41. "How To Live With Smog And Like It," *Los Angeles Times*, Oct. 20, 1954.

42. Los Angeles County Air Pollution Control District, Anti-Smog Inventions' Files, Archived by South Coast Air Quality Management District.

43. "Musician Claims Simple Smog Cure," *Los Angeles Times*, June 11, 1954.

44. Los Angeles County Air Pollution Control District, Anti-Smog Inventions' Files, Archived by South Coast Air Quality Management District.

45. Los Angeles County Air Pollution Control District, Anti-Smog Inventions' Files, Archived by South Coast Air Quality Management District.

46. Los Angeles County Air Pollution Control District, Anti-Smog Inventions' Files, Archived by South Coast Air Quality Management District.

47. "Vast Air Sanitation System Proposed As Smog Solution," *Los Angeles Times*, Dec. 14, 1954.

48. Morris Neiburger, "Weather Modification And Smog," *Science*, Oct. 4, 1957.

49. Morris Neiburger, "Weather Modification And Smog," *Science*, Oct. 4, 1957.

50. "Summary Of Evaluation Board Activities Calendar Year 1960" (Los Angeles County Air Pollution Control District, Jan. 1961).

51. "Ideas On Air Pollution Submitted To Evaluation Board" (South Coast Air Quality Management District, Sept. 1, 1978).

52. "Somebody Had Better Do Something About Smog," *Los Angeles Times* editorial, Aug. 2, 1958.

53. "Million Dollar Prize Urged For Auto Smog Solution," *Los Angeles Times*, Nov. 22, 1957.

54. "Missile Firm Working On Smog Muffler," *Los Angeles Times*, Jan. 17, 1958.

55. "Background Data Sheet On The Ramo-Wooldridge Anti-Smog Device," (The Ramo-Wooldridge Corp., Oct. 17, 1958).

56. Morris Deodorizers, Inc., Advertisement For "Electrostatic Fume Control System. Date unknown; believed early 1960s.

57. "New Gas Claimed Partly Smog-Free," *Los Angeles Examiner*, March 13, 1959.

58. San Gabriel Valley Motors, Advertisement For Automobile Exhaust Testing. Date unknown; believed late 1950s.

59. Puritron, Advertisement for Puritron Electronic Miracle. Date unknown; believed late 1950s.

60. S. Smith Griswold, Los Angeles County Air Pollution Control District, Correspondence With Automotive Electronics Co., Inc., Manufacturers Of The "Solar Volt All-Electronic Super-charger," May 6, 1959.

CHAPTER 6

1. Ann Scheid, *Pasadena: Crown Of The Valley* (Windsor Publications, 1986).

2. *"The Antitrust Case of the Century,"* Southern California Quarterly, Fall 1999.

3. Scott Bottles, *Los Angeles and the Automobile: The Making of a Modern City.* (University of California Press, 1987).

4. James E. Krier and Edmund Ursin, *Pollution & Policy: A Case Essay On California And Federal Experience With Motor Vehicle Air Pollution, 1940-1975* (University of California Press, 1977).

5. *"The Antitrust Case of the Century,"* Southern California Quarterly, Fall 1999.

6. "Plea To Car Builders," *Los Angeles Times,* July 30, 1969.

7. "A Peck Of Pickets," *Los Angeles Times,* Nov. 7, 1969.

8. "The Polluted Air," *Time,* Jan. 27, 1967.

9. "Anger And Disgust At Assembly Smog Hearing Here," *Los Angeles Times,* Feb. 25, 1968.

10. James E. Krier and Edmund Ursin, *Pollution & Policy: A Case Essay On California And Federal Experience With Motor Vehicle Air Pollution, 1940-1975* (University of California Press, 1977).

11. "Report On Trip To Detroit, Michigan," (Los Angeles County Air Pollution Control District, Nov. 18, 1954).

12. Krier and Ursin, *Pollution & Policy: A Case Essay On California And Federal Experience With Motor Vehicle Air Pollution, 1940-1975.*

13. John C. Esposito, *Ralph Nader's Study Group Report On Air Pollution: Vanishing Air,* (Grossman Publishers, 1970).

14. "APCD Complete Job–All Except Auto Exhaust," *Montebello News,* Nov. 7, 1957.

15. "Progress In Controlling Air Pollution 1959-1961, A Report To the People Of Los Angeles County" (Los Angeles County Air Pollution Control District, Issue date unknown).

16. Krier and Ursin, Pollution & Policy: A Case Essay On California And Federal Experience With Motor Vehicle Air Pollution, 1940-1975.

17. "Analysis Of Progress By APCD In Fulfilling The Recommendations Of The Governor's Report On Air Pollution Control (Beckman Report) Of Dec. 5, 1958" (Los Angeles County Air Pollution Control District, Aug. 18, 1958).

18. "The Automobile And Smog" (Los Angeles Air Pollution Control District, Jan. 16-18, 1960).

19. "Smog Fade By 1966 Predicted," *Los Angeles Examiner,* Oct. 15, 1961.

20. "1960 Called Beginning Of End Of Auto Smog," *Los Angeles Times,* Feb. 3, 1960.

21. Krier and Ursin, *Pollution & Policy: A Case Essay On California And Federal Experience With Motor Vehicle Air Pollution, 1940-1975.*

22. Jack Doyle, *Taken For A Ride: Detroit's Big Three And The Politics Of Pollution,* (Four Walls Eight Windows, 2000).

23. Doyle, *Taken For A Ride: Detroit's Big Three And The Politics Of Pollution.*

24. "Smog And Sewage: Crises Are On The Horizon," *Los Angeles Times,* Sept. 20, 1965.

25. "Bill Requiring Used Car Smog Devices Signed," *Los Angeles Times,* June 1, 1966.

26. "Autograms: School Bell Rings For Smog; New Car--$1,000 A Foot," *Los Angeles Times,* Dec. 8, 1963.

27. "'Smog Could Force California To Ration Gas,' Griswold Says," *Los Angeles Times,* Nov. 3, 1964.

28. "'Smog Could Force California To Ration Gas,' Griswold Says," *Los Angeles Times,* Nov. 3, 1964.

29. Krier and Ursin, *Pollution & Policy: A Case Essay On California And Federal Experience With Motor Vehicle Air Pollution, 1940-1975.*

30. Krier and Ursin, *Pollution & Policy: A Case Essay On California And Federal Experience With Motor Vehicle Air Pollution, 1940-1975.*

31. "Smog Board Flays Automakers For Appalling Delays On Controls," *Los Angeles Times,* Jan. 24, 1964.

32. "New Peril Seen In Car Smog Devices," *Los Angeles Times,* Nov. 16, 1966.

33. "Two 'Smog Fighter' Groups Wage War," *Los Angeles Times,* Aug. 14, 1962.

34. Al Wiman, "A Breath of Death: The Fatality Factor of Smog," KLAC-radio series, Oct. 1969.

35. Krier and Ursin, *Pollution & Policy: A Case Essay On California And Federal Experience With Motor Vehicle Air Pollution, 1940-1975.*

36. Krier and Ursin, *Pollution & Policy: A Case Essay On California And Federal Experience With Motor Vehicle Air Pollution, 1940-1975.*

37. *"The Antitrust Case of the Century"* Southern California Quarterly, Fall 1999.

38. "Smog: $11 Billion Cost To L.A. County In Last Twenty Years," *Los Angeles Times*, Jan. 20, 1965.

39. Krier and Ursin, *Pollution & Policy: A Case Essay On California And Federal Experience With Motor Vehicle Air Pollution, 1940-1975.*

40. Scott Wiman, "Breath Of Death," KLAC radio, Oct. 1967.

41. "Smog Uproar Over Automaker's Lobby," *Los Angeles Times*, Oct. 29, 1967.

42. Interview with Jim Birakos, Feb. 1, 2007.

43. "Carmakers Hit For Delays On Smog Controls," *Los Angeles Times*, Aug. 19, 1964.

44. "Smog Board Flays Automakers For Appalling Delays On Controls," *Los Angeles Times*, Jan. 24, 1964.

45. Doyle, *Taken For A Ride: Detroit's Big Three And The Politics Of Pollution.*

46. Bottles, *Los Angeles And The Automobile: The Making Of A Modern City.*

47. Bottles, *Los Angeles And The Automobile: The Making Of A Modern City.*

48. Bottles, *Los Angeles And The Automobile: The Making Of A Modern City.*

49. Bottles, *Los Angeles And The Automobile: The Making Of A Modern City.*

50. Doyle, *Taken For A Ride: Detroit's Big Three And The Politics Of Pollution.*

51. Bottles, *Los Angeles And The Automobile: The Making Of A Modern City.*

52. "Science Fiction Writer Sees Smog As A Killer," *Los Angeles Times*, July 30, 1964.

53. Tom Sitton, *Los Angeles Transformed: Fletcher Bowron's Urban Reform Revival, 1938-1953* (University of New Mexico Press, 2005).

54. "New Car Boycott Urged To Force Smog Device," *Los Angeles Times*, Jan. 1, 1959.

55. "Facing Up To Transit Problem," *Los Angeles Times* editorial, Feb. 3, 1963.

56. "Brown Calls Transit Leadership Disgrace," *Los Angeles Times*, Jan. 29, 1963.

57. "Brown Calls Transit Leadership Disgrace," *Los Angeles Times*, Jan. 29, 1963.

58. "A City Without Transit," *Los Angeles Times* editorial, July 26, 1965.

59. "U.S. Charges Automakers Plot To Delay Fume Curbs," *New York Times*, Jan. 11, 1969.

60. "Safety Council Laying Big Egg, Nader Claims," *Los Angeles Times*, July 6, 1966.

61. "Phlogiston To Smog: A History Of Burning," *Los Angeles Times*, Feb. 3, 1966.

62. Health Warning: Record Of Correspondence Between Kenneth Hahn, Los Angeles County Supervisor, And The Presidents Of General Motors, Ford And Chrysler On Controlling Air Pollution, 1953-1972, May 1972.

63. Health Warning: Record Of Correspondence Between Kenneth Hahn, Los Angeles County Supervisor, And The Presidents Of General Motors, Ford And Chrysler On Controlling Air Pollution.

64. "Consummate Lawyer Played Array Of Roles," *Washington Post*, May 9, 2005.

65. "County Sues Big Automakers For $100 Million Smog Damage," *Los Angeles Times*, Sept. 6, 1969.

66. Doyle, *Taken For A Ride: Detroit's Big Three And The Politics Of Pollution.*

67. "U.S. Settles Smog Suit Against Auto Companies Out Of Court," *Los Angeles Times*, Sept. 12, 1969.

68. Doyle, *Taken For A Ride: Detroit's Big Three And The Politics Of Pollution.*

69. Doyle, *Taken For A Ride: Detroit's Big Three And The Politics Of Pollution.*

70. *"The Antitrust Case of the Century,"* Southern California Quarterly, Fall 1999.

71. "Nader Raps Proposed Settlement," *Los Angeles Times*, Oct. 24, 1969.

72. *"The Antitrust Case of the Century,"* Southern California Quarterly, Fall 1999.

73. "L.A. Smog: 27-Year-Old Outcast Has Yet To Get Serious Padding," *Los Angeles Times*, Aug. 13, 1970.

74. "One Car To Family Proposed," *Los Angeles Times*, March 2, 1967.

75. "Statewide Smog Standards Revised," *Los Angeles Times*, Sept. 18, 1969.

76. Health Warning: Record Of Correspondence Between Kenneth Hahn, Los Angeles County Supervisor, And The Presidents Of General Motors, Ford And Chrysler On Controlling Air Pollution.

77. *"The Antitrust Case of the Century,"* Southern California Quarterly, Fall 1999.

CHAPTER 7

1. "Women's Group Joins Fight On Air Pollution," *Los Angeles Times*, Jan. 8, 1959.
2. Interview with Gladys Meade, March 3, 2007.
3. "Oil Industry Raps Smog Law Curbs," *Los Angeles Times*, Feb. 17, 1961.
4. "Smog Foes Take Aim At The Lone Rider," *Los Angeles Times*, Sept. 15, 1971.
5. "21st Anniversary Of State Smog Marked," *Los Angeles Times*, Nov. 17, 1964.
6. Afton Slade, letter to the *Los Angeles Times*, April 15, 1965.
7. "Stamping Out Smog Is Somers Family Project," *Los Angeles Times*, May 19, 1970.
8. "The Southland's War On Smog: Fifty Years Of Progress Toward Clean Air" (South Coast Air Quality Management District, 1997).
9. "Doctor Lists Smog As Factor In Man's Death, Raises Legal Issue," *Los Angeles Times*, Nov. 7, 1958.
10. "A Struggle For Excellence: One Hundred Years of the Los Angeles County Medical Association 1871-1971," (Los Angeles County Medical Association, 1971).
11. "Physician Tells Of Evidence That Smog Shortens Lives," *Los Angeles Times*, Oct. 13, 1953.
12. "Physician Tells Of Evidence That Smog Shortens Lives," *Los Angeles Times*, Oct. 13, 1953.
13. "Smog May Produce More Cancer Than Cigarettes, SC Professor Says," *Los Angeles Times*, July 26, 1957.
14. Betty Koster, *A History of Air Pollution Control Efforts In Los Angeles County* (Los Angeles County Air Pollution Control District, Aug. 31, 1956).
15. "Smog Seen As Possible Cause Of Cancer," *Los Angeles Times*, Oct. 1, 1955.
16. "Smog Called Important Cause Of Lung Cancer," *Los Angeles Times*, May 5, 1961.
17. "Doctors Offer First Proof On Smog Effects," *Los Angeles Times*, Dec. 6, 1958.
18. "Medical Research Or Control In Air Pollution" (Los Angeles County Air Pollution Control District, Nov. 2, 1951).
19. "The Effects Of Smog On Public Health, Draft #1" (Los Angeles County Air Pollution Control District, estimated release date: late-1950s.
20. "Smog Sickness Probe In Schools Demanded," *Los Angeles Times*, Nov. 21, 1954.
21. "Smog Not Danger To Health, Scientists Assure Gov. Knight," *Los Angeles Times*, Oct. 17, 1954.
22. "Assembly Smog Report Warns Of Catastrophe," *Los Angeles Times*, March 6, 1959.
23. "6,000 Animals Used In New War On Smog," *Los Angeles Times*, July 4, 1963.
24. "Standards Of Air Purity To Be Set," *Los Angeles Times*, Oct. 9, 1959.
25. "Smog Health Tests Planned On Patients," *Los Angeles Times*, Jan. 19, 1963.
26. "A Struggle For Excellence: One Hundred Years of the Los Angeles County Medical Association 1871-1971" (Los Angeles County Medical Association, 1971).
27. "Smog Can Cause Human Malignancies, Doctors Say," *Los Angeles Times*, April 5, 1957.
28. "Air Particles Called Smog Peril Boosters," *Associated Press*, Dec. 7, 1958.
29. "Smog: A Catastrophe Imminent For L.A.?" *Los Angeles Times*, Oct. 8, 1967.
30. "Smog Contributing Factor In Lung Disease," *Los Angeles Times*, May 30, 1963.
31. "Doctors Urged To Wage War On Air Pollution," *Los Angeles Times*, Sept. 7, 1967.
32. "Smog: A Catastrophe Imminent For L.A.?" *Los Angeles Times*, Oct. 8, 1967.
33. "Smog: A Catastrophe Imminent For L.A.?" *Los Angeles Times*, Oct. 8, 1967.
34. "Scenario For A Smog Disaster," *West magazine, Los Angeles Times*, Jan. 9, 1972.
35. "Suicide Blamed On Smog," *Los Angeles Examiner*, July 3, 1961.
36. "The Southland's War On Smog: Fifty Years Of Progress Toward Clean Air" (South Coast Air Quality Management District, 1997).
37. "No More Blue Sky: A Non-Progress Report On Air Pollution," *West magazine, Los Angeles Times*, May 31, 1970.
38. "Riverside Area Smog Problem In Sharp Gain," *Los Angeles Times*, Jan. 4, 1963.
39. "Smog Blown From L.A. To Arizona Line," *Los Angeles Times*, Sept. 30, 1969.
40. "L.A. Blamed For 40 Percent Of San Diego's Smog," *Los Angeles Times*, Oct. 15, 1963.
41. "Smog Affects Illini Team," *Los Angeles Times*, Dec. 27, 1963.
42. "L.A. Too Smoggy, Vikes Too Groggy," *Los Angeles Times*, Oct. 1, 1965.
43. "Detroit News Raps L.A. Bid For Olympics," *Los Angeles Times*, Feb. 15, 1963.
44. "A Peck Of Pickets," *Los Angeles Times*, Nov. 7, 1969.

45. "Smog Would Halt Bums' Night Games," *Los Angeles Times*, Sept. 18, 1957.

46. "Soviet Coach Agrees—Smog Undid His Team," *Los Angeles Times*, Aug. 6, 1964.

47. "Study Finds Greater Health Tolerance For Smog Among Southland Residents," *Los Angeles Times*, May 19, 1975.

48. "Schools' PE Classes Halted On Smoggy Days," *Los Angeles Times*, Aug. 11, 1969.

49. "Smog Playing Havoc With Prep Football," *Los Angeles Times*, Aug. 21, 1969.

50. "The Polluted Air," *Time*, Jan. 27, 1967.

51. "Here Comes The Smog," *Newsweek*, Aug. 19, 1970.

52. "Air Pollution Linked To Future Earthquakes," *Los Angeles Times*, Nov. 2, 1969.

53. "The Polluted Air," *Time*, Jan. 27, 1967.

54. "Air Pollution Linked To Future Earthquakes," *Los Angeles Times*, Nov. 2, 1969.

55. "The Polluted Air," *Time*, Jan. 27, 1967.

56. "Huge Dust Plumes From China Cause Changes In Climate," *Wall Street Journal*, July 10, 2007.

57. "Anti-Smog Campaign Pushed," *Los Angeles Times*, Sept. 17, 1968.

58. "Air Pollution Chief Assails His Critics," *Los Angeles Times*, Aug. 15, 1969.

59. "Blanket Smog Suit Dismissed," *Los Angeles Times*, Aug. 21, 1969.

60. *"The Antitrust Case of the Century,"* Southern California Quarterly, Fall 1999.

61. "L.A. Chamber Urges All-Out Smog Attack," *Los Angeles Times*, Dec. 10, 1967.

62. "Air Pollution Chief Assails His Critics," *Los Angeles Times*, Aug. 15, 1969.

63. "Applying Social Science To Air Pollution Control" (Los Angeles County Air Pollution Control District, Aug. 26, 1963).

64. "Mothers Charge Laxity In Smog-Control Fight," *Los Angeles Times*, July 17, 1969.

65. "Population Tied To Need For A-Power," *Los Angeles Times*, March 25, 1965.

66. "Smog Foes Taking Aim At Lone Rider," *Los Angeles Times*, Sept. 15, 1971.

67. "Drivers Sink Car-Pool Day," *Los Angeles Times*, Oct. 7, 1971.

68. "Will Blue Skies Smile On Los Angeles Once Again?" *Los Angeles Times*, Oct. 9, 1980.

69. *"The Antitrust Case of the Century,"* Southern California Quarterly, Fall 1999.

70. "'Poisoned Air Hits Public Apathy," *Los Angeles Times*, Sept. 20, 1966.

71. "Smog Documentary Stirs Public, Political Response," *Los Angeles Times*, June 23, 1969.

72. "Gasp! Batman Goes After Big Social Ills," *Los Angeles Times*, Dec. 19, 1969.

73. "U.S. Group Urges Tax On All Who Pollute Air," *Los Angeles Times*, Nov. 7, 1965.

74. "Scenario For A Smog Disaster," *West magazine—Los Angeles Times*, Jan. 9, 1972.

75. "Caltech Students' 'War On Smog' Creates Campus Stir," *Los Angeles Times*, March 4, 1968.

76. "We Wish You A Merry Smog Day," *San Bernardino Sun-Telegraph*, date unknown; believed to be early 1970s.

77. "Our Spaceship Home Is Getting Pretty Dirty," *Los Angeles Times*, July 11, 1966.

78. "Technology: Hero Or Villain," *Los Angeles Times*, June 4, 1967.

79. "Is Technology The Answer To All Our Problems," *Los Angeles Times*, Oct. 9, 1966.

CHAPTER 8

1. Dwayne Hunn, "Sonia Danielson remembers Ed," July 11, 1994, www.peopleslobby.hypermart.net/soniaremembersedhoyce94.htm.

2. "Edwin Koupal, Peoples Lobby Founder, 'One of God's Angry Men,' Dies at 48," *Los Angeles Times*, March 30, 1976.

3. Dwayne Hunn and Doris Ober, *Ordinary People Doing the Extraordinary* (The People's Lobby, 2001).

4. Hunn and Ober, *Ordinary People Doing the Extraordinary*. 5. Hunn and Ober, *Ordinary People Doing the Extraordinary*.

6. Roger Diamond, correspondence to Dwayne Hunt, Sept. 8, 1993.

7. Hunn and Ober, *Ordinary People Doing the Extraordinary*.

8. "Smog May Force Cities' Evacuation, Expert Warns –If One Can Leave Town," *Sacramento Bee*, July 9, 1967.

9. "Doctors Urged to Wage War On Air Pollution," *Los Angeles Times*, Sept. 7, 1967.

10. "Oh Say Can You Breathe?", *West Magazine*, May 31, 1970.

11. "Scenario for a Smog Disaster," *West Magazine*, Jan. 9, 1972.

12. "Scenario for a Smog Snafu," *West Magazine*, Jan. 9, 1972.

13. "Scenario for a Smog Snafu," *West Magazine*, Jan. 9, 1972.

14. "Scenario for a Smog Snafu," *West Magazine*, Jan. 9, 1972.

15. Interview with Jim Birakos, Feb. 1, 2007.

16. "Earth Day Observances Slated," *Los Angeles Times,* April 19, 1970.

17. Hunn and Ober, *Ordinary People Doing the Extraordinary.*

18. "Ninth Smog Alert Breaks 14-Year Record," *Los Angeles Times,* Oct. 2, 1970.

19. Bird, Jr., William, General Electric Theater, Museum of Broadcast Communications, undated, www.museum.tv/archives/etv/G/htmlG/generalelect/generalelect. htm.

20. "Our Environment Crisis," *Nation's Business,* Feb. 1970.

21. "Reagan: Errol Flynn of the B-movies," *The Age,* June 7, 2004.

22. Sierra Club, Norman Livermore, Man in the Middle: High Sierra Packer, Timberman, Conservationist, and California Resources Secretary, 1983.

23. "Governor Ronald Reagan," *California Journal,* Dec. 1970.

24. Governor Ronald Reagan , correspondence to Lee A. Iacocca, President Ford Motor Co., May 31, 1973.

25. "State Lags In Clearing The Air," *California Journal,* Oct. 1973.

26. "State Lags In Clearing The Air," *California Journal,* Oct. 1973.

27. Ben Lewis, Mayor of Riverside, correspondence and report to Governor Ronald Regan, June 1, 1972.

28. "State Again Delays Acting On 'Smog Emergency' Bid," *The Press,* Jan. 21, 1971.

29. Arie Haagen-Smit, Chair of the California Air Resources Board, correspondence to Larry Allison, Managing Editor of the Long Beach *Independent Press-Telegram,* Sept. 15, 1970.

30. Press Release, Office of Governor Ronald Regan, July 28, 1972.

31. "State Lags In Clearing The Air," *California Journal,* Oct. 1973.

32. Interview with Gladys Meade, March 3, 2007.

33. Interview with Gladys Meade, March 3, 2007.

34. Interview with Gladys Meade, March 3, 2007.

35. Interview with Gladys Meade, March 3, 2007.

36. Interview with Jim Birakos, Feb. 1, 2007.

37. "Armageddon in Air Pollution," *Cry California,* Winter 1972/73.

38. Interview with Mary Nichols, Jan. 26, 2007.

39. Interview with Mary Nichols, Jan. 26, 2007.

40. Address of Governor Ronald Regan to the Long Beach Joint Service Clubs, Long Beach, California, April 7, 1972.

41. Arie Haagen-Smit, Chair of the California Air Resources Board, correspondence to Robert Fri, Acting Administrator of the U.S. Environmental Protection Agency, July 9, 1973.

42. Testimony of David Calkins, U.S. Environmental Protection Agency, before the California Air Resources Board, Nov. 13, 1973.

43. Governor Ronald Reagan, correspondence to Senator Alan Cranston, March 26, 1974.

44. Robert T. Morgan, Executive Vice President of the California Manufacturers Association, correspondence to Governor Ronald Reagan, Sept. 20, 1974.

45. Address by Edmund G. Brown, Chair of the California Council for Environmental and Economic Balance, Oct. 2, 1973, before the Town Hall Forum, Los Angeles.

46. Interview with Mel Zeldin, May 1997.

47. South Coast Air Quality Management District Press Release, May 1997.

48. "Nader Task Force Blasts State Officials, Land-Use Practices," *California Journal,* Sept. 1971.

49. "Court's Ruling on Environmental Impact Reports Puts Pressure on Legislature," *California Journal,* Nov. 1972.

50. "Why California Stopped Building," *Business Week,* Oct. 21, 1972.

51. "California," *The Atlantic,* Nov. 1973.

52. Tom Bradley, Mayor of Los Angeles, correspondence to Governor Ronald Regan, Sept. 25, 1974.

53. "Freeway Era Draws To A Close As New Ways Are Sought For Moving People About," *California Journal,* June-July 1972.

54. News Briefs, *California Journal,* April 1972.

55. "A Cleanup Battle Jolts California," *Business Week,* Dec. 25, 1971.

56. Hunn and Ober, *Ordinary People Doing the Extraordinary.*

57. Hunn and Ober, *Ordinary People Doing the Extraordinary.*

CHAPTER 9

1. "Edmund G. Brown Jr. of California: The Counterculture Governor," *Fortune,* August 1975.

2. California Governor's Office, http://www.californiagovernors.ca.gov/h/biography/governor

_32.htmlwebsite.

3. Martin Schiesel, *Pat Brown: The Making of a Reformer* (Pat Brown Institute, California State University at Los Angeles, 2003).

4."Brown's Spending Rate Dips Below His Father's," *Los Angeles Times*, Jan. 21, 1978.

5. "'Era of Limits' Applies to Ecology, Too, Governor Tells Directors Of Sierra Club," *Los Angeles Times*, May 8, 1977.

6. "Edmund G. Brown Jr. of California: The Counterculture Governor," *Fortune*, Aug. 1975.

7. "Brown Will Keep Lights Burning Late at Capitol," *Los Angeles Times*, Nov. 24, 1975.

8. "Edmund G. Brown Jr. of California: The Counterculture Governor," *Fortune*, Aug. 1975.

9. "Ballad of Jerry and Linda," *Newsweek*, April 23, 1979.

10. "Brown Event Mixes Yogurt and Prayer," *Los Angeles Times*, Jan. 9, 1976.

11. "Jerry Brown: Learning to Live with Our Limits," *Time*, Dec. 8, 1975.

12. "Brown Makes Small Talk in London," *Los Angeles Times*, Dec.1, 1977.

13. "Governor Brown's Boy," *Esquire*, Nov. 1974.

14. Interview with Bill Sessa, Jan. 9, 2007.

15. Transcript of meeting between Arie Haagen-Smit and Governor Ronald Regan, March 22, 1968.

16. "In Search Of Blue Skies: The State Stiffens As The Feds Wilt," *California Journal*, May 1975.

17. Interview with Bill Sessa, Jan. 9, 2007.

18. Interview with Bill Sessa, Jan. 9, 2007.

19. "The Pressure Tactics Of Smog Boss Tom Quinn," *California Journal*, July 1977.

20. Interview with Gladys Meade, March 31, 2007.

21. Interview with Bill Sessa, Jan. 9, 2007.

22. Interview with Tom Quinn, Feb. 26, 2007.

23. Interview with Tom Quinn, Feb. 26, 2007.

24. "The Pressure Tactics Of Smog Boss Tom Quinn," *California Journal*, July 1977.

25. Interview with Tom Quinn, Feb. 26, 2007.

26. "California's New Hard Line On Smog," *Business Week*, April 7, 1975.

27. Interview with Tom Quinn, Feb. 26, 2007.

28. "Sohio Gives Up On West Coast-Texas Line," *Oil & Gas Journal*, March 19, 1979.

29. "Brown Wants State To Lead Solar Field," *Los Angeles Times*, August 20, 1977.

30. "Governor Jerry Brown: Reelection of a Politician Committed to Change," *Science*, Dec. 1, 1978.

31. Interview with Tom Quinn, Feb. 26, 2007.

32. Interview with Tom Quinn, Feb. 26, 2007.

33. Interview with Tom Quinn, Feb. 26, 2007.

34. Interview with Tom Quinn, Feb. 26, 2007.

35. Interview with Ed Camarena, Feb. 26, 2007.

36. Interview with Bill Sessa, Jan. 9, 2007.

37. Los Angeles Area Chamber of Commerce President Robert Dockson official correspondence with Senator Milton Marks, chair of the Senate Local Government Committee, June 23, 1975 .

38. April 21, 1975, association position paper.

39. Los Angeles County Legislative Representative Marvin Freedman official correspondence with Senator Milton Marks, chair of the Senate Local Government Committee, July 22, 1975.

40. Interview with Ed Camarena, Feb. 26, 2007.

41. LA Mayor Tom Bradley official correspondence with Senator Milton Marks, August 11, 1975.

42. Upland Mayor Abner B. Haldeman official correspondence with Senator Milton Marks, July 30, 1975.

43. Joanne Aplet and Gladys Meade, *Beyond County Boundaries to Clean Air,* report to the South Coast Air Quality Management District, January 23, 1992.

44. Interview with Ed Camarena, Feb. 26, 2007.

46. "Freeway Car Pool, Bus Lane Will Open Monday," *Los Angeles Times*, March 14, 1976.

47. "Freeway Experiment Jams Traffic, Angers Motorists," *Los Angeles Times*, March 16, 1976; "Diamond Lane Greeted by Raves, Pans," *Los Angeles Times*, March 16, 1976.

48. "State, U.S. Abandon Diamond Lane Fight," *Los Angeles Times*, Jan. 15, 1977.

49. "Street Accident Rise Blamed On Diamond Lane," *Los Angeles Times*, June 15, 1976.

50. "State, U.S. Abandon Diamond Lane Fight," *Los Angeles Times*, Jan. 15, 1977.

51. "Gunning for Brown," *National Review*, Nov. 25, 1977.

52. Interview with Bill Sessa, Jan. 9, 2007.

53. "A Leash On Man's Best Friend," *Los Angeles Times*, Aug. 18, 1982.

54. Interview with Bill Sessa, Jan. 9, 2007.

55. "New Industrial Construction In State Banned," *Los Angeles Times,* Aug. 25, 1979.

56. "New Chief Admits ARB's Shortcomings," *Los Angeles Times*, Sept. 18, 1979.

57. "Brown OKs Bill On Auto Smog Checks," *Los Angeles Times*, Sept. 1, 1982.

58. "Pollution Curbed, Reagan Says; Attacks Air Cleanup," *Los Angeles Times*, Oct. 9, 1980.

59. Interview with Tom Quinn, Feb. 26, 2007.

CHAPTER 10

1. "EPA Proposed Easing Air Pollution Deadline Plan Would Give L.A. Basin Up to 25 Years to Reduce Smog but Under Tougher Standards," *Los Angeles Times*, November 13, 1987.

2. Interview with Jim Lents, January 29, 2007.

3. "Clearing The Air On Los Angeles," *Scientific American*, October 1993.

4. Oral History Interview with Robert Presley. (2002-2003). Senator, 1974-1994; Secretary, Youth and Adult Correctional Agency, 1999-2003.

5. "AQMD Board to Fight Reorganization Move," *Los Angeles Times*, March 7, 1987.

6. "Air Pollution and the 1984 Olympic Games in Los Angeles" (South Coast Air Quality Management District, 1984). ; paper provided by Jim Birakos, former AQMD Deputy Executive Officer.

7. Interview with Jim Lents, January 29, 2007.

8. "The Path to Clean Air" (South Coast Air Quality Management District, 1987).

9. "AQMD Official Criticizes Agency On Air Pollution," *Daily News*, May 16, 1987; Interview with Jim Birkaos March 1, 2007.

10. "Air Quality Agency Falls Victim To Edifice Complex," *Los Angeles Business Journal*, Sept. 9, 1994.

11. "In Weighing The Costs Of Clean Air, Don't Omit The Value Of Each Breath," *Los Angeles Times,* August 11, 1989.

12. Interview with Jim Lents, January 29, 2007.

13. Interview with John Dunlap, April 12, 2007.

14. "A Role For Cities In The Battle For Cleaner Air," *Western City,* March 1990.

15. Interview with John Dunlap, April 12, 2007.

16. Interview with John Dunlap, April 12, 2007.

17. Interview with Curt Pringle, March 12, 2007.

18. Interview with Ed Camarena, February 26, 2007.

19. "AQMD's Legal Costs Zoom As It Flexes Its Enforcement Muscle," *Los Angeles Business Journal,* July 15, 1991.

20. Interview with Jim Lents, January 29, 2007.

21. "The First Woody's Barbecue Was Opened 31 Years Ago On Slauson Avenue In Los Angeles, California," *Black Voice News* online, July 13, 2006.

22. "Keeping the Clean Air Promise" (South Coast Air Quality Management District, November 1991).

23. "AQMD Makes Ride-Share Rule More Flexible," *Los Angeles Times*, April 15, 1995.

24. "Smog Agency Bows To L.A., Defers Some Stricter Limits," *Los Angeles Times*, September 10, 1994.

25. Bill Kelly, RECLAIM Program Adopted, AQMD Advisor, November 1993.

26. Chip Jacobs, Keeping Their Distance, Pasadena Weekly, March 28, 2003.

27. Pasadena Weekly, March 28, 2003.

28. Netherlands Ministry of the Environment an Automated Credit Exchange Conduct First-Ever, Rate-Based NOx Emission trading Simulation, *Business Wire*, Feb. 14, 2001

29. Pasadena Weekly, March 28, 2003; and Federal Affidavit of Ronald Modjeski, U.S. Environmental Protection Agency, 2004.

30. Chip Jacobs, Up in Smoke, Pasadena Weekly, May 1, 2008.

31. Pasadena Weekly, May 1, 2008

32. Interview with Curt Pringle, March 12, 2007.

33. Interview with John Dunlap, April 12, 2007.

34. Interview with Curt Pringle, March 12, 2007.

35. January 14, 1994 Letter from James Lents to AQMD Board; meeting minutes.

36. Interview with Jim Lents, January 29, 2007.

37. Form 625 filed by Layne Bordenave with the California Secretary of State.

38. Interview with Jim Lents, January 29, 2007.

39. Correspondence from William Burke, May 19, 2008.

40. Interview with Layne Bordenave, June 16, 2008. Willie Brown did not respond to calls and emails requesting comment on the incident.

41. "Ex-Chief Of EIDC Avoids Prison," *Los Angeles Times*, September 21, 2004.

42. "Ex-Chief Of EIDC Avoids Prison," *Los Angeles Times*, September 21, 2004.

CHAPTER 11

1. "Is there an electric car in your future?", *Design News*, April 8, 1996.

2. http://inventors.about.com, May 18, 2005.

3. "History of Electric Vehicles," US DOE, EERE, November 7, 2005.

4. "History of Electric Vehicles," US DOE, EERE, November 7, 2005.

5. "Defense Cuts To Hit Hard, Powell Says," *Los Angeles Times*, March 24, 1992.

6. "Aerospace Cuts To Devastate Area, County Study Says," *Los Angeles Times*, March 17, 1992.

7. "Group Seeks A Place To Park Electric Car Industry," *Los Angeles Times*, Jan. 20, 1992.

8."Advanced Electric Transportation Technology Commercialization: A California Plan" (Amerigon, March 25, 1992).

9. "Group Seeks a Place to Park Electric Car Industry," *Los Angeles Times*, Jan. 20, 1992.

10. "Northrup Checks Out Moves Into Transportation Projects," *Los Angeles Business Journal*, Feb. 10, 1992.

11. "Is There An Electric Car In Your Future?" *Design News*, June 23, 1997.

12. "It Whines. It's Fast. It's Fun," *U.S. News & World Report*, Sept. 30, 1996.

13. Interview with Jerry Martin.

14. Data supplied by the California Department of Motor Vehicles.

15. A.F. Burke, K.S. Kurani, and E.J. Kenney, "Study of the Secondary Benefits of ZEV Mandate," Prepared for the California Air Resources Board, August 2000.

16. "Lord of the Race," *LA Weekly*, March 5, 2004.

17. "Lord of the Race," *LA Weekly*, March 5, 2004.

18. "Lord of the Race," *LA Weekly*, March 5, 2004.

19. "Lord of the Race," *LA Weekly*, March 5, 2004.

20. "Lord of the Race," *LA Weekly*, March 5, 2004.

21. "Lord of the Race," *LA Weekly*, March 5, 2004.

22. "Lord of the Race," *LA Weekly*, March 5, 2004.

23. "Lord of the Race," *LA Weekly*, March 5, 2004.

24. "Lord of the Race," *LA Weekly*, March 5, 2004.

25. "Lord of the Race," *LA Weekly*, March 5, 2004.

26. "Lord of the Race," *LA Weekly*, March 5, 2004.

27. "Lord of the Race," *LA Weekly*, March 5, 2004.

28. "Lord of the Race," *LA Weekly*, March 5, 2004.

29. "Lord of the Race," *LA Weekly*, March 5, 2004.

30. "Lord of the Race," *LA Weekly*, March 5, 2004.

31. "Lord of the Race," *LA Weekly*, March 5, 2004.

32. "Lord of the Race," *LA Weekly*, March 5, 2004.

33. "Lord of the Race," *LA Weekly*, March 5, 2004.

CHAPTER 12

1. "Multiple Air Toxics Exposure Study In The South Coast Air Basin" (South Coast Air Quality Management District, Draft Report, January 2008).

2. "9 AQMD Advisors Quit In Protest Of New Smog Plan," *Los Angeles Times*, Aug. 9, 1996.

3. "AQMD Adopts Disputed Plan For Clean Air," *Los Angeles Times*, Nov. 16, 1996.

4. "Lord of the Race," *LA Weekly*, March 5, 2004.

5. "Environmental Justice Rising," *California Journal*, May 2003.

6. "Environmental Justice Rising," *California Journal*, May 2003.

7. "Air District Policies Have Allowed Chrome Plating Industry To Avoid Cancer Risk Standards In Los Angeles Area," *California Sustainability*, Nov. 21, 2002.

8. "Air District Policies Have Allowed Chrome Plating Industry To Avoid Cancer Risk Standards In Los Angeles Area," *California Sustainability*, Nov. 21, 2002.

9. "Air District Policies Have Allowed Chrome Plating Industry To Avoid Cancer Risk Standards

In Los Angeles Area," *California Sustainability,* Nov. 21, 2002.

    10. "Lord of the Race," *LA Weekly,* March 5, 2004.

    11. "Environmental Justice Rising," *California Journal,* May 2003.

    12. "Environmental Justice Rising," *California Journal,* May 2003.

    13. "Environmental Justice Rising," *California Journal,* May 2003.

    14. "Environmental Justice Rising," *California Journal,* May 2003.

CHAPTER 13

    1. "Clear And Present Danger," *LA Weekly,* September 23-29, 2005.

    2. "Clear And Present Danger," *LA Weekly,* September 23-29, 2005.

    3. Energy Information Agency, 2005 International Energy Annual Report, October 1, 2007, and California Energy Commission, Inventory of Greenhouse Gas Emissions and Sinks, 1990-2004, December 2006.

    4. "Stabilization Wedges: Solving The Climate Problem For The Next 50 Years With Current Technologies," *Science,* August 13, 2004.

    5. "Brown Announces Landmark Global Warming Settlement" (California Attorney General's Office, August 21, 2007).

    6. Federal Affidavit of Ronald Modjeski, U.S. Environmental Protection Agency, 2004.

    7. Memorandum to Howard Grobstein from Kathy Bazoian Phelps, EonXchange—"Analysis of Stolen Credits," Sept. 14, 2004.

    8. Fee Agreement, Air America Holdings, Inc., date unknown.

    9. Gold Ray Group Limited, "Procedures for Operation Bald Headed Eagle," June 29, 1998.

    10. Gold Ray Group Limited, "Hangar and Customs Requirements, July 22, 1998.)

    11. Gold Ray Group Limited, "Procedures for Operation Bald Headed Eagle," June 29, 1998.

    12. United Nations, Framework Convention on Climate Change, Conference of the Parties, Fifth Session, Bonn, 25 October–5 November, 1999," Nov. 4, 1999.

    13. "Ethanol Vehicles Pose Significant Risk To Health, New Study Finds," Stanford Report, April 18, 2007.

    14. "Driving Under The Influence," *Los Angeles City Beat,* Aug. 23, 2007.

    15. "Driving Under The Influence," *Los Angeles City Beat,* Aug. 23, 2007.

    16. "Air Board Makes Scarce Credits Available For Power Plants," *California Energy Circuit,* Aug. 10, 2007.

    17. "Air Board Makes Scarce Credits Available For Power Plants," *California Energy Circuit,* August 10, 2007.

EPILOGUE

    1. "The Southland's War On Smog: Fifty Years Of Progress Toward Clean Air" (South Coast Air Quality Management District, 1997).

    2. Rachel Carson, *Silent Spring,* (Mariner Books, 1962).

    3. "Think of Him When the Sky Is Blue," *Los Angeles Times,* March 6, 1977.

    4. "The Sins of Waste," *Engineering & Science,* Feb. 1973.

    5. "Save Earth from Warming by Using Pollution?" *MSNBC,* Nov. 17, 2006.

    6. "General Facts and Figures," driveclean.ca.gov, State of California. http://www.driveclean.ca.gov/en/gv/media/index.asp

INDEX